Writing in Dante's
Cult of Truth
From Borges to
Boccaccio

The Circle of the Lustful: Paolo and Francesca, 1827, William Blake, 1757–1827, National Gallery of Art, Washington, Gift of W. G. Russell Allen

Writing in Dante's Cult of Truth From Borges to Boccaccio

MARÍA ROSA MENOCAL

Duke University Press Durham and London 1991

Permissions appear on page 224.

© 1991 Duke University Press
All rights reserved
Printed in the United States of America
on acid-free paper ∞

Library of Congress Cataloging-in-Publication Data
Menocal, María Rosa.
   Writing in Dante's cult of truth : from Borges to Boccaccio /
María Rosa Menocal.
       p.   cm.
   Includes bibliographical references and index.
   ISBN 0-8223-1104-6 (cloth). — ISBN 0-8223-1117-8 (paper)
   1. Dante Alighieri, 1265–1321—Criticism and interpretation.
2. Dante Alighieri, 1265–1321—Influence.   3. Poetry—History and
criticism.   4. Poetics.   I. Title.
PQ4390.M547   1991   90-45998
851′.1—dc20   CIP

For Margaux, same vintage

Contents

Prologue:

Wilderness

Can a Poet doubt the Vision of Jehovah? Nature has no Outline:
but Imagination has. Nature has no Tune: but Imagination has!
Nature has no Supernatural & dissolves: Imagination is Eternity
—William Blake

The Voice of the Serpent
  dry hiss of age & steam
          & leaves of gold
                    old books in ruined
                        Temples
I will not disturb
I will not go
Come, he says softly
an old man appears &
  moves in tired dance
  amid the scattered dead
gently they stir
—Jim Morrison, *Wilderness*

I

ℐ have resisted—and unsuccessfully, for practical reasons—writing this preface because it seems to me that many, if not most, of the premises and functions of the introduction are antithetical to the historical constructs this book is grounded in. There has been no shortage of meditation on the problem of beginnings: Said's brilliant book of the same title; Vico, who frames and gives great proleptic life to Said's discussion; Derrida's highly influential "outwork"; even Hegel, who points out in his own preface to *The Phenomenology of Mind*[1] that it can be both inappropriate and misleading to begin by explaining the end the author had in mind (or, as perhaps few would admit, the end the author thinks she may have figured out after she has finally finished writing the book). A number of intimately linked classes of misrepresentation and misreadings are thereby encouraged: what is lyrical is flattened in explanation and clarification,[2] and retrospective light is made out to be guiding.

But the purposes of and the generally perceived need for introductions are clear: the material at the beginning neatly "restores" the harmony of diachrony that the writing process itself radically under-

1. In the edition I use I note the superb irony of the almost ridiculous number of introductions: the Introduction to the Torchbook edition, written by George Lichtheim; a Prefatory Note to the second edition by J. B. Baillie; a Translator's Introduction, also by Baillie; and a Preface and an Introduction, the last two by Hegel himself.

2. Hegel states this in his own philosophical terms: "Moreover, because philosophy has its being essentially in the element of that universality which encloses the particular within it, the end or final result seems . . . to have absolutely expressed the complete fact itself in its very nature; contrasted with that the mere process of bringing it to light would seem, properly speaking, to have no essential significance" (68).

mines. At some level we all hew to that polite and reassuring fiction that these bits of ordering somehow did and do come first. And in part this book is about the parallel and comparable fiction that is the cornerstone of literary history as we have been narrating it in the modern period: that almost unchallèngable notion that literary history actually works in a diachronic fashion. Indeed, we are inordinately enamoured of the construct of diachrony and the linear history that narrates it, and their presumed attendant clarities; we believe them to constitute the most fundamental heuristic and hermeneutic realities. But this book argues—indirectly, through the structures of literary relations it sets out—that this narrative-historical model actually distorts a far more important element of truth and reality. For literary history is itself not diachronic but rather synchronistic: time is all jumbled up everywhere, authors from different centuries and different universes sit one next to another and shape each others' work, both proleptically and retrospectively, as well as in the "normal" diachronic ways we are used to expecting and analyzing. Although one can hear the accusations already ("anachronism," "dehistoricization"), where is the historical truth, what contingency do we capture, in the retrospective linear order we impose? What reader, what writer, has ever read within an ordered history, much less written as part of it? Where is the falsehood in the history that tells us that Borges as a young man learned about literature not from the Argentine short story writers who preceded him (that, perhaps, is a different story) but rather as he was riding back and forth on the trolleys of Buenos Aires, sitting next to Dante and his *Commedia?* Literary history has all too often been an act of ordering and classifying, part and parcel of the strong scientific impulse from which philology was born and its many attendant post-Cartesianisms and positivisms. But why should we so strongly privilege the "reality" of diachrony and relegate other constructs of temporal relationships to a different and far less significant plane? One could easily argue that there is a far more compelling and influential reality in the orderings of personal histories—within which, for example, I first read Dante as an epigone of Eliot's, going from the *Animula* to the *Purgatorio*—than in other constructs. Thus, in part, this book is about the problems of writing literary history in a way that does not flatten the uncanniness of literature and does not imagine history to be either linear or clearly distinguishable from literature itself.

The model which underlies this work is thus something like what my colleague Giuseppe Mazzotta calls Viconian: "To the idea of history as a linear series of discrete rational units Vico responds with a view of history as an ever shifting configuration whereby time and space are simultaneously entailed and all periods are present." Clearly, it also shares with Vico's thought that anti-Cartesianism which would emerge, with a different texture, of course, in another renegade philologist, Pound. Pound's own "New Science," his radical departure from what philology had become at Pennsylvania in the first part of this century (starkly more Cartesian than Viconian), was both *The Spirit of Romance* and the *Cantos*. My own reaction inscribed in these pages is not only transparently anti-Cartesian but embraces what literary history, particularly in the age of positivism and rivalry with the other "sciences," has believed should be erased and banished: belief in what some may call the fantastical and respect for the compelling power of the most subjective elements: personal histories and personal visions. I thus rely heavily on two renegade models for temporal and literary relations: synchronicity and kabbalism.

My own understanding and use of the kabbala—which has both traditionally as well as recently been the object of vast scholarship—is very simple and limited: the kabbala is the master text, the writing of the universe, the telling of history in the cosmos. Like the Dante of the *Vita nuova*, we sit at our desks and ponder the stories and the texts and the inscriptions of our lives, lives whose viccissitudes and meanings are not knowable until, chapter by chapter, vessel by vessel, the writing, the passage of time, sheds light and tells us what the words meant the first time around. Jung's concept of synchronicity, unlike the kabbala, is far less well known. (While the kabbala has been left for the true believers and the literary historians to figure out and enjoy, Jung's work is, most of the time, subjected to the positivist scrutiny of a scientific community quite unlikely to revel in its darkest corners—of which there are, of course, many in Jung's extensive oeuvre.) Jung himself sets out the basic concept most starkly:

> All natural phenomena of this kind [acausal phenomena, other-wise called miracles] are unique and exceedingly curious combina-tions of chance, held together by the common meaning of their parts to form an unmistakable whole. . . . Synchronicity designates the parallelism of time and meaning between psychic and psycho-physical events, which scientific knowledge so far has been unable to reduce to a common principle. . . . The only recognizable and demonstrable link between them [parallel events] is a common meaning, or equivalence. (Jung, *On Synchronicity*, 517–18)

I understand this in terms that parallel my understanding of kabbala: they are both modes of describing the often uncanny relationship between self and universe, a relationship in which the universe speaks— at times indecipherably—to that soul which has become a central character.

I I

I can also describe this book in other ways. It is about the great fertility of Dante's meditations on what poetry ought to be, notions emblazoned everywhere throughout his work but most conspicuous at a number of key literary moments: at the heart of the conversionary *Vita nuova;* in the stunning scene of Francesca and her book; with the burning up of the "miglior fabbro" Arnaut Daniel at the summit of Purgatory. The extraordinary power of the Dantesque vision of poetry and its potential to reflect the Truths of existence are rooted in the marriage of literature and literary history that Dante effects. And in his aftermath, from the most immediate possible well into the various cycles of our own poetic era, Dante himself, variously and often very differently conceived, of course, becomes the critical prism and anvil for the musings on the same subjects of a stunning range of other poets. From Borges in a century and world hardly conceivable in fourteenth-century

Florence to the Boccaccio who first lectured there and then on the *Commedia,* Dante, his recastings of literary history, and his beliefs in the needs and duties of poetry—all strongly articulated within the literary enterprise itself, the *Vita nuova* and the *Commedia* particularly—in turn become the literary tropes for the later poets' recastings of both history and theory. The allusive Dantes in later literature, reshaped and recast in the mainstream of the literary history being constantly rewritten by poets, come out in many disguises, in the shapes of his own creations, or versions of them: Beatrices, Francescas, Cavalcantis, Arnauts.

It is, most of all, that Dante so intent on mastering the discourse of literary history, both before and after himself, who will be used again and again as a strongly evocative but also highly malleable token of poetry as a version of ideology. In the inevitable paradox, Dante has thus both succeeded and failed remarkably. While he is immensely powerful, the seemingly necessary element in the imaginative expressions of views on the ethics of poetry in the entire range of both Old and New World literatures, as essential a tool in Ezra Pound's catalogue as in the now obscure Silvio Pellico's, he is, no less than the poets he manipulates in his own works, the object of interpretation and manipulation himself, as much a vulnerable ghost, at times, as the Guido lurking about the tombs.

I have treated these issues in what seems to me the only viable fashion: episodically. Each chapter deals with an episode in this literary history of poetic literary histories and with one or more of the theoretical issues that that episode forces on us. The initial chapter is a reading of the *Vita nuova* itself as Dante's most excruciatingly naked vision of the relationship between Poetry and Truth. Silvio Pellico's now neglected *Le mie prigioni,* once the only text to rival the *Commedia* in international popularity, is in a number of ways exemplary of the often negative burden of Dante in an Italian canon unsure whether to join him or fight him. Pellico's various Francescas and his explicit rewritings of the *Commedia* constitute the key episodes explored in the second chapter, as well as the issues of autobiographical and conversionary structures and the possibility of univocal interpretations of texts so excruciatingly present in all the versions of the Francesca story that converge here. The central chapter of the book is an extended consideration of the apparently simple dedication to *The Waste Land:* the tribute paid by Eliot to his maker Pound, the same tribute paid by Dante to his maker Arnaut. The famous "miglior fabbro" epithet explicitly makes Dante a major player of a specific sort in the battles of modernism, and also sheds light on the nature of the literary history Dante was in the process of writing, a literary history Pound himself, a refugee from a Romance philology that served Dante too slavishly for Pound's tastes, will aggressively revise and even reverse. And Dante and Eliot, as the wielders of the ambiguous praise of the epithet, are conspicuously playing the role of poet-critic which they so relished, an issue which will surface as central in this chapter as well.

Two of the strongest visions and revisions of Dante emerge from great silences: Borges's always-dead Beatriz and Petrarch's conspicuous denial, the powerful unnaming of Dante that helps shape the *Rime sparse.* Chapter 4 deals with the most fragmentary and unnerving of rewritings, Borges's "The Aleph" and the eightieth of the three hundred and sixty-six poems of Petrarch's vernacular triumph, and with the issues of poetic ideologies and the anguishes of fame and posterity that are so explicitly confronted by both of these "rivals." Finally, in what I think of as an epilogue, the last chapter returns to the two most tantalizing figures glimpsed at the outset: the Guido who flickers briefly and brightly in the *Vita nuova* and the Francesca that obsessed Pellico (and, it sometimes seems, whole chunks of the nineteenth and twentieth centuries). But now they are part of a universe, that of the *Decameron,* remarkably close in time and space but also at what one might call an engaged distance: Boccaccio calls his own book a Galeotto, thus tying any interpretation of the *Decameron* to some interpretation of the *Commedia* (or at least of the Francesca episode), and at the same time dwells unflinchingly throughout on the enormous but inevitable and central difficulties of interpretation that are at the very heart of the literary and human enterprises. In what is my own attempt to avoid strict closure, I thus finish with Boccaccio's essentially subversive reading of the lessons of a *Commedia* which has metamorphosed from the transparency preordained in the

Vita nuova to the inadvertent and unwilling bearer of interpretative difficulty, that great example of the necessary relativism of texts and their readings, that is everywhere in the *Decameron*.

III

Many of the thousands of bits and pieces of this book, which existed as fragments of my teaching, a number of talks, and much of my endless conversation for about ten years before I had the necessary time and insights to shape it into a book, have been colored and shaped by an embarrassingly large number of people. I hope the insights from many, perhaps most, of those countless conversations are appropriately embedded and refracted in the chapters that follow; an attempt to recount them would be a far poorer acknowledgement than the reflections I think are everywhere in my text. Much "influence" is best left in its uncanny forms, and the acts of memory of a text are probably more honest and full than any long list, perforce dismissive, of names could conceivably be. There is a smaller crowd of individuals, however, whose presences have been so crucial to the very existence of the book that they can safely be named without diminishment.

Two extraordinary students, Linda Armao and Virginia Jewiss Campbell, both symbolize and embody the many and varied benefits and pleasures of the teaching half of our lives. In a different universe, Linda would have been co-author of an article that never took shape but that, in a substantially modified form, became the central chapter of this book on "Faint Praise"; to her I am indebted for not only the critical research assistance she provided in the initial phases of my inexpert thinking on Pound and Eliot, but far more for an unflinching loyalty and key, superb readings of the most difficult texts, both qualities which have sustained and encouraged me at crucial junctures in the writing of this text. Ginny, too, is the sort of student, and thus teacher, imagined in much sentimental pulp about teaching and learning, and which very occasionally comes to life with poignant immediacy. For this book, as it has evolved slowly from scattered readings in undergraduate survey courses at Penn to the synchronically ordered readings that fell into place at

Yale, and for many chapters that lie far outside this book, she has been the indispensable ally, the too-smart interlocutor, the loving recipient, blackboard and mirror, the dresser without whom the actress might well forget her lines.

Others have played crucial roles: George Calhoun rescues me daily from the many traps of banal domesticity and wields a meaner blue pencil than any other editor. He makes the articulations of my life possible and has always left the right books lying around for me to bump into. My debt to Giuseppe Mazzotta, aspects of which are conspicuous and detailed on most pages of this book, is actually mostly of the unacknowledgable sort: this is a book he encouraged and enabled, for the most part unknowingly, in hundreds of conversations and dozens of arguments about literary history and its articulations. Without his superb intellect and generosity I might not have dared to write such a book. And the magical Frances Howland has given all the alternates a perfect home these last four years. In far greater measure than she knows she makes my soul and intellect thrive in New Haven—and thus everywhere—and I have written this book basking in that sunshine.

But most of all, I think, this book would probably not exist without Roberto González Echevarría, who in many crucial ways practices what most people in our profession only preach. As the inimitably pithy Stanley Fish has most recently put it, being "interdisciplinary" is "so very hard to do"—mostly, to brutally reinterpret his argument, because interdisciplinarity is a theoretical posture that scarcely, if at all, affects disciplinary practices. In practice, of course, institutional pressures of vast proportions have in recent years essentially and functionally dis-membered the discipline of Romance philology—at least that version of it that one can see prefigured in Dante's *De vulgari* and that Pound rewrote in his *Spirit of Romance*—so that with the rare, usually aging exception, medieval literary studies in practice is now neatly divided into discrete linguistic and temporal packages that tag us—and largely delimit our work—as Italianists or Hispanists, as modernists or medi-evalists, as experts in the new world or the old. Within such a universe Roberto has unflinchingly encouraged and defended my own largely idiosyncratic critical practice and thus, given the imperatives of practical realities, made it possible. At the end of the day of my first visit to New Haven, Roberto quite literally threw himself into the middle of the street, directly in front of an oncoming cab which showed no interest in stopping until it confronted him—all so that I might not miss my train. The event, as Dante might say, prefigured the Truth; and for all his subsequent reenactments of that generous and fearless gesture, this book is, in part, a token of thanks.

I

Synchronicity:

Death and the *Vita nuova*

No snowflake falls in an inappropriate place.
—Zen expression

*That mankind has in this sense been cowardly has
done life endless harm; the experiences that are called
"visions," the whole so-called "spirit world," death, all
those things so closely akin to us, have by daily
parrying been so crowded out of life that the senses
with which we could have grasped them are
atrophied. To say nothing of God.*
—Rilke, *Letters to a Young Poet*

*A sleep trance, a dream dance, A shared romance,
Synchronicity . . .*
—Sting

I

The story of the *Vita nuova* is deceptively simple. The artist as a very young man falls hopelessly in love with an equally youthful Beatrice, and over a precisely marked period of years—the numbers will all turn out, in retrospect, to have been key markers—he acts out all the conceits of what we have come to call "courtly" love. In this endlessly suffering pursuit, hopeless beyond fulfillment, he sings the anguishes of such love and gives his readers a number of poems that are as lovely hymns to his ancestor troubadours as any those father figures ever wrote themselves. The living Beatrice in the first half of the book is thus the provocation of and the evocation in much marvelously self-serving and self-loving poetry, poetry that, in the strong vernacular tradition that fathered it, is primarily fascinated with itself and with the love object always just beyond its reach. The poetry itself is spun from that desire fueled and sustained by perpetual failure and endless seeking. The young poet playing the lover, then, indulges himself endlessly, has sleepless nights (some with remarkable dream visions), is physically ill, pines away . . . and sure enough, love poetry comes forth from the ordeal, as it is supposed to. All is well. Until, in a kabbalistically inscribed twist of events, Beatrice dies, and with her, for that young poet, so does inspiration. Without the absent object of desire, the young man is left without song—but he will not give in to such a fate. And it is Beatrice's death that provokes the realization that there is more to both life and poetry than that, than desire never fulfilled, than poetry that is its own center.

It is the dead Beatrice who is not only the focus of Dante's new life as a poet, but also, perhaps, a keen metaphor for his own first life and death as a poet. The new poet emerges from the crucible of her death a far abler reader of the text than the young troubadour who fell in love with Beatrice: he has turned to the truths that lie in the poetry itself, truths that were there before but that he could not read because he could not decipher the language they were written in. The centrality and necessity of death for this sort of revelation—a revelation rooted in both synchronistic and kabbalistic truths that taunt the modern reader—was keenly understood (and mocked, not so gently, perhaps) by Borges: his incarnation of Beatrice is a Beatriz who is not only dead but seems never to have been alive, but whose portraits reign over the house that shelters the Aleph, in the dark pit of the basement, that Aleph, that magic looking-glass that enables one to see, and thus write, the literature of the cosmos.

I I

It has been, at least in part, the tremendously authoritative power of Charles Singleton's reading of the *Vita nuova* as an authentic and all-powerful religious conversion that has kept us in the intervening years from seeing the full extent to which Dante's so-called prologue to the *Commedia* is first and foremost his manifesto of literary conversion. By this I mean—and this will be the point of this chapter—that the *Vita nuova* is first and last about writing, that other conversions and other "themes" are ancillary to this principal, *literal* story, that of the artist as a young man. I will argue, in fact, that to convince the reader of the literal truth of that story—a literal truth we have taken, by and large, as a metaphor—is the very point of Dante's narration of this remarkably failed love story. It is quite remarkable that one of the dominant clusters of themes of Dante criticism vis-à-vis the *Commedia* in recent years, that of tracing out the almost unending instances of self-reflection, literary conversions, literary invention reinscribed in the text, in sum, Dante's preoccupation with his work and his craft and his text, has been far less visible in readings of this text. This is true despite the fact that almost everyone views the *Vita nuova* as the important—if at times arcane and impenetrable—prolegomenon to the masterpiece. While a number of key critics have certainly understood and explored the metaliterary dimensions of the *Vita nuova*,[1] I want to suggest that what we call

1. The most innovative recent rereading is certainly that of Harrison, which will

metaliterary is, in the case of this text, the plainly literary as well, the
story at the surface as well as just below it, and that the combination,
which is a species of kabbalistic writing, has by and large evaded our
modern critical readings.

Clearly, on many points and at many key junctures, my reading of this
text will intersect and parallel previous readings, especially Singleton's
powerful and canonical model.[2] But the difference, I think, is funda-

---

be referred to further in the course of this chapter. Among the many earlier studies
that emphasize to some extent the metaliterary aspects of the text, the most lucid
are: de Robertis, a difficult philological piece that emphasizes the highly literary
background that is explicitly evoked and recounted in the *Vita nuova* by the
apprentice poet; Mazzaro (one of the numerous essays on the work; see Mazzotta
1983 for the curious phenomenon of the preponderance of essays on the *Vita
nuova*), a work akin to de Robertis in its detailed exploration of poeticoliterary
ambience in the work, with occasional (but never central) observations about the
work's metaliterary concerns; Mazzotta 1983, a pointed and brief sketch of the *Vita
nuova* as a "parable of poetic apprenticeship" (3) which will lead to the rediscovery
and reestablishment of the imagination as the essential feature of poetic language,
since only in the imagination of poetry does one find "the means of exploring the
world of the dead" (13) and the ability to bring them (the dead) back to life;
Mazzotta 1986b, a fuller and more complex elaboration of the role played by the
Vita nuova in Dante's elaboration of a poetics within which rhetoric is not separable
from all the other varieties of knowledge, including the theological; Brownlee
1984, which has as its focus *Paradiso* 25 but lays the groundwork with the poetic
genealogy evoked in chapter 25 of the *Vita nuova,* and notes the critical trans-
ference, in Dante's historiography, of authority, truth and revelation in poetic
identity from the classical tongue to the vernacular poet. Barolini 1984 addresses a
number of the same issues in the subchapter "Textual History" and provides a
thorough review of much of the critical literature on the subject. I hasten to add
that despite the intriguing and seemingly congruent title, Nolan's study is a strict
neo-Singletonian reading.

2. See the opening chapter in Harrison, "Critical Differences," which seeks to
break out of the Singletonian mold and tradition, although in the direct refutation,
of course, lies the trap of the paradigm. It is the paradigm, clearly, that explains the
proliferation of essays on the subject, and I suspect that it will remain regnant until
another strong reading—one that, like Singleton's *Essay,* dares to be written as if

mental, rather than merely one of emphasis or tone: to say that the story is about literature at the surface and that the conversion story is about a crucial change in an ideology of writing is apparently to situate the *Vita nuova* within a category of texts somewhat outside the bounds of conventional criticism. Indeed, this shift renders it highly accessible to the modern reader—precisely the opposite of what Singleton's reading does. The Christian conversion story, on the other hand, one in which an ideology of writing and literature is ancillary to the specific detail of Christian belief, is, as Singleton himself was the first to point out, profoundly distanced from us, from all readers since the Council of Trent, in fact, and remarkably difficult if not impossible to recapture (Singleton

---

there were a critical vacuum in *Vita nuova* scholarship—displaces it and becomes the reading to be refined and refuted, something that has yet to happen. Singleton's *Essay* was not, in fact, the first to suggest the kind of reading that we now credit Singleton with, nor was it even the earliest or most attractive nonphilological reading of this work: both Eliot and Pound had, as exemplary amateurs of Dante, strikingly important insights into the text, and I will explore these further below, both in this chapter and in chapter 3; Fletcher 1920 sketches out the major elements of a nonliteralist, allegorical reading which is dependent on the Augustinian structure of a spiritual autobiography, and explores the problems of truth values in theology versus poetry. (I note, additionally, that Fletcher is of particular value because it gives us a taste of the readings that precede him, including those of Grandgent, Vossler and others now forgotten or eclipsed. And it is not insignificant that Singleton's work on the *Vita nuova,* which first began to appear in 1945 and 1946 (the *Essay* itself is 1949), is carried out in what is essentially a dialogue with J. E. Shaw, whose 1929 *Essays on the "Vita nuova"* is the critical precursor in the essay genre, and who responds to Singleton 1945 and 1946 in his own pointed refutation in 1947. My own reading, elaborated in the remainder of this chapter, is no less dependent on many of the canonical constructs of the text: it will be apparent, for example, that virtually all points identified in the Singletonian *Essay* as critical elements of the theological/love conversion are the same points I identify, often for the identical reasons, with the literary conversion, and almost all the other secondary works I have mentioned have been critical to my own reading in identifying details of literary history embedded in the text, or instances of theoretical preoccupations in the *Vita nuova* I might not have seen myself.

1949, 3–5). However, Dante's story about arriving at strong—indeed, categorical—opinions about what is "right" and "wrong" in literature possesses a clearly transcendental importance and is readable within various historical constructs, including our own.[3]

In fact, Dante in the *Vita nuova* is unabashedly, shockingly concerned with texts and writing, with how one reads the text of life and then makes it literature. The work begins with the invocation of the *Libro della memoria* and the narrator's thus establishing himself as an author, a writer.[4] This explicit self-characterization, abundantly ratified through-

3. This discussion inevitably raises the thorny but central theoretical issue of the "historicity" of a given reading of a literary text. It is not clear to me how one would ever judge the degree to which one had succeeded in "recapturing" an "original" reading, and I believe the strength of Singleton's reading—and the reason for the canonical role it has enjoyed—resides primarily in its own coherence and in the fact that it seems to make a text that is otherwise puzzling, difficult, indeed inaccessible, as he notes, at a minimum a text that makes some semblance of sense, even if we are so far removed from it in terms of the theological detail that it remains essentially unsympathetic. It is a reading, however, which seems to me to be deficient in two closely intertwined ways: it shows little or no trace of, and does not account for, the very strong metaliterary concerns that are now indispensable elements of our readings—virtually any readings—of the Dante of the *Divine Comedy*. It is, in this reading, the sort of text that gives medieval literature a bad name: it becomes a literature which is undecipherable without specific keys, and the keys are, by and large, of no or little interest to anyone who does not share the same theological beliefs (and by "the same" here one means not just "Christianity" in the abstract but a precise, theologian's grasp of a number of issues on which the modern Christian is unlikely to have any opinion). It is, in sum, a reading that is persuasive because of its internal coherence (and which gives the *Vita nuova* itself a unitary coherence) and because one does, indeed, feel that Singleton has retrieved meaning long lost. It is thus rendered a peculiarly sterile text to serve as the annunciation of the *Commedia*—a *Commedia* which, despite its obvious theological underpinnings, is far from inaccessible to the modern reader in the same way.

4. Singleton's famous and widely accepted naming of him as a "scribe" who *at times* is a glossator is problematic on the face of it, because he must be at times one and at times the other. I see no reason why the narrator cannot be more simply named an author (or writer or poet), for to work with another book, another text,

out the work, is sealed at the end of the work, when the author-narrator reveals his future plans and tells us what he will write in the future—a future which is postconversionary, of course, because he learned how to read a certain language. One of the major effects of the prose-poetry format of the *Vita nuova* is the continual affirmation, with each poem "transcribed" from the old text to the new, that the protagonist is, of course, a Poet. The story of the Poet rises most consistently to the surface, presented without allegorical or symbolic intermediary. As Ezra Pound says, emerging from the critical/philological constraints of 1910 (not far different from our own in many ways), "Saving the grace of a greatly honored scholar, to speak of the *Vita Nuova* as 'embroidered with conceits' is errant nonsense. The *Vita Nuova* is strangely unadorned. . . . It is without strange, strained similes. . . . The 'Lord of the terrible aspect' is no abstraction, no figure of speech. There are those who can not or will not understand these things" (Pound [1910] 1952: 126).

Indeed, to believe in the literal truth of the literary story of the *Vita nuova* is, first of all, to begin to account for the otherwise unaccountably strange power of the story; it is rendered readable, what some might call "relevant" (if the latter had not become, in recent years, a term of opprobrium among so many), not just to the modern critic and reader but, crucially, to other writers, writers who, after Dante, struggled with his very deeply seated and in many ways very rigid views on the proper nature and function of poetry and literature. While the import of the

---

is in no way limited to scribes and glossers but is what all authors do, at all times. Clearly, this implies putting aside, rather than foregrounding, the more strictly medieval function of a glossator; but on the other hand, one could argue that this is precisely what Dante himself is urging on his readers, as I will suggest below. To understand the principal character in the story as a writer also resolves the problem of the times at which the "scribe" is "faithfully copying" (how in the world can we know?) versus the times he is, as "glossator," providing commentary that is, in many cases, in fact the supplying of privileged information—privileged because, indeed, the narrator is the author character. For a lucid discussion of the issue of the inconsistency of the "glossator" paradigm, see Stillinger 1988, a work whose analysis of the *Vita nuova* hinges on the *divisioni,* and which I will comment on below in my own consideration of these key sections of the narration.

specifics of an individual's faith may indeed, as Singleton recognized, dissolve into history, a strong poet's vision of poetry is never impenetrable or insignificant, even in its detail. In this text, then, as much as at the heart of the *Commedia*, Dante is a literary historian and theoretician; but here, in this more primitive story of his conversion, we have a starkly kabbalistic story as well, one in which the poet stands far less adorned, naked, vulnerable. The young artist has bared his soul and told us of his massive disappointments—his failures, really—and how he turns things around. As has been recently pointed out, Dantology has been a slave to Dante himself, a Dante who has convinced us, through the most remarkable rhetoric, of what his texts are about—and in this case, the authorially guided emphasis on the positive future has indeed obscured how much death and a dead past are the obsessions of a text thus deceptively entitled. In this, as in much else, Dante is a kabbalist, reading and interpreting "with excessive audacity and extravagance" (Bloom 1975: 125–26). What is at stake everywhere in the *Vita nuova* is the Book, its reading and its rewriting, and, of course, it is Beatrice's death that constitutes the indispensable heart of the conversion (and this is equally true whether we read it as principally poetic, theological or amorous). Above all, the *Vita nuova,* the story so charmingly called the "New Life," is in fact the story of the death—the purposeful and necessary death—for Dante of the old ways of reading and writing, the old kind of Literature, that had proved so disappointing.

I I I

The momentous break that marks the beginning of lyric poetry in the European vernaculars has been an obsessive fascination for critics since Dante himself first made it a legitimate object of study in his *De vulgari eloquentia.* It is one of a number of literary-historical subjects about which the braggart claim can be made that more has been written about it than about any other. Of the many entangled issues in this domain, I wish to single out the two major metaliterary ones that seem to me to have been of greatest concern to Dante the author of the *Vita nuova:* the issue of the "new life" or new beginning for poetry that is so starkly raised by the conspicuous establishment of the vernaculars of eleventh- and twelfth-century Europe as a new beginning in literary cycles, and the deeply solipsistic nature of that newly minted poetry itself.

One can, paradoxically, dispense with any extended review of the "origins" debate(s), for when and where the story of lyric poetry in the European vernaculars "actually" begins (a matter, of course, of some considerable dispute) is not nearly so important in this discussion as the fact that it does have a discernable beginning, that it is and was perceived as a major rupture vis-à-vis its "classical" antecedents. Indeed, whatever the provocations and contingencies at its beginning, the dénouement of the story invariably includes the remarkable invention that did indeed take place as part of the cluster of innovations conveniently tagged as "twelfth century": the vernaculars were born and prospered as literary languages, as the prime matter of a literature perceived (then, as well as now) as "new." It is difficult to overestimate the importance, difficulty, and implications of such an event, and it is supremely important to remember that, unlike the biological analogy that gives rise to the "birth" metaphor, a death is the implacable contingency of such creation: the displacement and substitution of a new language almost invariably constitutes, despite the wishes of many, the death of the one being replaced. Even more dramatically and with greater pain, of course, a number of paternal figures are supplanted by others. Dante, of course, was not only fully aware of these issues but both disturbed and fascinated by them: even his discussion of Latin as never having been a natural language at all but rather a *koine,* an artificial construct, smacks of self-justification, the defense against some unheard but deeply sensed reproach. His discussion of the inevitable evolution of natural and living languages, as opposed to those that are dead in their immutability—and the embarrassing but lurking hint that the same may hold for the poetry of such languages—leaves in no doubt his sensitivity to the issues of transitions and replacements that are both birth *and* death.[5]

5. Ironically, perhaps, the classicization of a language—i.e., the fixing of a

Thus, the specific historical conditions of the rupture are by and large irrelevant here. Almost any of the models that have been proposed for such origins share the characteristics that are critical for the perspective necessary for this reading of the *Vita nuova:* a linguistic rupture that involves the canonization of a language previously spoken but not canonized, and the concomitant invention of poetic norms for a complex written poetry springing, in different measures and ways, from

---

language such as Latin as an essentially unchanging entity—is a very distinct form of language death, although the language does not necessarily disappear, at least not immediately. In the *De vulgari,* Dante classifies Latin as an "artificial" language, a concept not far removed from (although considerably more delicate than) that of death; they are in comparable juxtaposition to the ever-shifting qualities of a vernacular, which is, by the fact that it does constantly evolve, a living language. Dante's observation about the artificiality of Latin has been of great interest to linguists, particularly in recent years when the very nature of "Latin" has been scrupulously questioned and largely redefined to the point where Dante's notion, once discarded as fanciful, can now be regarded as far more adequate a representation than the one that used to be commonly held, i.e., that the written literary language was, in some living and functional way, the normal spoken language of the Roman Republic and Empire. In the context of the *Vita nuova,* however, it is perhaps a key observation to remember, for it is, of course, Latin that Love speaks, at least some of the time—a fact that has led some critics to dismiss Singleton's valid assertion that he (Love) is a "troubadour." Singleton says that the Latin is meant to signify that his pronouncements are oracular, but at the same time, the Latin is perhaps meant to indicate the artificiality and inaccessibility of much troubadour poetry, poetry that had, paradoxically (and certainly ironically, from Dante's perspective), broken away from a dead Latin and was written in a "vernacular"—a *koine,* of course, one to which he thought literary Latin had, in fact, been comparable. But, clearly, the major thrust in the context of the *Vita nuova* is not the oracularity of the earlier poetry per se, but rather its unintelligibility (the two often being confused) and obscurity or hermeticism. It is this hermeticism, coupled with explicit falsehood (the gist of the second appearance of Love, where he is mediating for the different false lovers), that is finally repudiated in Love's third appearance: Dante accusingly and despairingly asks him point-blank why he speaks so obscurely, and Love, finally, replies in Italian. For more extended discussions see Singleton 1945 and 1946, Shaw 1947, and, more recently, Brownlee 1984.

both an oral tradition (the spoken and probably sung vernacular languages and songs) and a written tradition or traditions. Dante's descriptive metaphors of heritage are unambiguous: the mother's language (her lullabies and love songs alike, those models of sung and unwritten literature) is being elevated to the status of what is otherwise the father's, and the father's, the classical, is then, of course, replaced as the model by the child's, by this "new" language of poetry.[6] Of course, there is an important paradox in all of this: the establishment of this new form, when it is sufficiently entrenched to be considered canonical (as was certainly the case soon enough with both Provençal and Mozarabic lyrics, for example), itself becomes a new norm, a new canon, a new father figure to be either followed or replaced. Thus, a Dante acutely aware of the literary history of which he is a product (and out of which, in many ways, he is trying to write himself) has not one but two major ancestral historical forms that have given him birth as a poet: firstly, the classical, since he is still, of course, a reader of that tradition; and secondly, and no less critically, those first several centuries of the vernacular or "troubadour" writings which, by the turn of the fourteenth century, are themselves quite legitimately a tradition. Historical foreshortening should not obscure the fact that the latter was in its own right no less oppressively canonical for a writer like Dante. Dante, then, stands at what may be a unique kind of crossroads in terms of poetic ancestry: because he is still remarkably close to the Latin tradition, certainly enough so that it is a fundamental part of his linguistic and poetic upbringing, it has paternal authority and will constitute, when he writes in Italian, a model he is rejecting. But—and this is the peculiarity and perhaps the paradox—he has imbibed a considerable and powerful

6. It is, at a minimum, a revelatory coincidence that in the genesis and articulation of the Hispano-Arabic poetry (which some believe is an important model for the other new Romance poetries), the poetic voice in Classical Arabic is male, the vernacular (Romance) voice is female (and taken, explicitly, from the oral tradition), and the whole is, precisely because of the admixture of poetic types, a radically new hybrid that challenges the canonical standards that had previously excluded the vernacular voice altogether.

vernacular tradition as well (certainly the *De vulgari* is an homage, among other things, to that part of his ancestry), one which was itself eminently canonical and well established, in many crucial ways decaying and at an end, dead in the death of static and artificiality, by the time Dante began his writing career. Thus, although the extant vernacular tradition also defined itself, in great measure, as breaking from that same classical patronage, it too was a past for Dante; it too has been indispensable in his creation, and it too, inevitably, must be left behind.

If Dante embraces the first of the two salient characteristics of the troubadours, the substitution and recreation of a new poetic language deriving from the maternal tongue, ultimately he is deeply troubled by its second distinguishing feature, by what we insist on calling "courtly love" but is far more advantageously described as poetic solipsism. Dispensing, once again, with the seemingly interminable discussions of many often irrelevant ancillary aspects of the "courtly love" debate, and focusing on those readings that coincide with Dante's own interpretations of his antecedents, one can indulge in the simple assertion that the greatest obsession of troubadour poetry is itself. The poetry appears, on the first level, to be about an inaccessible love object; but when one apprehends, as most poets have, that the love is inaccessible because only then can the poetry be generated, then the true, the consummated objects of love are revealed: language itself and the music and poetry that are its receptacles. Given the historical nature of the dramatic linguistic break that is being executed and the new language that is being forged and molded as one goes along, it is scarcely surprising—perhaps even inevitable—that the creator will be more intrigued by his own creation than even normally. The circular and solipsistic (and some would eventually say sterile and pristine) nature of the poetic ideology is striking: since the generation and writing of the poem itself depends on lack of fulfillment, only an unfulfilled love can exist within the borders of this poetry—since poetry itself is the real desired object. The circle is a tightly closed one (as Zumthor has so well pointed out), the poetry often starkly hermetic, the love perforce a dead end, "sans issu," as the *Tristan* poet will tell us, and the ultimate adoration is of the lyrical form per se, of this poetic language quite literally in the making. While these features are abundantly clear from the earliest Provençal examples (one need only remember Guillaume's "Farai un vers de dreyt rien" [I will make a poem from absolutely nothing]), the phenomenon reaches its peak and glory in what is called, appropriately and in full recognition of the tight hermetic circle, the *trobar clus,* perhaps best rendered as *"self-enclosed poetry."* The master craftsman here is, of course, Arnaut Daniel, who, among other things, appears to have invented what is certainly one of the most difficult of lyrical forms, the *sestina.* The essence of Arnaut's accomplishment is best conveyed by the high priest of his cult in the modern period, Ezra Pound, who first learned about him in his truncated studies in Romance philology at the University of Pennsylvania, but who, shortly after abandoning that formal academic training, expended considerable independent effort on the translation of most of Arnaut's eighteen known extant songs, writing in 1918, "I have completely rewritten, or nearly finished completely rewriting all Arnaut Daniel" (quoted in Wilhelm 1982:64). Two years later Pound published his essay of admiration on "il miglior fabbro," delighting there in Arnaut's two salient characteristics: the stunning musicality of his verses and their hermeticism. Pound's translations, which are not, in fact, as complete as he had claimed, in turn also feast on these qualities of Arnaut's poetry (the very qualities which make him so perfect an exemplar, because of the high pitch of focus and the distillation—some might say exaggeration—of obsession with self and lyricism), and Pound's renditions are sparkling mosaics of almost meaningless beautiful sounds. As one critic of those translations has put it: "One winds up with the opposite of a literal trot: a free rendering that corresponds more with the original in terms of sound than in sense of imagery."[7]

7. Wilhelm 1982: 119. The essay "Il miglior fabbro" is part of Pound's famous and often-quoted *The Spirit of Romance,* which is Pound's version, in the throes of a heady rebellion against the academic philological tradition recently abandoned, of the birth-from-death history of the Romance literary tradition. Although it is probably almost never used in that way, Pound's text is nothing less than a new literary history to correspond to (and supplant) those from the formidable, no-nonsense Germanic tradition of *romanische Philologie* he had no doubt been fed as a budding philologist at Penn.

That, then, distilled through the later, far more iconoclastic philolo-
gist-become-poet, is the ancestor whom Dante too would hold up, in
the considerably different, retrospective light of the *Purgatorio,* as exem-
plary of the tradition that had preceded him and molded him, although,
crucially, the *tone* of Dante's apparent praise has not been much listened
to—a problem I will return to in a later chapter. But no matter, for the
time being: Dante's high estimation of Arnaut's craftsmanship and of the
essential apprenticeship provided by the full range of the vernacular
traditions is everywhere apparent. The *De vulgari,* certainly, makes it
abundantly clear that the Provençal corpus, and the Sicilian one closely
linked to it, constitute explicit role models, and from the opening pages
of the *Vita nuova* there is no doubt that a crucial part of the story told is
that the young Dante Alighieri has apprenticed himself to the rich (and
by then venerable, over two centuries old) traditions of the highly self-
reflective love lyrics of the Romance vernaculars. His own earliest
efforts are so unmistakably (and self-consciously) a part of that tradition
that they include, among other things, *sestine* to equal Arnaut's own best
examples of the *trobar clus.* But the young artist ends up being far from
satisfied with the poetics of predecessors who were once attractive, in
part, because they stood as revolutionaries with respect to their ances-
tors (who were Dante's own, at the same time), predecessors who
taught him, quite literally, how to write in the *parlar materno,* the mother
tongue. His conversion from their poetics to his own thus becomes the
meticulously chronicled story of the *Vita nuova;* this follows the arche-
typical structures of autobiographies in beginning at the end of the story,
a story which is that of how the author came to be able to understand
what he had already written and then go on to write his new kind of
literature—that literature of the New Life.[8]

8. Here lies, I sense, one of the crucial differences between my own reading of
this central aspect of the text and others', rooted, once again, in my acceptance of
the implied truths of the literary story line. Barolini, for example, in a number of
ways the most sophisticated of critics to deal with the issue of the historical layers
of writing present in the text, writes: "The lyrics thus chosen undergo not only a
passive revision in the process of being selected for inclusion, but also an active
revision at the hand of the prose narrative, which bends them into a new

The confusion here, in part, is that of the occasional doubling between historical author and the author who is the poet of the story of the *Vita nuova*. The role played out by the protagonist is that of authorship itself, and this conflation, a making explicit of what is always implicit, is part of Dante's kabbalistic enterprise: what is written is literally true and precedes any other reality. Among other things, that mysterious book from which the author Dante is taking his text is very much the kabbalistic text of reality. As in the *Commedia,* there is a tension between author and protagonist, the younger author, which is parallel to the tension between poet and pilgrim in the later text. After all, one is bent on usurping the other, quite literally taking his place, and the

---

significance consonant with the poet's 'new life.' The violations of original inten-
tion that occur result in certain narrative reversals; poems written for other ladies
in other contexts are now perceived as written for Beatrice . . ." (1984:15). In a
comparable tone, Holloway describes the procedure as: "In the *Vita nuova* Dante is
deconstructing his own earlier poetry, finding deeper layers of meaning to it than
he at first suspected were there . . . like some manuscript palimpsest" (105). In
these cases, as in many others far less noteworthy, there is a reluctance to believe in
(or at least voice belief in) Dante's naked statements of poetic revelation that made
him realize that, to take the critical example at hand, poems he thought he had
written for other women turn out, in fact, to have been (unsuspectingly) written
for Beatrice. Words and phrases such as "revisions," "bends," "violations of
original intention," "deconstruct," and "palimpsest" all work to distance the
modern critic from the very issue of belief in the Truth of revelation vis-à-vis
literature itself that Dante is focused on. The problem with this kind of distancing
is that it effectively denies the possibility of sincerity on the part of Dante (he
didn't "really" believe those poems were magically or mystically or kabbalistically
prewritten for Beatrice, he just cleverly constructed a text that says that because
that is an allegory for something else)—and perhaps it is in part the result of the
notion that in the acknowledgement and articulation of sincerity the critic would
be suspected of holding the same belief herself. It is also interesting that while a
critic may safely proclaim and document an author's belief in a canonical religious
Truth (no one, I'm sure, has ever thought twice about whether Charles Singleton
believed in the Christ himself), the language of both Barolini and Holloway
illustrates the typical critical aversion to Dante's statements about the Truth of a
literary revelation within which the real meaning of a text is never clear until the
reality it describes has been played out and consummated.

reader too suffers at least some of the anxieties and fears that naturally attend to such mergers of personalities within the self as we follow the not always gradual merger—at times a death struggle—between the two.[9] At the end, after an apparently full assimilation of the implications of the conversion, we have the new author as he sits down to—in this case—rewrite, copy, recount, the story of how the old life came to be the New Life—all, of course, inevitably, from the light of the New Life which has recast the meanings and intentions of what was read and written in the old. All, of course, rooted in the death of the old. Freccero, in words about the *Commedia* which are no less applicable to the *Vita nuova,* notes that "the paradoxical logic of all such narratives is that the beginning and end must logically coincide in order for the author and his persona to be the same" (Freccero 1986a: 263). In the case of the *Vita nuova* it is critical to note that the coincidence or convergence that unifies the beginning and end of the text is, furthermore, a congruence of emphasis on the process of writing: the first chapter gives us the author sitting down with a "book of memory" at hand and about to give the reader what we may best call a version of that text, and the last chapter ends with an invocation of a text to come, the text that is the logical and necessary result of the conversion just recounted—as it turns out, the *Commedia.*[10] And in the *Vita nuova,* it is

9. The problem of the multiple Dantes in this text is most charmingly described as "a small crowd" by Stillinger (55, n.31), and in the expression lies a significant insight: which voice is speaking from out of the crowd is, at times, not at all a sure thing.

10. It is perfectly just that the temporal authenticity of the extant text of the *Vita nuova* has always been a matter of (seemingly unresolvable) contention. See Harrison's final (fittingly, of course) chapter, "Vision and Revision," for a detailed discussion of the problem of the "original" ending of the *Vita nuova*—briefly, whether the text does originally end with the famous final lines announcing a new work devoted to Beatrice, or whether these are instead a *rifacimento,* a "touch-up" written some dozen years later. In the *rifacimento* view of the text, the original *Vita nuova* ends with Dante finding consolation for his grief from Beatrice's death in philosophy, allegorized in the *Donna gentile.* But this was an ending that had to be revised when Dante in fact found philosophy an inadequate consolation, aban-

worth repeating, the persona of the author, most markedly at the points of resolution and convergence, is the Poet. The conversion which is the fulcrum of change involves the movement, at least in theory a radical one, from poetry that serves itself primarily and a solipsistic love in the process, poetry as music and verbal hermeticism, in other words, to a poetry whose meaning and unequivocal truth exists *a priori* outside itself and its own frame of reference, a poetry preinscribed in the cosmos. The poet in this new universe is not the creator but the agent of revelation, at times even unknowingly so: the meaning of magic and sequences and visions may not be known until a startling revelation makes it transparent. This, of course, is exactly what is indicated in the recounting of the *Vita nuova*'s seemingly impenetrable first dream and in the author's annoying denial of an explanation for his puzzled readers, saying: "Lo verace giudicio del detto sogno non fue veduto allora per alcuno, ma ora è manifestissimo a li più semplici" (The true meaning of the dream I described was not perceived by anyone then, but now it is completely clear even to the least sophisticated [chapter 3]).[11] This is, from certain necessary perspectives, the story of a Platonic conversion: the harnessing of the primitive power of music—Poetry—to serve the needs of a kind of reason—Truth. But this is thus a species of reason that would be easily dismissed by almost any Platonist, for it is a reason which reflects

---

doned the *Convivio,* and turned to the *Commedia.* In fact, as Harrison notes, we do not have to decide (on the philological plane of pseudoscientific discourse) on the issue of *rifacimento* itself, only on its possibility—and, of course, one could practically describe the *Vita nuova* as being about *rifacimento:* "Revision remains a fundamental and always already operative principle. . . . The possibility of a later revision . . . remains plausible because of the revisionary agenda that sustains the work. . . . And what does the 'story' dramatize if not a series of corrections and revisions in the poet's search for adequate idiom?" (150). Again, I sense a difficulty of belief in critical language such as "the poet's search for adequate idiom," which seems to render both rational and linear a process which in the *Vita nuova* is both visionary and kabbalistic—but clearly Harrison's analysis of the thematic congruity of the *rifacimento* is very much congruent with my own reading.

11. All quotations from the *Vita nuova* are from Chiappelli, ed., and from the English version of Musa. Hereafter they will be referred to by chapters only.

not only transcendental Truths—which may or may not be true in an
Aristotelian paradigm—but which is grounded in a shocking belief in
the necessary truth of textuality itself and in the synchronicity that more
traditional rationalists squirm away from uneasily.[12]

I V

The major dramatic turn of events, what can be fairly described
as the literary conversion, in the Vita nuova is drawn out over nine
chapters, from 19 to 28, thus beginning just before the midpoint of this
text of forty-two chapters.[13] The first two of these contain two of the
poems generally described as "stilnovistic," "Donne che avete intelletto
d'amore" and "Amor e 'l cor gentil son una cosa," and even if we had no
other indicators, we might well suspect we are on the threshold here of
an important shift or event, because these are the poems in which
Dante's immediate poet-ancestors most starkly reverberate. If the
poems, as well as the actions narrated, of the first eighteen chapters are

12. Even Jung finally squirmed away and was uncomfortable with the discrep-
ancy between apparent versus provable truths, especially with the issue of causal-
ity; for the latter problem, see Popp, forthcoming. Still, his lucid expository
statements would not have made Dante uncomfortable: "No reciprocal causal
connection can be shown to obtain between parallel events, which is just what
gives them their chance character. The only recognizable and demonstrable link
between them is a *common meaning,* or equivalence. The old theory of correspon-
dence was based on the experience of such connections—a theory that reached its
culminating point and also its provisional end in Leibniz's idea of *pre-established
harmony.* Synchronicity is a modern differentiation of the obsolete concept of
correspondence, sympathy and harmony. It is based not on philosophical assumptions
but on empirical evidence and experimentation" (emphasis mine). "On Syn-
chronicity," 518, quoted here from the edition in *The Portable Jung,* ed. Joseph
Campbell.
13. See Harrison, 7–9, for a critique and reevaluation of the Singletonian
reading that places Beatrice's death at the mathematical center of the text. My own
interest is not in any external mathematical correspondence (i.e., in number
symbolism or numerology) but rather in the synchronistic correspondences, which
derive their coherence principally from internal correspondence.

reflexes of the earlier "courtly" traditions of Provence and Sicily, these two poems, following both chronology and taste, approach Dante himself: they are kissing cousins to and resonances of the poet's contemporaries and near-contemporaries, Guinizelli and especially the powerful and enigmatic Cavalcanti, to whom the *Vita nuova* is dedicated and who is called here the "primo amico." In the chronology of a poetic autobiography, then, the alert reader would anticipate a threshold: narrator and protagonist must soon merge, since the last of the poetic antecedents, those still lurking about in the authorial present, are rapidly falling behind.

But from a narrative, structural point of view the text is still at this point adhering to the initially established (preconversion) format. One must pause here to consider carefully the peculiar structure of this text: "Everyone knows" that the *Vita nuova* is a prose-poetry text—and it is then described as either a hybrid or a *sui generis*. But far fewer seem to have noticed that what is of utmost importance is the variable nature of the prose-poetry relationship, the shifting relationship of three different voices vis-à-vis each other that is of interest, since in fact a major formal conversion will occur in this central cluster of chapters as well. The first part of the text is composed so that those chapters that contain poems (not all of them do, of course) include two very different prose voices which frame the lyric voice between them. There is the initial narrator, who has been telling us the story all along and is the generally unchallenged voice in the structurally simpler chapters that contain no poetry. This is the voice which is the autobiographical "I," necessarily already knowing the outcome but attempting to narrate the events "innocently" as he goes along, with a sense of fidelity to his preinscribed text. (This narrator appears also to have an often acute sense of the reader's expectations of suspense and dramatic outcome from something that has been marked off in the preexisting text and announced as the point at which a new life began.) This Dante narrates the events which, in these chapters at least, occasion or inspire a poem, introduced at the end of that chapter's events and following immediately thereafter. And these poems are—and here lies, finally, some considerable strangeness—in turn followed by a brief and usually completely straightfor-

ward and formal description of the poem itself, that poem that has just
been presented. This second prose section of the chapter is normally
called a *divisione*.[14]

Thus, in the first movement of the text, roughly its first half, in each
chapter that presents a poem (or more than one poem, as is the case in
some chapters), there are three formally distinct presentations of what
might be crudely described as the "same material": a prose narration of
"what happened"; the poem(s) that formed the lyrical reaction to the
event(s); and finally, and most mysteriously for almost all critics, a
pseudoscientific and remarkably banal explication of the poem's struc-

14. Almost all studies of the *Vita nuova,* including the major ones discussed in
the preceding notes, include at least some attention to the structural properties of
the work, including the disposition of narrative prose, framed lyric, and *divisioni.*
Other studies that focus more specifically on this aspect of the work include
Hollander 1974 (with a characteristically exhaustive bibliography) and D'Andrea,
which sees scholastic commentaries as the source of the *divisioni.* See also Barolini
1989, where the structure of the *Vita nuova* is explored in terms of that of
Petrarch's *Canzoniere.* Pipa makes the unusual revisionist argument, based on a
strongly politicohistorical reading of the work, that the heart of the *Vita nuova* is
not the poetry but the prose, which is read in part as political allegory. Most
recently, the Stillinger dissertation includes a lengthy and lucid chapter devoted to
the formal structures of the work, a formal structure which is "governed through-
out by divergent formal principles" (61) and within which ever-variable *divisioni*
play different kinds of roles. Although in great measure this work (which only
came to my attention when this book was in its final stages of preparation) is quite
different from my own in approach and conclusions, at least one aspect of
Stillinger's reading of the *Vita nuova* seems to me to be harmonious with my own:
he believes that the relationship between poetry and narrative prose in the text
may be understood according to the text's own internal model, i.e., the poetry is
Beatrice, the narrative prose is Dante. As he notes, this model is appealing because
"it is satisfyingly concrete. It is strange, too, in a way that I think is faithful to the
spirit of the *Vita nuova.* . . . My own similitude might be expressed with similar
cryptic boldness: in the *Vita nuova,* the prose is Dante and the poetry is Beatrice"
(70). I differ from Stillinger here, however, in that he identifies what seems to me
the unflinching equation of the literal truth of textuality and being of the "Beatrice
is a nine" revelation as a part of "sweeping[ly] analogical thought" and a "person-
ification of abstract thought."

ture and "divisions" (i.e., its formal fundamental formal characteristics—that is why these blurbs are called *divisioni,* of course). In the invariable order of these three components, this last is a miniature and accurate, but essentially quite primitive, *explication de texte.* The first problem in knowing just what to make of these little expositions of the poems that precede them is their transparent limitations: they rarely go beyond telling the reader what he can see for himself (even "li più semplici," as Dante would have it). Traditional criticism has scarcely gone beyond pointing out the conspicuous similarity these *divisioni* bear to mechanical scholastic procedure—and Boccaccio, as editor of the *Vita nuova,* acts out this reading by shifting these highly formal and starkly positivistic glosses to the margins.[15] But there is a no less puzzling feature, one that seems largely to have gone by the wayside in most readings: these unadorned little expositions, beginning about halfway through the text, are either eliminated altogether or are fully integrated into the quite different voice of narration that *precedes* the poem. The text's second movement is thus substantially altered, structurally and tonally, from its first: after chapter 27, in which the *canzone* stands starkly alone, without any *divisione,* each chapter that houses a poem finishes with that poem—and the voice of mock Scholasticism, that droning voice of the self-evident gloss, the simple student at his rote best, is either gone altogether or transformed, absorbed into the "crowd of Dantes" of the storyteller. But I am getting ahead of the story here.

In chapters 19 and 20 we are still playing by the old rules: Dante has given us his remarkable "philosophical" or *stilnovista* poems and the reader is still given a *divisione* after each. The subsequent chapter, 21, exists almost exclusively to give us yet a third sonnet in what would be called the "sweet new style" in the retrospective clarity of the *Purgatorio,* and it too is followed by an exposition of its outward form. But the action of the story starts to pick up again in chapter 22 when Beatrice's father dies, a prefiguration of the more significant death that is to follow. If, however, Beatrice alive is in part an emblem of the old poetry, then her father's death is much more than mere foreshadowing of her own,

15. See Stillinger, especially 83–113, for a full and provocative discussion.

since the death of the old poetry's father is a literalization of transparent significance. In chapter 23, Dante dreams that Beatrice herself has died, and once again there are at least two layers of textual truth that mark events: the "annunciation" of what is "really" to happen and the literalization of the dream itself, the synchronicity playing itself out. And, in a relentless accumulation of images destroying the past, Dante's multiple literary pasts, there is yet another death—or, more appropriately, a disappearance—in chapter 24, in which we see for the last time the figure of Love.

Love had played a significant role in the first half of the book, the literally personified metaphor for Love as a separate entity and persona.[16] His fourth and last appearance here is both spectral and ex-

16. Love has appeared four times in the *Vita nuova,* in chapters that, retrospectively, have alluded to the harmony with Beatrice's own "nineness":3, 9, 12, 24 [1,3,4,6]. In his first three appearances, all of which, of course, precede the conversion, Love is explicitly and emphatically the protagonist's master—the young writer, the poet, is portrayed by the older and wiser author, the narrator, as having been pathetically at Love's mercy. Provisionally, it is also worth noting that this Love first appears in chapter three (and, of course, at synchronistically appropriate hours) and is thus the provocation not only for Dante's first poem (a love poem, of course) but also for his establishment of a relationship with Cavalcanti and other poets which, within the parameters of the story we are told, consists exclusively of exchanges of poems and opinions on the same. That first poem is that "recounting" or lyrical version of the vision in which Love has held Beatrice in his arms, held her flaming heart in his hand, forced her, apparently against her will, to eat it, and then dissolved in tears before disappearing, with Beatrice still in his arms, into the heavens. The confusing (and one might add, confused) dream, lyricized, is sent out for reactions from other poets, to no avail— and it is then that Dante, who clearly wishes to prolong the reader's confusion, ends the chapter with the maddening, "The true meaning of the dream I described was not perceived by anyone then, but now it is completely clear even to the least sophisticated," quoted above, and this persistently enigmatic dream will be discussed further below. It is nevertheless true that a considerable amount of ink has been spilled on the question of just exactly who this Love is, although I think the question is only a complicated or difficult one as long as one is assuming the issues at hand are theological rather than primarily poetic. See the extended discussions in Shaw, Singleton and Musa. Singleton's identification of him as the

plicitly intended to clarify that he is disappearing because there is no longer any need for him, no longer any call, in the development of the artist's poetic ideology, for this kind of poetic prop. The narrator tells us that Love himself clarifies his own insufficiency, and quotes him as saying: "E chi volesse sottilmente considerare, quella Beatrice chiamerebbe Amore per molta simiglianza che ha meco" (Anyone of subtle discernment would call Beatrice Love, because she so greatly resembles me [chapter 24]). It is of considerable significance that this revelation comes on the heels of Beatrice's first death, so to speak, for that is what one must make of Dante's first knowledge of her death in a dream. Beatrice herself is no longer that dying kind of love poetry any more, the kind that needed agents like Love, elaborate and mediated poetic imagery, to be meaningful. It is crucial to remember here that the older, the first, the now-vanishing Beatrice had such needs, and in that purposefully cryptic first dream, with that engaging but teasingly difficult sequence of the burning and then eaten heart, she had exhibited some awareness of the nature of her limitations, at least in life. It is perhaps at this point, and not at the end of chapter 3, when Dante taunts us with the "obviousness" of the meaning of that numerically critical dream, that we can speak with some modicum of assurance about what it might in fact have so "obviously" signified. But again I get ahead of the story, for the

---

"Troubadour god of Love" is certainly the closest, although the use of the word "god" here is problematic and ultimately probably misleading. If we do assume that in his retrospective on his period of poetic training Dante is dealing with literary issues and history principally, then the figure of Love personified that appears four times in the text is that poetic *conceit* of Love which, indeed, the troubadours canonized. It is a Love defined in such a way in the cumulative canon that it is, as we have noted above, highly solipsistic. Musa's argument that in Provençal poetry love is never personified misses the point: Dante, in some measure for the sake of an acting out of his conversion, personifies the earlier lyrical construct of love that emerges from the poetry from which he is himself evolving. Hollander 1974 also grapples with the issue: "One of the aesthetic and rational problems of the *Vita Nuova* is Dante's rather confusing treatment of Amore. It is a problem which he himself partly acknowledges in the brilliant if self-serving twenty-fifth chapter of the work"(6).

meaning of the dream is explicitly dependent on the revelations of the conversion.

Returning, then, to the dismissal of Love from the story, the reader is left to conclude that mediation and metaphor in poetry have flown out the window—and in case it was not clear from Love's dramatic last annunciation and bowing out of the scene, Dante devotes the following chapter, the liminal twenty-fifth, to a clear prose discussion of the nature and purposes of poetry. It is a passage which includes a round dismissal of his vernacular antecedents, saying, "E la cagione per che alquanti ebbero fama di sapere dire, è che quasi fuoro li primi che dissero in lingua di sì" (The reason why a few ungifted poets acquired the fame of knowing how to compose is that they were the first who wrote poetry in the Italian language [chapter 25]). Even more to the point, the chapter ends with the following succinct statement on what real poetry ought to be: "Però che grande vergogna sarebbe a colui che rimasse cose sotto vesta di figura o di colore rettorico, e poscia, domandato, non sapesse denudare le sue parole da cotale vesta, in guisa che avessero verace intendimento" (For, if anyone should dress his poem in images and rhetorical coloring and then, being asked to strip his poem of such dress in order to reveal its true meaning, would not be able to do so—this would be a veritable cause for shame [chapter 25]). Once again, one is compelled to remark on the extent to which the Dante of the *Vita nuova* is cultivating varieties of transparency; here, certainly, masking is not only dropped, it is denounced. (There is thus some irony in noting that so much criticism of the work has remained attached to the language of metaphor that is being banished from the "new life": in fact, the details of the "love story," paradoxically, start to fade and are increasingly subservient to the reflections on the nature of writing and literature that are at the core of this story of the "new life".) At this critical turning point we glimpse a Dante who has figured out the simplest solution to an impossibly complicated problem: how to limit and control the insufficiency and treachery of poetic language. The "solution" is, however, not an invention but a revelation, the kabbalistic insight that Truth is already there to be read and then rewritten—and it is only then that poetry can have any kind of exactitude of meaning, that it can say the Truth.

This revelation goes a very long way to explaining the meaning of the mysterious *divisioni* themselves, which, like the figure of Love, are no longer necessary in the new life. The last of the old-life *divisioni,* in fact, will appear in the next chapter, 26. (This, of course, is the number that will resonate strongly in the cantos of the *Purgatorio* devoted, once again explicitly, to poetic theory. It seems to me an exemplary case of the kind of synchronicity, as opposed to numerology, that Dante is involved with, for chapter 26 is important in the texts because of their internal harmony and correspondence, rather than because of any externally determined other "meaning.") The narrator tells us, from his perspective of knowing how it all came out and how it all fit together, things he could barely discern while he was living through them: Beatrice actually dies while Dante is writing the *canzone* that will stand alone in chapter 27—and we remember that in its transparency this becomes the first poem in the book not to have to be followed by a simple gloss, a poem that seems itself to reject the empty formal conceits of Scholasticism. Chapter 28, when Dante finds out about Beatrice's death in the original sequence of events, follows, and this is the last of the nine in this liminal and conversionary sequence. It is followed, appropriately, by the famous chapter that sets out the meaning of the number nine and concludes with the observation, rather precious for the modern reader, that Beatrice *is* a nine:

> Ma più sottilmente pensando, e secondo la infallibile veritade, questo numero fue ella medesima . . . questa donna fue accompagnata da questo numero del nove a dare ad intendere ch'ella era uno nove, cioè uno miracolo. . . . Forse ancora per più sottile persona si vederebbe in ciò più sottile ragione; ma questa è quella ch'io ne veggio, e che più mi piace.

> If anyone thinks more subtly and according to infallible truth, it will be clear that this number was she herself . . . then this lady was accompanied by the number nine so that it might be understood

that she was a nine, or a miracle. . . . Perhaps someone more subtle than I could find a still more subtle explanation, but this is the one which I see and which pleases me the most. (chapter 29)

It is thus that in this seemingly bizarre chapter we find what is perhaps the most direct, the most unabashed and naked presentation not only of "what Beatrice means to me" (to paraphrase Eliot's famous essay on Dante) but, far more importantly, of what Dante has become; he has become a simple reader of the simplest truths inscribed, pre-inscribed, in a universe that can make sense only when we can become such readers. Then, at that point of breakthrough, the sense is complete, almost too simple, for the good reader—he who is not subtle, who has discarded the mediations and the conceits of all those other poetics. Initially, in fact, Beatrice's death leaves the Dante trained in the classical traditions, that earlier poet, stunned and poetryless. As Mazzotta has noted, "Now that she is physically dead, the metaphors for her seem to be another empty fiction. If the question while Beatrice was alive was whether she is and how she is unique, now that she is dead the question is finding the sense of metaphors that recall her" (1986b:156). Once again, the problem can be reduced, at least initially, to one of the nature of expression chosen and the rejection of an expressive mode, a poetics, that was insufficient to deal with fundamental truths that are inscribed in texts we must first learn how to even read. What Mazzotta is calling rhetoric here I have called poetics, but the fact that they might indeed be taken for the same thing is exactly what Dante has in mind: the elimination of both or either as a category of expression separate or separable from other categories of truth and knowledge. There is a certain pathos, I think, in realizing that it is exactly when the poet's soul is most naked, when he reveals the most outrageous of truths, that his readers, at least in this century, have thrown the most elaborate of veils on his simple revelations. She *was* a nine, she *was* a miracle—no likes about it.

The differences, then, between the old life and the new life include the fact that poems in the new life, after the living Beatrice's death, need no *divisioni* or pseudoscientific explication, as did those in the old, now discarded days and poems once reigned over by an inaccessible love object, the living Beatrice, and a mediating Love figure. In those old days the author was just like all the other poets, in other words, all those in the tradition from which he came, a tradition within which, according to the *Vita nuova* (and as a follow-up of sorts to the *De vulgari*), poems need the prop of commentary in order to have any really unassailable "truth value"—those things that are measurable and provable such as the number of stanzas and the kind of rhyme and where the first part ends and the next begins. The old poetry adored that empty glossing of form, but in the aftermath of death and its revelations, in the aftermath of the conversion—and in some great measure that *is* the conversion— it is clear that for him who can read and then rewrite the universe the poems themselves have absolute truth value, they are stripped of the trappings that begged for that kind of commentary and made it neces- sary, and they are so simply and so clearly about transcendental other truths that they can and must stand by themselves. Beatrice *is* love. Poetry *is* truth. The old Beatrice is dead, and the new writer, forged by the pain of the failure of his first Beatrice, will now revel in the vision of a Beatrice who will need no Love as a figure to mediate between her and the absolute value of love itself. And just as she *is* a nine, as the newly converted Dante loses no time in telling us, so poetry, real and worth- while poetry, is as rationally true as what others call scientific language. Here, clearly, is the merger between the disparate components charac- terized in the preconversion part of the text by the three different and incomplete voices: the narrative, the lyric, and the commenting. These observations, of course, have been made by a number of critics vis-à-vis the *Commedia* and its development of the notion of the inseparability of theology and poetry, but the *Vita nuova*'s explicit turning to the primary truth of (certain kinds of) texts has been far less recognized, although, oddly enough, it is expressed with an embarrassing directness that has faded in the *Commedia* itself. Freccero's observation that, contrary to what Auerbach maintained, "the theological principles that seem to underlie Dante's formal pattern are themselves in turn derived from literary principles" (1986a: 269) is, if anything, even more applicable to the *Vita nuova,* where at the most literal level—which is the level now invested with absolute truth value—the writer and his literary texts are invariably primary. This, then, is a new life indeed, and in the last half of the book, in the chapters remaining after the banishment of the past, we see an author preparing for the full significance, only partially divined (for that is the very nature of such belief in the kabbala of writing), of his newfound faith and practice. This is succinctly put in the famous last paragraph, of course, as "io spero dicer di lei quello che mai non fue detto d'alcuna" (I hope to write of her that which has never been written of any other woman [chapter 42]). Here all the components come together in the terseness and incantatory repetition of a synchronistic text: the hope that the revelations will continue and that the writing, the saying of the truths of the universe that is the poetry, will flow from that.

V

Poi che fuoro passati tanti die, che appunto erano compiuti li nove anni appresso l'apparimento soprascritto di questa gentilissima, ne l'ultimo di questi die avvenne che questa mirabile donna apparve a me vestita di colore bianchissimo, in mezzo a due gentili donne, le quali erano di più lunga etade; e passando per una via, volse li occhi verso quella parte ov'io era molto pauroso, e per la sua ineffabile cortesia, la quale è oggi meritata nel grande secolo, mi salutoe molto virtuosamente, tanto che me parve allora vedere tutti li termini de la beatitudine. L'ora che lo suo dolcissimo salutare mi giunse, era fermamente nona di quello giorno; e però che quella fu la prima volta che le sue parole si mossero per venire a li miei orecchi, presi tanta dolcezza, che come inebriato mi partio da le genti, e ricorsi a lo solingo luogo d'una mia camera, e puosimi a pensare di questa cortessima. E pensando di lei, mi sopragiunse uno soave sonno, ne lo quale m'apparve una maravigliosa visione: che me parea vedere ne la mia camera una nebula di colore di fuoco, dentro a la quale io discernea una figura d'uno segnore di pauroso aspetto a chi la guardasse; e pareami con tanta letizia, quanto a sé, che mirabile cosa era; e ne le sue parole dicea molte cose, le quali io non intendea se non poche; tra le quali intendea queste: *Ego dominus tuus*. Ne le sue braccia mi parea vedere una persona dormire nuda, salvo che involta mi parea in uno drappo sanguigno leggeramente; la quale io riguardando molto intentivamente, conobbi ch'era la donna de la salute, la quale m'avea lo giorno dinanzi degnato di salutare. E ne l'una de le mani mi parea che questi tenesse una cosa la quale ardesse tutta, e pareami che mi dicesse queste parole: *Vide cor tuum*. E quando elli era stato alquanto, pareami che disvegliasse questa che dormia; e tanto si sforzava per suo ingegno, che le facea mangiare questa cosa che in mano li ardea, la quale ella mangiava dubitosamente. Appresso ciò poco dimorava che la sua letizia si convertia in amarissimo pianto; e così piangendo, si ricoglia questa donna ne le sue braccia, e con essa mi parea che si ne gisse verso lo cielo; onde io sostenea sì grande angoscia, che lo mio deboletto sonno non poteo sostenere, anzi si ruppe e fui disvegliato. E mantenente cominciai a pensare, e trovai che l'ora ne la quale m'era questa visione apparita, era la quarta de la notte stata; sì che appare manifestamente ch'ella fue la prima ora de le nove ultime ore de la notte. Pensando io a ciò che m'era apparuto, propuosi di farlo sentire a molti li quali erano famosi trovatori in quello tempo: e con ciò fosse cosa che io avesse già veduto per me medesimo l'arte del dire parole per rima, propuosi di fare uno sonetto, ne lo quale io salutasse tutti li fedeli d'Amore; e pregandoli che giudicassero la mia visione, scrissi a loro ciò che io avea nel mio sonno veduto. E cominciai allora questo sonetto, lo quale comincia: *A ciascun'alma presa*.

A ciascun'alma presa e gentil core
nel cui cospetto ven lo dir presente,
in ciò che mi rescrivan suo parvente,
salute in lor segnor, cioè Amore.
    Già eran quasi che atterzate l'ore
del tempo che onne stella n'è lucente,
quando m'apparve Amor subitamente,
cui essenza membrar mi dà orrore.
    Allegro mi sembrava Amor tenendo

meo core in mano, e ne le braccia avea
madonna involta in un drappo dormendo.
    Poi la svegliava, e d'esto core ardendo
lei paventosa umilmente pascea:
appresso gir lo ne vedea piangendo.

    Questo sonneto si divide in due parti; che ne la prima parte
saluto e domando risponsione, ne la seconda significo a che si dee
rispondere. La seconda parte comincia quivi: *Già eran.*
    A questo sonetto fue risposto da molti e di diverse sentenzie; tra
li quali fue risponditore quelli cui io chiamo primo de li miei amici,
e disse allora uno sonetto, lo quale comincia: *Vedeste, al mio parere,*
onne valore. E questo fue quasi lo principio de l'amistà tra lui e me,
quando elli seppe che io era quelli che li avea ciò mandato. Lo
verace giudicio del detto sogno non fue veduto allora per alcuno,
ma ora è manifestissimo a li più semplici.

    After so many days had passed that precisely nine years were
ending since the appearance, just described, of this most gracious
lady, it happened that on the last one of those days the miraculous
lady appeared, dressed in purest white, between two ladies of
noble bearing both older than she was; and passing along a certain
street, she turned her eyes to where I was standing faint-hearted
and, with that indescribable graciousness for which today she is
rewarded in the eternal life, she greeted me so miraculously that I
seemed at that moment to behold the entire range of possible bliss.
It was precisely the ninth hour of that day, three o'clock in the
afternoon, when her sweet greeting came to me. Since this was the
first time her words had ever been directed to me, I became so
ecstatic that, like a drunken man, I turned away from everyone
and I sought the loneliness of my room, where I began thinking of
this most gracious lady and, thinking of her, I fell into a sweet
sleep, and a marvelous vision appeared to me. I seemed to see a
cloud the color of fire and, in that cloud, a lordly man, frightening
to behold, yet he seemed also to be wondrously filled with joy. He

spoke and said many things of which I understood only a few; one was *Ego dominus tuus*. I seemed to see in his arms a sleeping figure, naked but lightly wrapped in a crimson cloth; looking intently at this figure, I recognized the lady of the greeting, the lady who earlier in the day had deigned to greet me. In one hand he seemed to be holding something that was all in flames, and it seemed to me that he said these words: *Vide cor tuum*. And after some time had passed, he seemed to awaken the one who slept, and he forced her cunningly to eat of that burning object in his hand; she ate of it timidly. A short time after this, his happiness gave way to bitterest weeping, and weeping he folded his arms around this lady, and together they seemed to ascend toward the heavens. At that point my drowsy sleep could not bear the anguish that I felt; it was broken and I awoke. At once I began to reflect, and I discovered that the hour at which that vision had appeared to me was the fourth hour of the night; that is, it was exactly the first of the last nine hours of the night. Thinking about what I had seen, I decided to make it known to many of the famous poets of that time. Since just recently I had taught myself the art of writing poetry, I decided to compose a sonnet addressed to all of Love's faithful subjects; and, requesting them to interpret my vision, I would write them what I had seen in my sleep. And then I began to write this sonnet, which begins: *To every captive soul.*

To every captive soul and loving heart
    to whom these words I have composed are sent
for your elucidation in reply,
greetings I bring for your sweet lord's sake, Love.
The first three hours, the hours of the time
of shining stars, were coming to an end,
when suddenly Love appeared before me
(to remember how he really was appalls me).

Joyous, Love seemed to me, holding my heart
    within his hand, and in his arms he had
    my lady, loosely wrapped in folds, asleep.

> He woke her then, and gently fed to her
> the burning heart; she ate it, terrified.
> And then I saw him disappear in tears.

This sonnet is divided into two parts. In the first part I extend greetings and ask for a response, while in the second I describe what it is that requires the response. The second part begins: *The first three hours.*

This sonnet was answered by many, who offered a variety of interpretations; among those who answered was the one I call my best friend, who responded with a sonnet beginning: *I think that you beheld all worth.* This exchange of sonnets marked the beginning of our friendship. The true meaning of the dream I described was not perceived by anyone then, but now it is completely clear even to the least sophisticated. (chapter 3)

If we follow Dante, and we have reached a certain level of clarity and vision, then, as he suggests tantalizingly, here and there throughout the work, certain things are now perfectly clear. First and foremost among the mysteries that ought to be clear now is that of the first dream, that garbled and vaguely terrifying vision that produced the first of the text's poems. Dante's almost taunting line about even the "simplest" of readers "now" (in the light of revelation) grasping it clearly still resonates— and a leery reader, a would-be interpreter remembers that none of the other poets appealed to at the time, not even the great Cavalcanti, got it right.[17] In fact, it is fair to say that it is a problem more often avoided

17. Very much in passing one must remember that the nature of the relationship with Cavalcanti is immensely complicated and exploring it fully here would constitute too great a detour. But several aspects of it are relevant to the perspective I am trying to establish for the *Vita nuova,* a text, incidentally, in which "il primo amico" plays an explicitly central role (as opposed to the *Commedia,* where it is Cavalcanti's absence that is explicit). The *Vita nuova,* however, is dedicated to Guido, who became his friend, we are told in chapter 3, *because* of the exchange of poems subsequent to that problematic first dream-cum-poem, and because, we are led to believe elsewhere, Guido is clearly a kindred soul poetically, in a number of ways; this is most noteworthy in the chapter on poetry, of course,

than not, despite its excruciating interpretative problem of the discrep-
ancy between the enduring opacity of the dream and the assertion that,
in a visionary light, it would become transparent. Certainly none of the
interpretations offered to date gives one that "bingo" smart of recogni-
tion that a dream's "transparent" decipherment should certainly pro-
voke, although the most recent meditation on it by Harrison is other-
wise satisfying in its richness and density, thus mimicking appreciatively
the text's and the dream's singular qualities.[18] But Dante's dismissive
little line invites us to call his bluff.

We must view the dream retrospectively, of course, realizing first and
foremost that the Love who is the mysterious protagonist in that first
dream has been utterly abandoned. That Love who once was verging on

---

where the dedication occurs. But even with Guido, perhaps especially with Guido,
Dante is in the process of distancing and establishing himself as different: the first
chapter, with its evocation of the *libro della memoria* is, as Mazzotta has noted, an
unequivocal echo of Cavalcanti's masterpiece, *Donna me prega,* a poem that estab-
lishes the imagelessness of love. "Guido's steady effort in the poem is to unsettle
any possible bonds between *poetic images and love,* or love and the order of the
rational soul" (Mazzotta 1986b:153, emphasis mine). Dante's poetic truth, of
course, will be radically different, and from this insightful reading we are drawn to
the conclusion that not only is what is at stake primarily the poetic articulation of
love, since it is the articulation which gives it meaning, but also that, as one might
have suspected, the overt praise of and association with Guido, his foremost rival
for poetic achievement and mastery, is one that is ultimately a difficult and
antagonistic one, fueled by the desire on Dante's part to distinguish clearly among
what seem to him clearly distinguishable alternatives in the realm of poetic
ideology.

18. For earlier "interpretations," many of which are mere restatements of
Dante's own assertions and/or the unconvincing (because it is so incomplete)
notion that it is a prediction of Beatrice's death, see DeBonfils Templer 1973 and
Harrison. The latter provides cogent and satisfactory insights into the dream itself
and the central issue of the discrepancy: "No one saw the "true meaning" of the
dream at the time. We may say, then, that a blind spot lurks at the heart of this
visionary experience. . . . While Dante suggests that time opens the vision's
meaning to full view, after some seven centuries we still are not able to see what he
had in mind when he declared as much" (21).

omnipotence for the struggling young poet, that tradition, as Singleton so aptly named it, has been banished from the scene, quite effectively killed off. In his second appearance, Love was the spokesman, a mediator, in fact, among several explicitly false "loves," the *donne schermo,* thus making his association with the older poetry as explicit as possible.[19] It was Love who wept once again in his third appearance, one in which he was explicitly aware of his imminent banishment: he weeps, as does any lover who knows he is about to be abandoned, but he is also gracious enough, in Dante's depiction, to urge a new sincerity in Dante's poetry—thus, of course, sealing his own doom and final departure in chapter 24, as we have already seen. But this Love, this conceit of a spiritually solipsistic tradition and often intensely hermetic poetry, is still at the peak of his powers in the third chapter, in the dream and its retelling, a sequence of events provoked by the drunken ecstasy of Beatrice's greeting. In fact, since in the story that is the moment at which the young artist, overcome by classic first love, will write his first poem, Love's power could be no stronger—he is the poetry revered and emulated by the virtually mad young man about to write his first poem. Madness was her greeting and its revision in his provocatively difficult dream.

The first "obvious" interpretation, then, is that the author's statement, made in the light of the most severe kind of disdain, is subtly ironic: what is obvious to him when he has buried the poetics of Love is precisely that the dream has no meaning—certainly no "clear" meaning. One can, of course, point to all sorts of the bits and pieces of the dream that are true and that are interpretable: the color symbolism, the mysterious Latin, the burning heart, and so forth. One can talk about

19. Klemp, in an elaborate argument, maintains that the function of the *donne schermo* is rooted in Dante's role as revisionist: first he leads us astray and then he helps us discover the truth (186). But at least in part the *schermo* function fairly traditionally and simply as part of the autobiographical and conversionary pattern, which requires confession and expiation of earlier sins, of the wrong path at first taken. Moreover, the most compelling point about the "screen ladies" is precisely that they are the false inventions for a false love poetry.

the young, misguided poet's heart being burned by Love and eaten by his Lady—i.e., step by step the original artist is destroyed by the trappings of his ancestors' poetry. One can, in fact, construct a number of more or less elaborate and more or less sophisticated interpretations of the dream—but none that is or would have been transparent and obvious, let alone to the most simple. The only thing that is transparent and obvious, especially to the simple, is that the vision *qua* vision—or *qua* prophetic dream—is a garbled one. Inevitably, the poem written to reflect the incoherent vision is able to be formally lovely without shedding any light, any meaning, on the puzzle of the dream vision. And in much of this there is little question that it derives from that fine troubadour tradition of self-referentiality and obsession with the poetry itself, beginning with the evocation of an audience that is (what else?) exclusively other poets. That the "message" of the poem, beyond the evident interest in poetry and its encoding and decoding, should be hermetic is the best possible "proof," I believe, of Singleton's claim that this Love is a troubadour, and that the lyrics of the preconversion *Vita nuova* are meant to be seen as examples and specimens of that parent with whom he had such a love-hate relationship. Finally, it is imperative to note that this is an incoherence that Dante as author is ascribing to a poetic history which he has clearly renounced for himself. What is it that we can always see so clearly at the end of the road? Our mistakes, of course, and the shallowness of so many a first love.

There can be little question, in the cruel light of that early morning, that dawn from which Dante is recounting his past, that his first love was, indeed, a failure. And since his persona, his character, was explicitly that of the artist as a young man, the Poet in the making, rather than independently or primarily a lover, then, crucially, it is not that the change in love drags with it a change in poetry, but rather that a change in attitude about what poetry is will necessarily entail writing about a different kind of love. The love written about and dictated by trou- badour poetry is what the young Poet is in the *Vita nuova:* self-serving, self-involved, self-pitying, unproductive of anything other than a love poetry, which may be marvelous in its forms—the cherished object of the structural gloss—but which is not a part of a larger universe of meaning.[20] But for Dante such poetry and such a lover were simply no longer sufficient—in fact, were never sufficient or rewarding in the first place. One of the dark undercurrents of the *Vita nuova*—detected by Borges in the resonances of the *Commedia*—is the great chasm of Beatrice's insufficiencies. In a particularly moving passage of his *Essay,* Singleton says that Dante is rejecting a love which knows no rest or satisfaction, necessarily a hopeless love, a love without possibility of peace. "Troubadour love was really always that—a love without peace" (99).

This is precisely the case, of course, except that it is critical to note that this is because it is an explicitly and hermetically literary concept of love. It may, because of the charms of the writing of it, the seduction of its expression in lyrics, go on to influence people, of course—but the poets themselves do not hold it up as anything more than poetic, certainly not as a sociological or a theological theory of love developed outside the context of the need for poetic inspiration and production. It is a theory of love which transparently serves artistic needs primarily and social ones secondarily, if at all, and a broad range of readers would argue it is highly negative and destructive when it is applied as a social principle. And that too is the story of the *Vita nuova,* the failure, the heartbreak, even the tragedy of transferring what can only be lyrical to all other parts of life, including the narrative: garbled dreams, dead young women. And the point, finally, is that Dante rejects it as a literary principle as well because his young love of Beatrice was so catastrophically painful; but instead of retreating to a novelistic stance, he moves forward to the kabbalistic vision within which realities and lyricism cannot be separated from each other and literature functions in a moral universe that is no different from the moral universe of

20. Dante is in some ways anticipating the argument that DeRougemont would make in the twentieth century about the largely negative effects of Provençal poetry: that in its glorification of an asocial and unproductive love, a love of the beauty of form(s), it actually creates such love—or the expectation and glorification of it—in individuals whose emotional states are, in some great measure, conditioned by the love poetry they read.

individuals. Literature, writing, is *real*. Beatrice *is* a nine. The Book of Memory *exists*. The ideology rejected is a poetics that does not recognize this, that cannot read or accept these truths about texts and their relationship to life—an ideology that is founded on a notion of fiction as something that has its own rules and that is epistemologically different from reality. Dante, a kabbalist in this sense as well, rejects such a notion and kills off Love and the rather foolish and weepy young man who believed in him, a false god indeed. And Beatrice, finally, most painfully, had to go as well; she will be written about again when a Dante fully liberated from the old traps and trappings can both fully decipher and then say what she can mean in the newly revealed universe. The newly minted Dante has many hints which he has dutifully passed on to us, but he has a great deal more contemplation to go until all the harmonies and all the congruences, all those nines, are clear enough to be reinscribed. He licks his wounds and bides his time.

Alas, the modern reader, with few exceptions, cannot accept the radical notion that Beatrice is a nine as anything other than a literary statement, understanding literature as a construct that is starkly different epistemologically from the construct we privilege as "reality."[21] This is so despite the fact that the statement is delivered in the *Vita nuova* precisely as an example of how poetry is *not* fiction but rather the ultimate, the very expression of Truth—mystical, kabbalistic, perhaps, but Truth nevertheless. If we were not, for better or worse, so deeply entrenched in a universe of reason and positivism and their derivatives, we would be less inclined, perhaps, to talk about the fiction of not being a fiction, to remember that most famous of lines about the *Commedia,* but rather about the destruction of fiction and the elevation of Truth as the principles of Poetry. That too is what the *Vita nuova* is about. The severe difficulty lies in determining whether we must deal with all of this as a fiction, whether, to put it differently, we reject the most fundamental

21. In some ways Bloom's most recent articulation of his reading of Dante as prophetic poet and Beatrice as the center of his idiosyncratic gnosis is, I think, congruent, although far from identical: "at once true poet and peculiarly favored by God" (Bloom 1989:49).

premise of Dante's text by interpreting it as a fiction. But Dante himself is trying to reconcile something which we, as heirs of a remarkably powerful positivism and rationalism, are greatly tempted to call mysticism, with a belief in the possibility not only of writing the Truth but having such written truth be revelatory and even conversionary for others. Thus, the "miracles" he describes in the *Vita nuova* are miracles for him, true for him and part of what he is trying to tell us: that there is (or can be, if we can learn how to read it) great transcendent Truth in what the unbeliever and the blind might take to be pedestrian "reality" or reduce to the banal parameters of the "factual" or "nonfactual." Moreover, in the writing of the events and the experiences, the "facts" are turned back into the Truth (a Truth we are unable to account for outside of literature) they once were in the first Book. There are thus three separate "versions" of the events, of any event: those that are written kabbalistically, those that take place, which may seem to be pedestrian and unexceptional, and the third reinscribing in a literary text. The latter must be the right kind of literary text: that which is written by someone who is first and foremost a strong and able reader, able to properly interpret the events of the life that is lived "factually" as manifestations of events that in fact are already inscribed in the first Book, and then is able to write a text that lets us see the truth of one through the other. This is an experiencing and subsequent writing of a reality and Truth that cannot be understood, let alone described and rewritten, in positivist terms, in the terms that require an "understanding" that is limited by either rationalist discourse or precepts.

Dante, in other words, is a full step ahead of the many philosophers—all postmedieval, of course—who have said that when the truth is understood it can no longer be said. Dante, prewriting Vico, believed that when the truth was understood it could be said—it must be said—and in a poetry that is more truthful than any facts can be. I believe his answer to the belief in the unsayability of truth would be that that is true only in a system that has classified the mystical and the "real" inappropriately, divided them from each other inappropriately. What is True, in a text such as the *Vita nuova* (and since the story of it is held up to be exemplary, by sheer dint of being True, in all texts), is that which lies between the pedestrian and ultimately meaningless "facts" of any possible encounters with a Bice Portinari—or any other woman, for that matter—and what renders such facts true and meaningful: how they reveal to us and act out what was and is always written in the greater text. The literary text, then, is the expression of the interpretation of one through the other. That is the lesson about writing and Truth—which ought, in fact to be inseparable—that Dante learns in the trials and tribulations recounted in the *Vita nuova.*

Synchronicity is everywhere strewn along those paths, and that, first and foremost, is the meaning of such things as numbers and their obvious, if at times problematic conjunction with each other and with other meanings. Although the "meanings" of numbers according to external systems of symbolism are undeniably there and potent, though sometimes difficult to pin down and decipher in any absolute or neat system, the meanings of such coincidences of numbers is, more importantly, internal—markers along Dante's path that critical events or revelations are at hand, deeply personal, ultimately, and perhaps not fully interpretable according to formalized, external systems of numerology. They are, however, unmistakably and intensely meaningful personally, and they are inscribed in the text and in the universe of Truth precisely because there is an intersection between the details of a personal life and its potential banalities and cosmic Truth, on the one hand, and sense and order on the other. But neither the inattentive nor the unbeliever will be able to read such Truths. And the elaborate constellation of numbers which in part seem to make "sense" and in part do not is part of that greater text manifesting itself, leaving its markers in real life, although they can only serve as such markers if and when someone can read them. It is clear, for example, that even the "obvious" correspondence of the number nine with Beatrice's appearances and her very person are not perceived or understood by Dante until after the revelation is at hand; it is then, retrospectively, that he is able to understand that she was marked in certain specific ways as significant, unusual, a recurring indicator of the way his writing must turn. The additional fact that there are unavoidable links thus established between Beatrice and Christ caused modern critics some consternation, until Singleton was able to explain the ways in which, in an earlier mode of Christianity, such a tie between personal and universal salvation was in no way blasphemous. But one is also tempted to add, of course, that in many, if not most non-Western religions (and, not surprisingly, in the more universalistic, mystical branches of the Western ones, including the Christianity of the Gospels), the discovery of God within the individual is not only not blasphemous but altogether expected, the revelation that is actively sought in a lifetime. But because Dante is difficult to classify as a mystic, according to the ways in which we have come to label mysticism—i.e., principally by an assumption of a lack of linear coherence—we have discarded this as an additional interpretation of the facts set out in the *Vita nuova*—that Beatrice is, for him, the Christ, and that Christ, rather than Beatrice, is the metaphor. And yet, Dante clearly is setting out for us in this text a mode of first reading and then writing the Truth that lies at the far end of the traditional and caricatured view we have of the mystical experience as unsayable, but is, if anything, even further removed from that positivist dichotomy of fact versus fiction with which we perforce operate in our times and in our culture. In the new life, when the old gods and the first loves are dead, Truth is strange, and it is everywhere to be read, and poetry is its handmaiden.

II

Bondage:

Pellico's Francescas

O that you would kiss me with the kisses of your mouth!
For your love is better than wine,
Your anointing oils are fragrant,
your name is oil poured out;
therefore the maidens love you.
Draw me after you, let us make haste.
The king has brought me into his chambers.
We will exult and rejoice in you;
we will extol your love more than wine;
rightly do they love you.
—Solomon's Song of Songs,
verses 2–4

I

*J*n literary canons almost by definition fraught with idiosyncrasies and major discrepancies between literary works' standing in different historical periods, few works can rival the decline in fortunes of Silvio Pellico's *Le mie prigioni.* First published in November of 1832, this work, now normally labelled as "memorialistic" (when it is referred to at all, as it in fact rarely is), quickly became one of the most successful books of the nineteenth century and, internationally, of Italian literature: reprinted innumerable times, translated into more than forty languages within a matter of years. In France, for example, there were five translations in 1833, the first year after publication; the first American translation was published only a few years after that, in 1836, a sure sign of a best-seller, given the logistical difficulties involved. Apparently, it was immediately seen as the principal source of inspiration—political, ideological, spiritual—coming out of the Risorgimento. Even more significant, perhaps, in terms of some "standard" of literary import, Pellico's generically ambiguous work was and is something of an insider's "classic," and writers of all manner of prison literature from Stendhal to Solzhenitsyn consider Pellico not only a kindred soul but his book the—modern, at least—prototype of a depiction of a prison as the locus of spiritual liberation.[1]

1. For fuller accounts and citations of Pellico's status among fellow writers see Brombert 1978, 14–15, 75–77: Solzhenitsyn, in *The Gulag Archipelago,* writes: "It has been known for many centuries that prison causes the profound rebirth of a human being. The examples are innumerable, such as that of Silvio Pellico" (Brombert 1978:15). Stendhal, in Brombert's assessment, was even more profoundly influenced by Pellico's work, whose literary qualities reverberate throughout the *Chartreuse de Parme:* ". . . the urge to write, to make contact; the secret signals; the fancies of the imagination; the prisoner's walk; the relations with the jailer's daughter. . . . Count Mosca thus refers to the Spielberg as a "pleasant abode" (*lieu de plaisance*) where one's legs risk gangrene: an obvious allusion to

Despite both its massive international fame during the nineteenth century and its past and enduring status among a number of highly influential writers, *Le mie prigioni* has fallen to a level of remarkable obscurity and disregard among all potential publics; its most prominent exposure in the last several decades is that it is read, in abbreviated and simplified form, by Italian schoolchildren as part of the study of the Risorgimento itself.[2] Hard times have clearly befallen Pellico's once adored and much-studied work: *Le mie prigioni* has been unambiguously relegated to the category of nonliterary works whose importance, past and present, is exclusively tied to the historical event whose vicissitudes both "inspired" it and gave it prominence.[3] Whatever literary merit a writer like Solzhenitsyn sees in it has fallen out of sight among almost all students of Italian literature. Pellico and this work of his must thus certainly stand as the Italian author and text with the most dramatic

---

Pellico's friend Maroncelli whose leg had to be amputated" (76). Among the French writers alone, one can also count both Nerval and Verlaine as acutely aware of the specifically literary merits of a work more popularly read otherwise; see also Mombello for ties with Verlaine and Nerval, as well as de Musset (who wrote a poem by the title *Le mie prigioni*) and for the general history of the *fortuna* of the text in France. (One must note that the *Prigioni* is certainly not the only work whose literary merits appear to be visible almost exclusively to other writers: a far more famous case is the recently "rediscovered" *Les Liaisons dangereuses,* whose merits were first recognized by other creative writers while scholars had only previously seen the text's biographical and sociological material, for a long time a standard critical procedure towards eighteenth-century texts in particular; see Cherpack.)

2. There is no standard or definitive edition, and the text has a predictably poor record of publication in the twentieth century; see the preface to the 1983 Longanesi edition, which provides a detailed history of the text's editions and publications, a history clearly seen as tied to variable politicohistorical vicissitudes. Ironically, it is not a first-rate edition itself, even at first glance: it omits Pellico's prologue, cited below.

3. Bertacchini's encyclopaedic work can be used as exemplary (a bit better than most, in fact) in terms of the nature of the Pellico citation: invariably brief, invariably with a reference to its monumental importance, invariably described as "memorialistic" (or some variation thereof) and thus never discussed in literary terms.

decline in standing: from international classic to obscure pseudohistorical text, dished out in appropriate pablum form to children to convey to them something of the pathos of the Italians' long-ago struggle for liberation from the Austrians. But literary history is no exception to other histories: it is full of unfairnesses, and none of this would bear any second thoughts if it were not for the fact that *Le mie prigioni* is so very peculiar a literary text if one reads it outside its imprisoning historical memorialistic framework, at least for an initial moment of imaginary suspended disbelief.

I I

You are handed this text to read without being given any information about it other than the self-evident: it is in Italian, and you assume it to be a part of the Italian literary tradition with which you are more or less familiar. As you read, the following characteristics stand out: the work is divided into one hundred parts, a preface and ninety-nine chapters; moreover, there are three principal divisions within the text, clearly marked by the three different prisons to which the protagonist is sent.

In the preface there is an interpolative gloss of two of the key phrases of the opening terzina of the *Divine Comedy:* "nel mezzo . . . mi trovai"— the kind of allusive gloss Dante both reveled and excelled in.[4] It is also

4. After an epigraphic citation from Job ("Homo natus de muliere, brevi vivens tempore, repletur multis miseriis") the preface begins: "Ho io scritto queste memorie per vanità di parlar di me? Bramo che ciò non sia: e per quanto uno possa di sè guidice costituirsi, parmi d'avere avuto alcune mire migliori:—quella di contribuire a confortare qualche infelice coll'esponimento de'mali che patii e delle consolazioni ch'esperimentai essere conseguibili nelle somme sventure;—quella d'attestare che *in mezzo* a' miei lunghi tormenti *non trovai* pur l'umanità coiì iniqua" (Has my motive for writing these memories been vanity, a desire to speak of myself? I hope not, and in so far as any man may set himself up as judge of his own actions I feel that I have had some better ends in view. I wanted, that is, to help console some unhappy creature by this account of the evils that I suffered and of the consolations that, as I know from my own experience, a man can find amid the greatest misfortunes; to bear witness that in the course of my own long sufferings I

immediately clear that an earlier version of the narrator is the protago-
nist, and that the story narrated belongs to the conversion type: how the
narrator/protagonist found truth in moments of deepest darkness, how
in truth there was comfort, and that the purpose of telling the story in
the first place is precisely to provide the same kind of comfort for
others.

The day and hour on which the protagonist begins his journey into
what will be ten years of imprisonment and the concomitant acquisition
of truth and knowledge are identified as three o'clock on a Friday
afternoon, referred to as "quel povero venerdì." The first textual
identification of the protagonist comes from another character in the
story, rather than from the narrator himself, and he is named not only as
an author but more specifically as the author of a work whose title is the
name of one of Dante's most famous characters, Francesca of Rimini. In
fact, this specific form of identification is repeated on several occasions,
a reasonably clear indication of the sort of identity the author either
believes he has or wishes to have.

In what appears to be a key scene, the protagonist, in danger of
succumbing to the temptations of a young woman who waits on him in
his jail cell, refuses to read to her, as she has requested, passages from the
Song of Solomon. The narrator makes it clear at this juncture (without
appearing to need a more direct allusion to the Francesca scene, a
version of which he himself has written) that the reading aloud of a text
which includes some sexual revelation is most likely to lead the man and
woman reading that text into the same sin as the text describes.

I I I

Even a casual first reading of this text, the *Prigioni,* reveals this
panoply of parallels between Pellico's text and Dante's, most so obvious

---

did not find humanity so wicked [this and all subsequent citations from the 1986
Jacomuzzi edition and in English from the Capaldi translation]). This is similar in
effort (if not in accomplishment) to the kind of allusive "rewriting" of Cavalcanti's
Donna me prega we find in canto 10 of the *Inferno.*

they cannot fail to be intentional—although the nature and precise
intent of that conspicuousness are much harder to decipher. The revela-
tions are muted, of course, by our expectations, and since we have come
to expect Pellico's text to be a memorialistic text from the politically
explosive nineteenth century (when the many national revolutions
produced all manner of correlative texts, a considerable number of them
autobiographical, in fact[5]), the almost excruciatingly obvious attempt
Pellico appears to be making to link his text with Dante's has been
completely missed. There are, however, compelling reasons to explore
these further, beyond the fact that they are indeed there: The unavoida-
bly purposeful associations between a (politically and literarily) once
important nineteenth-century political-spiritual "memoir" and Dante's
Commedia tell us a great deal about the power of Dante's engagement, his
fusion of what in most other spheres, political and spiritual, are consid-
ered separate categories. Moreover, Pellico's insistence on the manifold
difficulties of writing and especially of reading and "correct" interpreta-
tion, played out in a virtuous rewriting of the Francesca episode, should
both alter our canonical perspective on the Prigioni (removing from it
tags such as "naive" and "straightforward") and ultimately explain in
some measure why the text has failed canonically, why it was unable to
sustain its contemporary critical acclaim. It is, in fact, in Pellico's failure
to convincingly carry out Dante's program of truth and engagement that
we may glimpse its enormous difficulty—for, unlike other writers,
Petrarch and Boccaccio among them, who reject Dante's programs in
one way or another and end up writing either against them or around
them, Pellico is a true believer and an epigone.

We are rather easily fooled by the classification of "memoirs" or other
scientific-historical type tags that prevent us from seeing both the
strongly fictive (i.e., intertextual) structures of the work and its strong

5. The most helpful recent study is Fernández 1988, which, although focused
on the early nineteenth-century biography in Spain, provides numerous far-
ranging insights into a number of related topics: the explosion of autobiographies
in the post-Rousseau period and the correlation between births of nations (and
their coming into a "modern world") and a strong interest in the autobiographical
form, including the spiritual autobiography.

links to one of the most imitative of literary categories, the spiritual autobiography. While the strongly literary nature of the autobiographical form has become so widely acknowledged in the literary profession as to be almost an unproductive cliché, far less is understood about the precise relationship between such literary structures and specific concepts of truth in an author such as Pellico, who is deeply intertwined with both Dantesque structures and those of spiritual autobiographies far more widely read in Pellico's lifetime.[6] It is a readily understandable "paradox" that the highly introspective autobiography should flourish—both for writers and readers—precisely in the age in which revolutionary and political upheaval reached a fever pitch. In fact, the question literary historians might well ask about *Le mie prigioni* is whether it succeeded as political memoirs, as a text that testified to and for the most moving aspects of the Italian Risorgimento, or whether its vast popularity makes of it one of the most exceptionally successful of religious conversion stories.

The first-person narration of a religious conversion, the spiritual autobiography, is a critical subcategory of the autobiography, clearly marked by various kinds of exceptional literary imitation as the backdrop against which the author develops the "story" of what is presumably the most subjective of personal experiences. In his lucidly authoritative work in this area, Bowman has noted that the strong markings of literary imitation in these texts is evident in at least two fundamental presences: that of a clearly visible model-prototype (the *Confessions,* for example, being the most frequently used) and the more than occasional

6. On the other hand, one must also acknowledge the considerable critical conservatism of the Italianist branch of the profession and note that many even today would agree, explicitly or not, with the perceptions voiced in Wellek and Warren's 1956 *Theory of Literature* excluding autobiography from the category of "literature." Of course, recent immense critical interest in the autobiographical form and its highly literary echoes and structures is a phenomenon that is datable, at least roughly, to the year of publication of Wellek and Warren's classic study; see Olney's detailed introduction to the history of scholarship. To continue to grossly categorize Pellico's work as "historical" or "memorialistic," and thus nonliterary, is a far different problem.

citations from or allusions to the Bible.[7] Within this tradition, in fact, it is precisely in the high visibility of the imitation, in the strong and frequent markings of an overt and, to the modern eye (although not, perhaps, a postmodern one) heavy-handed and inescapable intertextuality, that the text acquires its validity: "C'est le recours même à l'imitation qui est la preuve du texte . . . l'autobiographie spirituelle y voit, à ses origines, validation et donc signification" (Bowman, 317). Once we begin to perceive the innumerable ways in which Pellico almost slavishly follows this model and his unrelenting evocation of the texts he believes he must rewrite ("copy" in a Dantesque, *Vita nuova* sense), we are struck more forcefully than ever by the fact that this most intimate of all possible relationships with Dante is so absent in the literary history we have read and written. In fact, Pellico's text is remembered for something resembling the opposite: a naive and simple attachment to "fact" or "history" (these, of course, understood as having an existence objectively independent from textuality itself) and thus a conspicuous lack of attachment to fixed or previous literary structures.[8] Finally, the astonishingly strong imitative features of the *Prigioni* have almost completely disappeared from sight when viewed, as the text has consistently been, through the critical prism of the purported "naiveté" and "sincerity" of the Romantics, and—because of

7. "Ainsi, l'autobiographie spirituelle est imitative d'une manière plus marquée que la plupart des genres littéraires, et cela malgré le fait, ou peut-être à cause du fait, qu'elle veut représenter une expérience personelle et intime. C'est cette conjonction d'un extrême degré de littérarité et de subjectivité qui crée son statut exceptionellement intéressant" (316).

8. Wilkins, although "obviously" outdated, in fact provides a cogent statement of the views presented in most other histories, studies, and introductions, including almost all written much more recently, and he allies *Le mie prigioni* rather strictly with the Italian Romanticism of its times: "But its most essential characteristic was a pervading sense of liberation from traditional formalism of any sort: there had come into literature a new conviction that the individual writer, however restrained by his own concepts of artistry, was free to seek and find inspiration in his own life and in the life of which he was a part, and to choose and create his own forms of expression" (413).

Pellico's overt and lachrymose sentimentality in parts—as if "true sentiments" were only expressible agenerically or in something "authentic," by which, I surmise, one must mean "original."[9]

But there can be no doubt, in fact, that at the most basic structural level Pellico's text is a casebook example of this otherwise rather fluid genre, the spiritual autobiography—with the more than merely interesting detail, of course, that it is Dante who provides the unmistakable prototype. I say Dante here because it is an amalgamated "Dante" who serves as the model text, a Dante who is the author of the *Commedia,* to be sure, but of other texts as well, including especially the *Vita nuova.* Pellico begins his text with a quote from Job and follows with a recounting of the day of his imprisonment that cannot help but draw any reader (of Italian, particularly) into the *Commedia.* In the preface, moreover, as well as repeatedly throughout the text, the narrator makes absolutely clear, protests to the nth degree, that his work is not of a political nature—despite the unmitigatedly clear political circumstances of his imprisonment. These were circumstances which would have been amply known to every contemporary reader and which, in turn, in a perhaps false act of historical contextualization, every introduction to the work, every blip about *Le mie prigioni* makes clear—although this spelling out of "background" almost invariably and probably inadvertently succeeds in strongly foregrounding a seemingly impersonal "history." As the first of many invocations of Dante, sacred text, makes clear,

9. DeSanctis firmly categorizes Pellico's work as part of the "ciclo letterario che fu detto romantico, un romanticismo italiano, che facea vibrare le corde piú soavi dell'uomo e del patriota" (a literary cycle called romantic, an Italian romanticism which played on the most sentimental chords of men and patriots) (966). In far more recent criticism of or allusions to Pellico, the tags of "sentimentality" and "lachrymose" are more frequent than not: "Ma adesso abbiamo una corrente memorialistica che pur accogliendo la superiorità del sentimento, finisce non solo per deformarlo in sentimentalismo. . . . Esempio particolarmente chiaro del memorialismo sentimentale-religioso sono *Le mie prigioni*" (But now we have a memorialistic school that, although it acknowledges the superiority of feelings, manages to transform that into sentimentality. . . . A particularly clear example of sentimental-religious memoirs is *Le mie prigioni* [Forti-Lewis:146]).

he has written the text for four reasons: to comfort others in similar circumstances of suffering and need; to bear witness that in the worst of circumstances human beings are not as bad as we think they are ("in mezzo a' miei lunghi tormenti non trovai pur l'umanità così iniqua, così indegna d'indulgenza, così scarsa d'egregie anime, come suol venire rappresentata" [to bear witness that in the course of my own long sufferings I did not find humanity so wicked, so unworthy of forgiveness, so devoid of excellent souls as it is usually made out to be]); to invite others to put aside hate and turn the other cheek; and to affirm (ridire) an old truth often forgotten, that religion and philosophy (by which he means, of course, faith and reason) are one.

Small wonder that Gramsci, for whom Pellico's "prison memoirs" (as Italian literary histories have it) ought to have had enormous importance, ignores the Prigioni altogether: it is of no more interest to him than any other spiritual tract and recounting of a conversion away from political life was likely to be. In this, at least, Gramsci, in his conspicuous silence, was a better literary historian than DeSanctis, who sees Pellico as more or less typical of the liberals of his time, fundamentally political creatures whose language nonetheless reflected a rhetorically expeditious fusion of religion and politics: "a quel modo che i liberali trasferiscono a significato politico parole scritturali, come l'apostolato delle idee, il martirio patriotico, la missione sociale, la religione del dovere" (in that way, liberals gave a political significance to scriptural passages, such as the evangelization of ideas, patriotic martyrdom, the social mission, the religion of duty [DeSanctis:943]). The first paragraph of the narration proper by Pellico ends with the charming "Simile ad un amante maltrattato dalla sua bella, e dignitosamente risoluto di tenerle il broncio, lascio la politica ov'ella sia, e parlo d'altro" (Instead, like a lover who has been ill-treated by his beloved and who is determined to maintain an attitude of dignified aloofness towards her, I intend to leave politics alone and speak of other matters). Like most spurned lovers, Pellico is in part bluffing, and his "postpolitical" memoirs cannot be free of the memories and the strong traces of the earlier love. But like the Dante he has conjured from the first page as his explicit model, he is intent on transforming a failed love in one arena to the revelation of more proper love in a different one. This is a far cry, certainly, from DeSanctis's faintly cynical suggestion that the rhetoric of one cause is potentially useful in a different one, and a clear reversal, moreover, of that canonical perception (at least vis-à-vis Pellico) that it is the political engagement and "contribution" that marks the text as worthwhile for posterity.

To speak of spiritual autobiography—or any kind of biography, perhaps—is to invoke a conversion almost automatically, for as Freccero has so convincingly (and now canonically) noted in the realm of the *Commedia,* there can scarcely exist an autobiography until after a conversion has taken place; otherwise, the text at hand would have little possible focus and value. Pellico seems intent that we grasp the point: not only does he hint from the outset that a conversion—and a specifically religious one, at that—is the point of his text, but he explicitly chooses as his prototext a Dante he reads, in turn, as a text of conversion. One of the critical scenes in the *Prigioni,* in fact, is that clear rewriting of the Francesca scene. More of that below, but for the time being it is important to note that while Dante's Francesca is both unconverted and unrepentant (of course), Pellico's, following a far different pattern and tempo of conversion, is converted *avant la lettre.* It seems quite clear why it is not only inaccurate but also damaging to condemn *Le mie prigioni* to the status of "mere" prison or political memoirs: to do so is to risk missing the fact of the explicit reading of Dante that constitutes the basic structure of the work, and in turn, the explicit evocation of a conversion narrative—with all its literary peculiarities and built-in significations, all its powerful allusiveness to the entire canon of conversion texts. To miss the insistent and obsessive rewriting of Dante is also to ignore what may be the strongest example of the political appropriation during the Risorgimento of early Italian writers such as Dante, among others, in the difficult efforts to paint Italy as a nation. And to miss the conversionary and thus autobiographical structure of the text (and replace that, in our base reading, with the relatively static structure of "memoirs") is, finally, to miss the text's entire point—to blink and not see that crucial convergence of aesthetics and history.[10]

In the case of Pellico there is a second category of texts also automatically evoked, that of the recounting of prison and imprisonment. This, unlike the spiritual autobiography, has not gone unnoticed by the few critics who have dealt with the text, although it is not altogether clear to me (in part because the critical tradition is so slim and fragmentary) whether it has been grasped that Pellico's prison is the focus of his conversion. The irony—although this is perhaps too common a paradox to be an irony—is that the conversion provoked is in almost all ways one that has turned the narrator away from the kind of political engagement that landed him in prison in the first place. Political, i.e., nonspiritual engagement is, in the end, the lover who

10. That convergence is, of course, both aim and example in the Dante who here is become sacred text, and it is also explored suggestively by de Man in his brilliant meditation on autobiography. I have also found useful, for this essay, van Slyke, who (in part) distinguishes between memoirs and autobiography on the basis of the degree of presence of a "narrataire" or narratee, noting that the stronger the presence the more likely an autobiographical reading of the text is to be revealing. Not only is the narratee a strong presence in *Le mie prigioni,* but the relationship between that fictive or intended reader and the narrator is unmistakably of the type signaled by van Slyke as constituting one of the most powerful ones in the history of autobiography, that which can certainly trace its origins to the Augustinian *Confessions* (and which for any Italophone would smack of Dante): that of teacher and pupil. Pellico's stated goal, from the outset (and alluded to repeatedly throughout the narration), as quoted above, is to teach a series of lessons, and the typological descriptions provided by van Slyke could hardly ask for a better example than *Le mie prigioni:* "Ce narrataire occupe, du moins provisoirement, une position inférieure à son narrateur, qui se charge de lui inculquer une vérité d'ordre général, réligeuse, politique, ou intellectuelle" (27). The point, finally, is not only that to speak of memoirs is to strongly evoke an exteriorized genre and to speak of autobiography (of whatever subclassification) is to alert the reader to the interiorized properties of the text at hand, but that the narrative structures and motivations (the latter most apparent in the narrator-narratee relationship) of an autobiographical text tie it strongly to other literary texts and other literary genres—ties that are, in the case of the Pellico text, critical for any reading that might transcend the most superficial.

spurned him—and who is finally recognized as unworthy, although her great merit is of course to have thrown him into a situation where a more transcendent truth could be recognized. From pain and rejection come light and truth; but what makes this story peculiar, at least as long as we continue to read it in a political context, is that pain and rejection, inflicted, of course, by political enemies (in the context of Pellico's earlier frame of reference), do not make Pellico see more clearly or believe more fervently in the virtues of the cause of independence and unification. On the contrary, in pragmatic terms this is a radically apolitical text, a text that in many ways should have been the bane of the Risorgimento rather than, as we are now led to believe, one of its textual banners, for, as he says at the outset, the story aims to teach a far different politics: the testamental Christian virtues of charity, turning the other cheek, loving one's enemy, giving up hate.[11] And although the history of the Italian Risorgimento is by far not one of the bloodiest of its time or any other, it was no more guided by proto-Gandhian principles than any other—except, perhaps, in raising Pellico's *Le mie prigioni,* after its publication in 1831, to the status of one of its sacred texts, a somewhat disingenuous banner of how the war was won.[12]

11. There is considerable testimony, in fact, that while the text was fabulously popular from the outset, Pellico's political friends and others engaged in the Risorgimento were appalled by his complete retreat from the kind of political engagement they believed was necessary to defeat the Austrians. See the introductions to various editions.

12. It is instructive, for example, to browse among the various (relatively) contemporary introductions to translations of the *Prigioni.* The introduction to an American English edition of 1885 (although the frontispiece creates some confusion by also including a date of 1867), by one Epes Sargent, who had met Maroncelli, includes the following very telling assessment of the "value" of *Le mie prigioni:* "Widely celebrated as it was while the political ideas for which the author suffered called forth rebuke and bitter persecution from the government in power, the book merits a more extensive welcome, now that those ideas have become the inspiration of awakened Italy; now that the despotism of Austria, in her last Italian stronghold, has collapsed and passed away; now that the flame has been kindled that is not likely to be extinguished till the last vestige of an ignominious serfdom has been consumed. Surely this is the moment to revive, with more honor than

But prison, or prisons, as Pellico quite markedly makes it in his title, are those stretches of space and time—like exiles and sojourns in the desert, mournings and painful marches through the Bolivian jungles— that forge belief. Just as long and (physically) painful meditation is meant explicitly to do in Zen practice, for example, and as obviously correlative medieval monastic practices did, exiles and imprisonments are certainly among the premier, albeit involuntary, crucibles in the literary tradition, and especially in the political-textual branch of that tradition.[13] And archetypically there are two principal outcomes of such trials, of those forty days in the desert: The first is that greater strength-ening, that forging of the indestructible spirit and instillment of irre-pressible determination that we see in those who either remain or become politically and ideologically deeply engaged in the aftermath. The second is in many ways the apparent polar opposite, for it results in a retreat from any sort of external engagement and in a turning inward to contemplate the self, the necessary (or at least desirable) contingency of which is a retreat from the vicissitudes of the external world.

The difficulty lies in the fact that so many examples of what appear to be the latter—from the Christ story itself and including, certainly,

ever before, the remembrance of those heroic spirits who spoke a word for Italian independence, when so to speak was to incur the risk of the dungeon or the scaffold" (v–vi). Further on there is an indication that while the enemy is scarcely alluded to, and this is not a vindictive work, moreover, a hardly more fitting vindication against that enemy could be found. These statements do not read the *Prigioni* outside an explicitly political context (as the narrator has urged us) but rather in a context within which the very "Christianity" of the narrator is perceived explicitly as an extraordinary political tool.

13. I note in passing that the second volume of Manchester's monumental biography of Churchill is structured precisely around the years of "exile," of Churchill's almost complete enforced isolation—needless to say, very unwelcome to him—from open political life. And the literate can well guess the morality tale implicit in the structure of the narration itself: it prepares the protagonist in a number of different spheres, hones him for the severe tests he will face when he returns, triumphantly of course, from that desert. The subtitle of the volume (the title remains the same for the entire multivolume series) is, simply and tellingly, *Alone.*

Pellico's text—are so readily interpretable and frequently held up as examples of the former. This is true not only in literary hermeneutics but in political practice, since it is abundantly clear that the nonviolent resistance movements of both Gandhi and King (both of whom spent politically and spiritually productive periods incarcerated, of course) are based precisely on that kind of reading of texts such as the New Testament. For them (and for many other readers of far less historical importance), the "lesson" lies precisely in the open paradox: the retreat from direct force and its largely negative (violent, vindictive) manifestations is ultimately the most effective weapon against the political enemy. This is a reading, a lesson (in the scriptural sense) that would certainly be rejected by those who come out of the comparable forging process with the greater conviction in their ideology, a Gramsci, a Guevara—and perhaps, were they given the chance to rebut, by those whose story is being thus interpreted, the Christs, the Pellicos. The discussion must ultimately transcend intent or even "reading" in the absolute sense of the word since, as these cases clearly demonstrate, and as Pellico himself will realize and explore within his text, there are invariably multiple interpretations, even radically contradictory ones. But in order for the discussion to even get that far—and this is my simple point here—it is indispensable to recognize that Pellico's text is very much, very necessarily of this conversionary type, the type for which he himself believes Dante is the most compelling prototext. Moreover, one senses in Pellico's association of his own incarceration with Dante and his exile the resonance of a strong reading of the *Commedia,* one in which, as Mazzotta has put it, in words that could as readily describe Pellico's *Prigioni,* exile itself is the most necessary of conditions: "The poet's sense of his mission could hardly be overstated. Exile is the condition in which his voice rises, but the displacement does not entail a complacent isolation within a world largely indifferent to the private truth the poet witnesses. . . . Like the prophets, Dante makes of exile a virtue and a necessary perspective . . . he also acknowledges that the truth he communicates, paradoxically, is that which alienates him further from the world he has already lost" (Mazzotta 1984:650).

Indeed, from this perspective and the corollary one that in the end the *Commedia* itself is a text which can be and is read according to both schemes, the political and the spiritual, it is Dante who provides the key inspiration and the necessary prism for Pellico. In the end, the Pellico of the *Prigioni* never really forsakes altogether the abandoned lover and his role in politics and history. But his ten years of exile, which produce the central text of his lifetime and career, give him a sense of clarity of vision and perspective, as his indispensable little prologue makes clear.[14] The results include, of course, a version of the paradox spelled out by Mazzotta: his acquisition of a sense of harmony with the surrounding universe, so palpable throughout the *Prigioni,* especially the latter half, will dismay and discourage those who saw in him the staunchest of political allies. But in the end, the success of his work as an anti-Austrian manifesto, which it specifically denies being, will have made him a powerful and successful revolutionary.[15]

The multiple, plural prisons of Pellico's unusual title ("le mie pri-gioni" sounds, initially, just as awkward in Italian as "my prisons" does in English) succeed in evoking the plurality of types of prisons the character Pellico will deal with. It is literally true, and an important set of markers within the text, that the prisoner passes through three different jails: Santa Margherita in Milan, the Piombi in Venice (which Casanova, a libertine perhaps taken for a liberal by the Austrians, had already made famous), and the infamous Spielberg. But in the tradition of other prison conversions out of which Pellico is writing, the more significant prisons are both those to which the structure of the text itself has alluded, i.e., of those preceding texts, and those metaphorical

14. Pellico was released from the Spielberg, the last and most infamous of the various prisons, in September of 1830, and apparently began writing the work the following year at the "suggestion" of his confessor and spiritual advisor, the Abbot Giordano. It took him less than a year to write and was first published in November of 1832.

15. In 1834 Pellico realized full well the double isolation that his text had provoked: "Two kinds of fanatics are against me—those who imagine they are Liberals and want at all costs popular and anti-clerical revolts, and those who imagine they are saints and want at all costs persecutions in the name of God" (Quoted by Capaldi, xvii).

prisons from which the protagonist himself can finally escape, given the enforced meditation and introspection of incarceration. Both the textual tradition, which includes many texts but most notably Boethius and Cellini, and the philosophical revelations within those texts revel in the pseudoparadox of the happy prison, the liberation—spiritual, philosophical, intellectual, even political—that results from the physical entrapment. Even those whose incarcerations result in greater commitment to political action bless the lucidity that originated in the damp and dark—and if Cellini has the chapter "In lode di detta prigioni" in his *Vita* (note again that it is critical to see the autobiographical structure, as opposed to the "memorialistic"), Pellico has a clearly and charmingly Dantesque version of the same: his extensive recounting of the graffiti—with the hint, of course, that it is kabbalistic inscription— he finds, reads, and transcribes (chapter 9). The writings on the wall of one of his cells (it is quite helpful for the narrative that Pellico was not only moved from one prison to another but often enough from one cell to another), which he calls *iscrizioni,* include such learned ones as quotes from Pascal; but the one that draws Pellico is the "humble" one, "Benedico la prigione, perchè m'ha fatto conoscere la ingratitudine degli uomini, la mia miseria e la bontà di Dio" (I bless this prison because it has made me know the ingratitude of man, my own misery, and the goodness of God).

The condemned Pellico could scarcely have found a better motto for the desired and desirable spiritual state to be developed in that or any incarceration; the handwriting was certainly on the wall. And, to drive the point further, he tells us that next to this inspiring inscription was one he cannot or will not reproduce, one blaspheming God and cursing fate. But it is not only that our narrator will not legitimize it by writing it down for us; one of the jailers comes in and scrapes it off the wall with a knife because its author, in a madness (we scarcely need be told) produced by profound despair and lack of spiritual well-being, had been condemned to death for murder. The murder itself resonates of Ugolino, of the deepest pits of an inferno: the "povero diavolo," unable to kill his enemy, had killed the innocent son of his intended target instead, "il più bel fanciullo che si desse sulla terra" (the most beautiful boy on earth). And *Inferno* 33 echoes back the prison, the horror. Our horrified Pellico is left alone in his cell with the words of horror scraped off the walls—a palimpsest awaiting—and the sayable inscriptions, those blessing the place and the goodness of God, to watch over him. Pellico is both awed and horrified by the power of words, of the written, intelligible word—a state both appropriate for and debilitating to an author—and nowhere will this be more evident than in the scene he will use to both tie and sever him to both texts he worships, both of the texts which have guided virtually every word of his own from the very first: the scriptural Dante and the Bible.

I V

FRANCESCA THE VIRTUOUS

Paolo: Insiem leggemo
        "di Lancillotto come amor lo strinse
        Soli eravamo e senza alcun sospetto . . ."
        Gli sguardi nostri s'incontraro . . .
        Il viso mio scolorossi . . .
        Tu tremavi . . . e ratta ti dileguasti.
Francesca: Oh giorno! A te quel libro restava.
Paolo: Ei posa sul mio cuor.
        Felice nella mia lontananza egli mi fea.

Paolo: Together we were reading
        "Of Launcelot, and how Love held him in thrall.
        We were alone, and without any dread."[16]
        Our eyes met . . .
        My face colored . . .
        You trembled . . . you vanished.
Francesca: That day! You kept the book . . .

16. I have cited Binyon's translation of these two verses from *Inferno* 5. The rest of the translation is my own.

Paolo: I laid it on my heart
And far from you it made me happy.

(Pellico, *Francesca da Rimini,* act 3, scene 2)[17]

Francesca, daughter of Guido of Ravenna, was married to Lancelot of Rimini, but it emerges that the hate she professes for her husband's brother, Paolo, is really a passionate (but fully "innocent") love, conceived before she was married, that she would have carried to her tomb as a secret had the unwitting Paolo not come to visit his brother. Throughout five scenes Francesca struggles valiantly (and, in the end, vainly) to flee the scene where she would even have to face Paolo, and even when they are thrown together twice, she remains not only chaste but desperate to avoid even being in his presence; for, although she loves him, she is tormented by the infidelity to an indulgent and compassionate Lancelot involved in so much as listening to her brother-in-law's declarations of love.

In the middle of one such encounter—placed in the central act 3—the heart of *Inferno* 5 is replayed with Paolo, now, describing the moment of their falling in love: they were reading about "the other" Lancelot and Guenevere, their eyes met, and she trembled, rose, and fled, leaving the book, which he has carried around ever since, in his hands.

The final scene, in fact, is set up when Francesca summons Lancelot to say goodbye and beg his forgiveness (she is fleeing to Ravenna to avoid having to be anywhere near her "lover"). A maddened Paolo, who had dreamt damage was being done to her, runs into the room. Inevitably, as Francesca desperately tries to get rid of him, Lancelot appears and murders both brother and wife—but is prevented from turning the sword on himself by Francesca's father, who has witnessed the scene.

FRANCESCA THE PURE

Non sempre per verità i suoi baci cadeano a proposito, massimamente se capitava aprire il Cantico de' Cantici. Allora, per non

17. This and subsequent citations are from the edition in Finocchiaro Chimirri, the most recent and far and away most complete study of this work.

farla arrossire, io profittava della sua ignoranza del latino, e mi prevaleva di frasi in cui, salva la santità di quel volume, salvassi pur l'innocenza di lei. . . .

Actually, her kisses were not always well directed, especially if she happened to open the Book at the Song of Songs! When this happened, to prevent her blushing, I took advantage of her ignorance of Latin and used words and phrases to safeguard the holiness of the Scriptures, and her innocence. . . . (Chapter 31)

The prisoner has just been moved to another, grimmer prison. But he soon discovers an unexpected pleasure in this new place: the jailer's daughter brings him his coffee every evening. It is only when she, with extraordinary loving care, makes him his coffee that he is then able to write at nights. And she, who identifies him as the author of the then famous and very much *au courant Francesca da Rimini,* quickly cultivates a teacher-pupil, confidante relationship with him. The young girl tells him daily about her "amante," with whom she has a difficult relationship; the prisoner looks forward to the visits and starts to realize she is not as unattractive as he had first thought. She appears, from his description, oblivious to the seductiveness of her behavior, invariably "innocentissimo" but also intimate, affectionate, confessional: "Ella aveva una semplicità ed un'amorevolezza seducenti. Mi diceva: 'Sono tanto innamorata d'un altro, eppure sto così volentieri con lei! Quando non vedo il mio amante m'annoio dappertutto fuorchè qui' " (Her simplicity and kindness were a delight. "I'm so much in love with another," she would say to me, "and yet I do like to be with you! Whenever I can't see my lover I get bored everywhere except here" [chapter 29]).

He struggles with an increasing attraction to her and a decided ambivalence about what he can be to her; without ever saying it, it is clear he cannot imagine actually having an amorous relationship. Chapter 30 opens: "Queste carte sarebbero certamente più dilettevoli se la Zanze fosse stata innamorata di me, o s'io almeno avessi farneticato per essa. Eppure quella qualità di semplice benevolenza che ci univa, m'era più cara dell'amore. E se in qualche momento io temea che potesse nello stolto mio cuore mutar natura, allora seriamente me n'attristava" (These pages would no doubt be more intriguing if Zanze had fallen in love with me, or if I, at least, had become delirious over her. Yet that simple affection which united us meant more to me than love, and if at times I was afraid that it might in my own foolish heart change into something else, I became sincerely upset at the thought).

After pages and pages of this impending and remarkably indirect (but nonetheless transparent) seduction, the girl ever more dedicated and affectionate (including physically so) and the prisoner ever clearly more infatuated with her (at a certain point he is glad he is so physically uncomfortable in the infernally hot and mosquito-infested cell, for perhaps nothing else would keep him from acting on his feelings), we reach the climactic scene: they are speaking about God and religion, something the prisoner, in his role as teacher, often spoke of to her. "E talvolta, troncando ad un tratto un ragionamento frivolo, prendeva la Bibbia, l'apriva, baciava a caso un versetto, e volea quindi ch'io glielo traducessi e commentassi. E dicea: 'Vorrei che ogni volta che rileggerà questo versetto, ella si ricordasse che v'ho impresso un bacio'" (There were times when she would suddenly break off some frivolous argument, take up my Bible, open it and kiss by chance a verse, which she would then ask me to translate and comment upon for her. Then she would say: "I wish that every time you read this verse again you may remember my kissing it" [chapter 31]). But in fact, he knows that her kisses on the Book at times, even often, fall in difficult places, especially on the Song of Solomon. The pupil, the vulnerable girl who thinks she is in love with someone else, kisses the pages of a Song of Solomon she cannot even read herself and begs to have it read and translated and explained to her. And the prisoner? He refuses the text, he mistranslates the scripture, a scripture which would clearly be too seductive, which, one is sure by this point, would mean the end of innocence and reading that day, mosquitoes and heat and all.

The next chapter, 32, begins "Nulla è durevole quaggiù! La Zanze ammalò" (Nothing is lasting on this earth. Zanze fell ill). After a few more days, during which she is clearly in pain and in distress, she disappears, mysteriously, to the country, under the cloud of suspicion and gossip that she had been "seduced"—and the prisoner never sees the girl again.

V

These are Pellico's two versions, two rewritings, of *Inferno* 5: the first is the story he develops in *Francesca da Rimini*, a five-act play written in 1815 for which he became mildly famous. The second is a central and critical section of *Le mie prigioni*—which of course made him fabulously, internationally famous. The two are linked to each other explicitly: the first, the *Francesca, tragedia,* is used as the key identification for the prisoner throughout *Le mie prigioni,* for the Pellico who identifies himself not only as a writer (rather than a political prisoner or anything else) but as the author of the *Francesca.* Both versions interpret and recast Dante's ethics of reading and writing in ways which are typical not only of the Romantic period of which he was a part, but more importantly in ways which reflect, painfully, the difficulties writers have had in Dante's wake, the painful impossibility of following his agenda, of carrying out his program, of, quite simply, following in his footsteps. Both readings and recastings reveal the same concerns, the same "yes, but . . ." when faced with a Dante who says that Truth and History and Literature and Text are all the same thing, whose incomparably influential text is a scripture of a logology. And the difficulties are crucially interrelated: how can drama survive innocence (or, perhaps, how can innocence be dramatic)? and how can writing—or, more accurately, its interpreta-tion—be unambiguously correct? In Pellico's struggle with these ques-tions, in his unmasked rewriting of the master text, we confront a host of problems that are at once peculiar to those who write in the wake of the *Commedia* but that are also, in fact, common in all literary traditions or periods when there are strong Truth Texts, Bibles and Qur'ans.

Francesca da Rimini is an early and in some ways simply innocent attempt to grapple with the problems at hand, and it is undoubtedly a part of an interpretative tradition of *Inferno* 5 within which Francesca's fundamental innocence and concomitant tragic misfortune is a given, a tradition which is typical of the Romantics (although certainly far from exclusively so).[18] Although in the last decade or so the far more common understanding of the text and Francesca's role and culpability focuses on her severe and ultimately deadly failures as a reader, the exegetical tradition, which has from the outset been riveted by and worshipped the canto, has often worshipped its heroine as well and found it essential, and probably easy, to cast her as victim. What both direct criticism and the sort of interpretation implicit in rewritings like Pellico's *Francesca* have done is quite simply to believe Francesca, to take her "Galeotto fu il libro e chi lo scrisse" line at absolute face value and condemn the book and/or the sort of unhappy misfortunes and misunderstandings that Pellico so vividly portrays: the suspicious husband walking in as Francesca is trying to banish the lover, but alas it is misunderstood. . . .[19] The difference in Pellico's treatment, in both

18. This primarily in the sense that it was an Italian version, perhaps the first, of the sort of popularization of myths and of classics (Dante fills both slots in the Italian panorama) that English and German writers of the period had been engaged in as part of that Romantic endeavor. It would appear that the *Francesca* was the first such endeavor in explicitly and unambiguously rewriting a portion of the sacred *Commedia,* and for Pellico it appeared to be a risky business, although the eventual success of the play certainly broke the ice and set the precedent. It is reported that Foscolo advised Pellico to burn the *Francesca* when he read it— although it remains unclear whether the advice came from a revulsion at Pellico's taking on such a taboo or from his sense of its literary limitations. See Finocchiaro Chimirri for a detailed recounting of the history of the play.

19. For a fuller exposition of interpretations of canto 5 see chapter 5, below. In this context, however, it is not so much academic or learned criticism of Dante that is the appropriate context as the manifold artistic versions of the canto that surround Pellico's versions, a tradition which in a number of art forms appears to have been particularly rich in the nineteenth century, with numerous visual depictions, almost all of which convey considerable sympathy for the lovers. (Often this is made clear by depicting the swooned Dante as well.) It is a pictorial tradition so strong that its painters in the nineteenth century alone include Blake, Delacroix, Dante Gabriel Rosetti, Watts, and Beardsley, among others. Of the literary reworkings, the one that achieved greatest prominence and eventually completely surpassed Pellico's theatrical version in popularity and critical signifi-

rewritings, is at once apparent: Francesca is *literally* (as well as in terms of fate or intent, say) quite innocent.

What stands out in Pellico's tragedy is, indeed, the complete lack of consummation, even that which might have taken place offstage and merely recounted. His Francesca is guilty only of the most minimal possible sin under the circumstances: that of a desire almost fully repressed and controlled—a desire, moreover, that had its very brief moment of awakening before she was even married, before it could thus have been even tainted with culpability. She is from the outset unflaggingly repentant of even that suggestion of premarital lust, and her every behavior throughout the five scenes is motivated by the equally virtuous wish to place herself beyond any temptation and to protect her husband and his honor—a husband, curiously enough, named Lancelot by Pellico, perhaps suggesting he bore some peculiar unnamed guilt, even before the murders at the end. Perhaps, too, he is not only recalling the Lancelot of the kiss of *Inferno* 5 but the Lancelot who stepped onto the shameful cart, that other prisoner—of an irrational and shameless love for Guenevere.

But the Francesca of *Francesca da Rimini* is the other possibility. She is passionate really in only one sphere and really has only one fear and desire: she is almost hysterically afraid of actually having the love passion that she senses her character is supposed to have, that her character knows is in her ancestry, but that in this manifestation the author has ordained is strictly forbidden. The hierarchy and textures of the charac-

---

cance is D'Annunzio's *Francesca da Rimini* (originally written as a vehicle for Eleonora Duse), adapted for the opera by Zandonai. D'Annunzio's far more successful version is clearly cast in the mold and tradition of dramatically tragic love stories where the love itself is not eschewed but consummated, however discreetly: the Romeo and Juliets and the Tristan and Isoldes, where, in sum, it is understood that the root of the tragedy necessarily lies, first and foremost, in the consummation of the love. (The D'Annunzio/Zandonai version is so strongly Wagnerian, in fact, that the lovers are reading not the Lancelot but the score of *Tristan und Isolde,* a transposition that reflects in crystalline fashion at least some of the textual issues involved, those of genres and the ascendancy of highly influential master texts.)

ters in *Inferno* 5 are reversed: those who were silent there (the unnamed lover and the presumed or imagined husband) are here the creatures of passion and the driving forces behind almost all the action, whereas Francesca, who was in complete control, narrator, heroine, the only star in her own universe, is largely silent except to express her frantic desire to escape, to flee action, the possibility or hint of passion. Even the earlier, unseen Francesca, the one who had the fleeting moment of love, is the white of Dante's black, for in a reversal whose implications are inescapable it is not only Paolo who, reminiscing, narrates the scene during which they were reading together, but Paolo too who hangs on to the book after a horrified Francesca flees the scene, afraid of the results of their eyes meeting.

The critical scene, then, the scene that is the core around which all else is built and all other action must revolve, is not only removed by Pellico—it is known to have taken place only because it is recounted by Paolo—but critically and tellingly omits the sin of the moment, the kiss brought on by the reading. If we did not have the testimony of the sister scene in *Le mie prigioni* we might think this merely excessive prudery on the part of the playwright. But the scene during which Pellico the prisoner mistranslates scripture in order to avoid the sure temptation of a kiss—that kiss already planted on the book itself, kisses like those of Solomon for his bride, no doubt—sheds considerable light on the literary preoccupations that have so radically altered both the theatrical and the autobiographical versions. In both cases, in fact, what Pellico has done, at least at one level, is to completely deny and contradict Dante: Truth and Text cannot, at least in some cases, coexist—we cannot read certain texts without assuming their guilts. Francesca is guilty of the simplest act, not of the interpretation that followed her reading, but of the reading in and of itself.

That anyone, even an author, would not only hold but write and inscribe such a view is not peculiar in and of itself; this is, after all, one of the tenets of certain versions of what we call "fundamentalism," and all sorts of ideological positions vis-à-vis reading—and the need to abstain therefrom—are rooted in the same or a comparable belief. This is also, in many ways, a version of a common enough reading of Dante's

Francesca scene, that interpretation being that the culpability lay in reading a pornographic text. But here Pellico is taking all of this a considerable step further, and his reading, as manifest in his two texts, is both far more radical and, for a man whose own definition of himself is insistently that he is a writer, far more problematic in its implications. The nightmarish problem that emerges for and in Pellico is, finally, that no text is exempt from misconstruction and misreading, that there is, finally, no text so liminally clear and true that it is really sacred: in the end, both the Bible and the *Commedia,* texts he has held up explicitly (and not just by cultural heritage and implication) as sacred, must be denied, must be held back, must be undone. In the *Prigioni,* besides the multiple citations and allusions to both sacred texts, some of which I have already pointed out, it is in chapter 6 (in the English translation, so appropriately entitled "Consolation from the Scriptures") that we get the most forthright setting out of the status of the two texts for the Prisoner: "Ben mi si permise ch'io avessi una Bibbia ed il Dante. . . . Imparava ogni giorno un canto di Dante a memoria, e questo esercizio era tuttavia sì macchinale, ch'io lo faceva pensando meno a quei versi che ai casi miei. . . . Questo divino libro [referring to the Bible]. . . . Se non che, ad onta del buon volere, spessissimo io leggeva colla mente ad altro, e non capiva" (It is true that I was allowed to have a copy of the Bible and of Dante. . . . I used to learn a canto of Dante by heart every day, but even this exercise was so mechanical that I carried it out with thoughts less on those verses than on my own misfortunes. . . . This divine Book. . . . Even so, however, in spite of my good will I used to read it very often with my mind on other things, and did not understand it).

Following the familiar pattern of a spiritual autobiography, one text serves as a (textual) guiding light (the *Commedia*) and the other as the source of exemplary quotations (the Bible), and the privileged status of both is evident in their being the only ones he is permitted to actually keep with him (one is, in an irreverent moment, tempted to say that under such circumstances they were likely to become sacred even if they had not been so before the fact). But in both cases even Pellico is a far from perfect reader, and the question of whether there can be a text sufficiently transparent to have perfect readers is, clearly and painfully, just beneath the surface. In both cases a reader is likely to be thinking of himself or of other presumed irrelevancies while reading; in both cases the sanctity of the text, in fact, does very little to guarantee a perfectly devoted reader. However, the depths of the problem are not obvious until the reader reaches the series of chapters that recount the overcome passion with Zanze, the guard's daughter who made the coffee that let him write all night—and perhaps it is this scene's highly charged atmosphere, that anticipation of revelation, that made it reverberate for Stendhal in the *Chartreuse de Parme*. It is there, finally, in the scene when she asks him, kissing the sacred book, to read her that scripture so relentlessly erotic and tempting, that Pellico, himself playing a Francesca as pure and converted as the one on the stage that had made him famous, must deny both sacred texts in one fell swoop and one disappointingly anticlimactic moment: no reading, no temptation, no kissing, no sin, no Dante, no Bible.

An extraordinary position, one is forced to note again, not, perhaps for some anti-intellectual illiterate, but certainly for a man who cannot name himself except as a writer, and a writer of unambiguously literary texts[20]—the kind of text most likely to be construed in the most radically contingent fashion, interpreted as the reader will see fit at the moment of reading—and for whom no writing is as precious as the two texts he has just put aside, purposefully mistranslated, denied. Moreover, in the final analysis, in this almost complete denial of the possibility

20. Pellico in fact continues his work as a writer while he is imprisoned—it ends up being a major pastime and consolation. See chapter 28, for example, where he gives a partial list of works composed in prison: "Ivi io scriveva di cose letterarie. Composi allora l'*Ester d'Engaddi* e l'*Iginia d'Asti*, e le cantiche intitolate: *Tancreda, Rosilde, Eligi e Valafrido, Adello*, oltre parecchi scheletri di tragedie e di altre produzioni, e fra altri quello d'un poema sulle *Lega Lombarda* e d'un altro su *Cristoforo Colombo*" (There I wrote literature. It was then that I wrote . . . and the poems entitled . . . besides the outlines of several tragedies and of other works, among which were a poem on the Lombard League, and another on Christopher Columbus). I note that in the Capaldi translation, which has added chapter titles that are nonexistent in the original, chapter 28 is called "Literary Distractions."

of "innocent" reading, at least under certain circumstances, Pellico is saying it makes little difference whether it is the Lancelot or Solomon's Song—and in this he is ratifying the canonical Catholic view that had removed the reading of scripture from the provenance of those not "authorized" to do so, the clergy. It is not difficult, in fact, to add this second layer of interpretation to this scene: the young girl not only cannot understand, literally, the language of scripture, but even if it were translated she would almost undoubtedly be unable to interpret its difficulties correctly, she would take Solomon's love songs too liter-ally—shades of Boccaccio's characters, here, a faint memory of an Alibech's literal acceptance of the suggestion to "put the devil in Hell." The difficulty (and, at times, impossibility) of interpretation is every-where and threatens the reading of any text: Francesca and her lover-to-be might just as well have been reading a bit of the Old Testament. But Pellico is a poor apologist for the Church's draconian textual prohibi-tions, for he himself clings to the forbidden text almost as a talisman: he reads it endlessly, even when he himself is aware he is not doing it justice, he quotes it, he memorizes it as he does Dante's *cantos*—all of these consolations at least in principle denied others. Pellico is thus painfully aware of both the potentially damaging contingencies of inter-pretation and the innocent and virtuous values of reading under other circumstances. There will be times, he says—and in this he is breaking with Dante, perhaps even with the Bible—when one will have to choose between text and truth, when even the sacred texts will turn their backs on the devout reader.

One remarkable aspect of this entire scene in the *Prigioni*—and I believe it reflects back on *Francesca*—is the extent to which Pellico is aware that in the complete suppression of the sin, or of any sin that the reader can read about, there is a considerable diminishing of literary interest. The opening of chapter 30, quoted above, confesses that the work he is writing would be far more "dilettevole," enjoyable, if there had been a consummated grand passion in the story of Zanze. Love stories, seduction stories, are far more "dilettevoli" than a story such as the one he has told, where nothing other than virtue comes of such an encounter, where the kiss on the Bible is never picked up and (blasphemously, perhaps) transferred to the would-be lover (reversing and replacing the obviously repressed object of desire), where Francesca herself has fled in horror, even in a "mere" recounting, at the idea that a kiss would follow a reading. The scenes in both texts are, from a dramatic point of view, thwarted or compromised by the overriding requirements of an uncompromising virtue: Pellico as author clearly felt that a choice needed to be made between the delights of reading (and its concomitant carnal sins) and the possibilities of a longer-term redemption, and he chose the latter—although not without some obvious trepidation and regret.

The interest for us lies in great measure precisely in the dilemma Pellico has perceived and played out, particularly in the later prison scene, where he is at the same time commenting for us on his earlier rendition of *Francesca:* he has struggled to little avail with Dante's precepts, those embodied in the *Commedia,* and he simply cannot make out how one can either read or write within such a system, even if one has faith, as he does. (Perhaps, more properly, the problem arises, in his view, precisely when one has faith.) He is, as I have said before, a true believer, both in the scripture and in Dante, but even so, he knows that the kiss from the girl's lips to the (for her) indecipherable words of Solomon would have gone the next step, would have followed the path of Francesca—not his Francesca, finally, but Dante's. There is no way, he tells us in considerable distress, to have literature work under such circumstances, to have texts say one thing and mean another, to have Francesca sin and those reading her not, to write the adulterous kiss and not thus be adulterous. Pellico the author of *Francesca* and Pellico the reading prisoner in the *Prigioni* (and one is explicitly identified as the other, let us not forget) feels and is trapped by the principles of sacred texts that, in his literary tradition, are the standards at both ends of the sacred-secular spectrum, a spectrum that is, in the case of this tradition, in fact circular. He seems to be saying that there must be a different standard, for faith, for writing, for interpretation, for mere mortals— mere mortals like Francesca and like Silvio Pellico. Mere mortals have to choose between sin and not-sin, between reading and not-reading, between sacred and profane—and when they take on, when they follow their sacred models, even in a state of piety and reverence, they must do so with awe and caution and most of all with an appreciation of the vast differences between them: Dante's Francesca can do things Pellico's cannot. And Borges will be the next century's Dantista to fret most about these limitations of mere mortals, mere poets, and that blinding light thrown off by Dante: how can we write the Aleph?

From this perspective, then, Pellico's spiritual autobiography and conversion is even more profound than one might have at first suspected, for he is renouncing, at a very fundamental level, not only politics and history—neither of which one suspects was ever that interesting for him in the first place—but also that lover who so mistreated him. He is renouncing the possibilities, the passions, the success, of seductive literature: "Queste carte sarebbero certamente più dilettevoli. . . ." For a writer so enamored of his tradition, this second sacrifice was undoubtedly infinitely more painful—as painful, no doubt, as the choice to mistranslate the Old Testament to the girl sitting next to him in that infinitely lonely cell, a girl, after all, who had been the only one able to make him coffee just so, so that he was able to write his tragedies of virtue all night long.

V I

The text we were handed turns out to have more than just the passing overt markers that link it to Dante, especially to the *Commedia;* it constitutes a highly marked re-creation within which its author, Pellico, can explore and articulate his own conversion, one which could not have taken place, one surmises, without the helping hand of the earlier text. One of the most intimate characteristics shared by the two texts— and here and elsewhere there can be little doubt that Pellico is purposefully duplicating the tenets of the master text—is that they are not only the products of conversion(s), but are, in the purest "good news" tradition, meant to serve as conversion texts themselves, texts that will spark or finalize a conversion in a reader. In this sense, at least, the *Prigioni* is a fitting tribute to the *Commedia,* each a textual guide through its own dark wood, that of incarceration and that of writing: the convert pays homage to the text that was essential to his own conversion by reproducing it, by writing a different version of it, which will, he clearly hopes, serve the same functions of comfort, consolation, conversion. If Dante personified Virgil, author of the *Aeneid,* as his guide, then Pellico leaves the question in a rawer state, and merely hangs on to the book itself.

While inevitably one links Pellico's text with other meditations born of imprisonments, it is also necessary to link it—unlikely or contradictory as this may seem at first—with the sort of voyage narration of which the *Commedia* is exemplary. Pellico's narration in the *Prigioni* of his ten years of imprisonment—echoes of epic time, here—has limited affinity, in the long run and in the end, with the more static, philosophical revelations and discourses that are characteristic of the enforced isolation and meditation (including physical immobility) of cell life. On the contrary, despite all sorts of moments when the narrator gives us his reflections on what has happened or is happening, Pellico's prison is not a quiet locus for memory. Far from it, in some ways: the condemned man himself is almost always on the go, in transit from one cell to another, from one prison to another, meeting literally hundreds of characters as he goes through.

In this way too Pellico pays tribute to his literary master: sprinkled among the characters he meets are private and public citizens alike, from famous literati and patriots of the time (Maroncelli being certainly the most notable among these) to deaf and dumb fellow prisoners, a prostitute named Magdalen, jailers of all varieties—in sum, a remarkable panoply of the human race that serves both to educate the narrator and to provide a variety of experiences in a circumstance more commonly noted for the opposite. It is also true that Pellico is far from isolated from the "outside" world: the variety and quantity of communications from others is considerable, again ranging from the philosophical and other inscriptions on cell walls to letters he receives (licit and otherwise), visits, and all manner of other interactions with those outside the already teeming and highly mobile walls of his different cells and prisons.

The overall effect then, is far closer to that of the *Commedia* than one might have expected from something described as memoirs from prison, for the narrator, who, like that of the *Commedia,* has already been to the other side of the mountain and is recounting the trip so that the reader may share in the revelations that lead to conversion, is really recounting a trip and a highly instructive exposure to a broad range of human beings—exemplary and otherwise—and their experiences. The prisoner's relationship with Zanze, the girl who kisses the desired pages of the Bible, is in that sense far from unique or isolated—he will have relationships with thieves and murderers, saints and madmen alike, and he stores away these nuggets, not always understanding what they mean at the time. For this text, like the one that guided him, is in the end a contemplation of the present rather than the past—and it is a text obsessed with how it can be written.

But it is important to insist strongly on these almost obsessive textual affinities of every variety precisely because in the end, as perhaps with all rewritings, it is the difference implicit in the interpretation and rewriting (what we so facilely call a "misreading," with its troubling implication of a "correct" reading) that is crucial and instructive. In this case the departures stand out as vividly as the detailed, almost cartoonish imitations. In many ways, too, Pellico's departures from his guide may be precisely the features that have made his text difficult to absorb in the canon, a canon haunted by Dante, enslaved to him, committed either to rewriting him limpidly and unfalteringly or to writing him away—these are standards that few texts have managed to overcome. Pellico's narrative failure, particularly if we use Dante as the standard—as Pellico himself has set us up, inexorably, to do—is that we never sense quite how lost he might have been, we never have that gradual but sure sense of progression that the *Commedia* lures us into. The Francesca episode is instructive in that regard as well: the converted Pellico does not know how to sin, not even through falling into surrogate temptations, and this not only diminishes the potential narrative drama and interest (as he himself understands full well) but undermines the kind of conversion narration he has embarked on, the kind Dante gave him. The narrator and the protagonist are too often and too early converged, and

Pellico cannot (or chooses not to) neatly separate out the "I"'s at the beginning that will converge at the end.

This choice, this failure (again, by the yardstick Pellico himself has forced on us) is part and parcel of Pellico's reading of Dante, of that interpretation and revisionism that I have already explored. It reflects, of course, the same doubts about the possibilities of sacred, ever-truthful writing and guaranteed good reading: Pellico fears that when the story is retold even the surrogate temptation from which he can turn back and recover, from which he may well emerge purer than at the outset, will itself be far too powerful. Paradoxically, the nature of Pellico's reservation about Dante's principles is that writing is too powerful, too much of a wildcard, to ever be tamed, to ever be made to be and to create great Truth. And, not surprisingly, whereas Dante has turned from his "private" interests to history, and from texts that speak to themselves to those that speak truths universally, Pellico is in fact moving in something resembling the opposite direction, eschewing both history and dangerous literature for the apparently safer, or at least more comforting, consolations of a private truth. Francesca never even kisses Paolo, not even offstage, in the telling of it.

VII

The strikingly unambiguous intertextuality of the sort we see in Pellico's text(s) is almost invariably an explicit and purposeful marker of literary continuity. Especially in a spiritual autobiography—but in fact in any text unembarrassedly rewriting another, especially a "master text," as for example the *Francesca da Rimini*—the "role models" serve in the same way language itself does, as the basic communal property within which any and all individuality or originality must be expressed. It is true, in fact, that Pellico's critical differences with his mentor texts are all the more salient and inescapable precisely because he has in other ways so unhesitatingly recalled his authorities, and precisely because at key moments, when the master text would take us in one direction, the other version takes us elsewhere: I imagine most readers would expect a different dénouement when Pellico starts to tell the story of how he used to read the Bible to Zanze. Thus, the questions that remain to be addressed, it seems to me, are how it has been possible to completely overlook something so loudly crying out to be noticed and, following that, whether our evaluation of a text such as *Le mie prigioni* is substantially altered once we have so completely changed its critical and ontological status. In other words, why did Pellico's text fail so badly after so dramatic an initial success? And does knowing it is very far from what we thought it was, a sort-of-political memoir, make it more readable, more worthy of restitution to the canon?

It is difficult to piece together with any real authority what kind of reading *Le mie prigioni* had during its years of unrivaled popularity; while most sources indicate it was a success tied both textually and historically to the trials and successes of the Risorgimento—in other words, to the lover who spurned him and whom he would in turn cast out of his life—these are almost invariably the same sources that believe the text to be just that, a political memoir of a particularly sentimental and lachrymose bent. Without extensive archival work in dozens of countries— a task well outside the purview of this study—it is hard to do anything other than speculate on the subject of whether, for instance, its spiritual-autobiographical properties were more readily recognized in the middle of the nineteenth century, and whether this in turn might have contributed to a more positive reading of the text than it has had in recent years. Even the sort of research that would inventory contemporary reviews of the text would most likely yield very inadequate results, since published criticism and reviews would reflect a far more sophisticated and "learned" perspective than the sorts of views and tastes that bought the book and made it an international best-seller—the critics' perceptions may have had little to with the public's, then as well as now.[21]

21. One has to wonder, in passing, for example, what will be made in the future of the great international popularity of Eco's *Name of the Rose* a few years ago, and can only too easily imagine the danger of leaping from the pronouncements in reviews of it in the *New York Times Book Review,* say, to the reason(s) so many

But one can make several observations in this realm of reception with some degree of certainty. Firstly, as I have already emphasized, the *Prigioni* was and has continued to be a text whose strongly literary features have always been apparent to other writers, even while the political-historical veil of "context" has by and large clouded them for academic critics. It is also true—and this may be of some relevance— that during the nineteenth century there was a great upsurge in both the writing of and the readership for autobiographies, and that many of these, like Pellico's, were born of starkly historical-political circumstances and yet retreated to privacy and the self. In the wake of Rousseau's indisputable influence, the temptation is to look in that direction for both the inspiration and the popularity of the autobiographies of the nineteenth century. But it is no less viable to note that in a period of great turmoil, when an individual's relationship to history is most starkly set out—and the Risorgimento explicitly conflates the difficulties of personal and national identities—both writers and readers regularly retreat from history itself.

Given this, it is precisely the literary-spiritual structure of the *Prigioni* that may have appealed—especially to the mass audiences. The everyday workings of history in crisis, after all, are far from beneficial to those not in the center of the whirlwind, and it is not so much the almost excruciating sentimentality of the *Prigioni* that was likely to make it a contemporary success but the spectacle, so to speak, of the retreat from the center and the assertion of the value of the individual spirit that Pellico so unabashedly represents. But most importantly, that shift in historical circumstances from past to present that makes footnotes to all of Pellico's characters as well as general historical introductions necessary has obscured the dramatic gossip of much of the text, the abundance of *People* magazine material. The amputation of Maroncelli's leg, Pellico's sister's becoming a nun, the parade of state prisoners going through the Spielberg, on and on, these people, famous, notorious, or merely fascinating for the public, were not remotely part of an archaic

---

Americans had it laid out on their coffee tables. Ultimately, many of these kinds of questions remain unanswerable.

History but rather a very mobile and vivid part of a present about which, in the end, they had had fairly little news. Thus, the text "worked" in its own historical context in great measure because that "context" was a given rather than a framework imposed from without, and because the interest of that material—whatever purpose Pellico may have intended it to serve—was intrinsically strong. Finally, as I noted above, in the context of the many rewritings and appropriations and contemplations of Dante that in the Risorgimento were the special and ubiquitous markers of a wide variety of patriotisms, a legion of Italian readers would perhaps have seen the transparent dependence on the *Commedia*—and found it unremarkable. Others, who did not expect to read Dante as a basic subtext of almost anything else, would not have been as aware of the sounding-board effect in terms of the single specific case, but to judge from the introductions to some nineteenth-century translations, it is clear that the conversion structures did not go altogether unnoticed. It is interesting, as I noted above, that an important interpretative lesson drawn from the text was a kind of pre- or proto-Gandhian one, that the spiritual resistance to Austrian brutality and denial of the rights and independence of Italians was the best of all possible resistances. Of course, it might also be that, remembering the bloodletting of the last years of the Terror, many may have felt some relief that in the wake of the Italian revolution-*cum*-independence a famous prisoner who had suffered a brutal ten years' incarceration was urging Christian charity and forgiveness. It is also possible, finally, that contemporary readers would not have had the difficulties with a text that is at once sacred and profane that seem to plague us both as common readers and as critics.

It seems to me that the blindness of more recent criticism—and by this I mean everything from DeSanctis on—to the strictly literary characteristics of this work is in at least some measure a product of the secularization and historicization of Italian literary studies, codified by DeSanctis and ratified by Croce and Marxists alike. It is a text that has been relegated to obscurity by DeSanctis himself—and in the vacuum of history, there is no externally generated interest to provide any kind of "opposition" or alternative readings. Significantly, as the notes to this chapter reveal, the *Prigioni* is far more likely to be cited with sensitivity to its literariness in a study on French spiritual autobiographies, or by a comparatist, than it is in a comparable study of Italian autobiographical texts. Thus, Pellico's text, cut off from its structuring ties to a tradition of sacred texts, has been left to fend for itself in the secular and historical universe within which whatever meaning and value it can have is rooted in its historical circumstances: the Risorgimento, most likely, and perhaps Italian Romanticism. The possibility that this is also, or instead, a text grappling quite directly with the Truth, engaging itself quite intimately with the tradition of sacred texts (as opposed to merely voicing some fairly banal and standard Catholic spirituality), does not emerge easily in this context.

Not surprisingly then, the canonical view emerges that this is a text *of* the Risorgimento, i.e., mostly about that historical moment, from the vantage point of one of its political prisoners who was never out of touch with others also involved in the political upheavals, and tainted with a sentimentality and religiosity that is part of the (again, historical) context of a Romanticism that rejected models and imitation in favor of authenticities of feeling, barings of the soul, and so forth. This is a secularized reading that the *Prigioni* will to a great extent sustain: the narration is, as I have noted, filled with contacts with the outside world, as well as with other prisoners, many of whom were also political. *Le mie prigioni,* like the *Commedia,* can be read for its political insights and historical values. Moreover, Pellico's expressions of Christian charities and virtues, his almost naive horror at the ways of the political world, his cheek-turning and forsaking of historical involvement, can then be taken as the Romantic component of the work, another side of the coin that is Foscolo. But I believe that the critical and canonical failure of *Le mie prigioni* is due in large measure, ironically, to this status it has acquired, this tagging of it as a memorialistic text of this turbulent historical moment. Anyone picking it up to read a more or less exciting narration of at least certain aspects of the Risorgimento—written by one of its most famous prisoners, no less, who was a professional writer besides—or expecting the sort of memoirs from jail that have the makings of the great novels of the nineteenth century would unfailingly be disappointed. That reader may not know she is in fact reading a spiritual autobiography (a genre that has never claimed great popular readership) and may not be fully cognizant that a rewriting of the *Commedia* is the real agenda, but she is certainly aware that, in terms of how it is billed, it falls fairly flat.

The question, then, is whether it is only or even primarily this sort of false advertising, this raising of inappropriate expectations, that has caused this dramatic fall in fortunes, and thus whether a revision of those expectations would change that *fortuna* substantially. It is the final paradox, I think, that by redefining the text as a spiritual autobiography and understanding it as I have suggested, as one author's grappling with the problems of engagement and Truth that Dante handed down to all his successors, Pellico's text is likely to be even less read than before—even a mediocre memoir of the Risorgimento might well seem to be a more likely hit on a survey course reading list. The benefits of the alteration in generic classification (and thus expectations) are simple and limited: we are reminded, as Rilke says, that we have crowded out of life—and much literary criticism—that whole "spirit-world" that is, in fact, an integral component of meaning itself, if not for us as individuals, for a vast number of writers whose work is then that much less than coherent. One might even say that the principal benefit here is that we uncover in *Le mie prigioni* an entire interpretative system for Dante, one that reveals either a misreading or a correction—depending on one's own reading of the *Commedia* and the *Vita nuova*. But in saying that, we also understand that this is one chapter—far from isolated and, historically, far from insignificant—of the many where gifted authors wrestle with the problems of sacred texts and literature as history, problems posed most uncompromisingly by Dante. And Pellico's struggle, in the end, is more than worth recognizing and reading as such—not just because it is in a number of ways exemplary of the difficulties of writing within the Italian tradition, but because his open and drawn-out acknowledgement of failure in terms of the standards set by the Master is in a different way a great triumph Dante might well have approved of, the triumph of painful, rather than glorious Truth.

III

Faint Praise and Proper Criticism:
The *miglior fabbri*

It's its usual pristine self. And it's good, in its genre.
But they're like craftsmen—they've decided they're gonna make
this particular wooden chair that they designed, and each one
will be very beautifully made, but it will be the same
chair. . . . They're craftsmen.
—David Bowie commenting on a German
rock group, *Rolling Stone,* April 23, 1987

I

Ieu suis Arnauts, qu'aimas l'aura
E chatz la lebbre ab lo bou
E nadi contra suberna.
Arnaut Daniel

Aye, I Arnaut, pluck the wind's traces
On ox, hunt hare, helter skelt
And I swim 'gainst torrent's beating
Ezra Pound as Arnaut

*J*n one of his finest ironic moments in the *Commedia,* Dante fully transforms the most hermetic of the Provençal poets, the Arnaut Daniel who reigns over the *trobar clus.* The poet who reached the height of achievement in the art of self-enclosure will face his new creator and master here and uncover himself utterly. He will claim, in a Dantesque version of the Provençal *koine* he had written in, that he neither can nor will conceal himself:

Tan m'abellis vostre cortes deman,
qu'ieu no me puesc ni voill a vos cobrire.

So does your courteous request please me that I neither can nor would conceal myself from you. (*Purgatorio* 26, 140–41).[1]

And in the age, regnant until relatively recently, when poets were the most powerful and canonically influential literary historians, an Arnaut

1. This and all subsequent quotations (unless otherwise noted) from the *Commedia* are from the edition and translation of Charles Singleton.

who would otherwise have remained quite hidden among his dozens of Provençal cohorts receives here, in the *Purgatorio,* the first push to greater fame as a greater poet. But Dante's *rifacimento* would in and of itself probably have served only to make Arnaut one of the better known of the troubadours among students of the *Commedia* and of the ever rarer ones of the Provençal lyric itself.

But there eventually came a second push, that into a veritable stardom that some might judge incommensurate with his limited and rarified corpus of some eighteen poems. A young Ezra Pound, engaged in his own *rifacimento*—a conscious and purposeful making it new—of the literary history then called Romance philology, brought Arnaut back from the dead by using him as one of his many masks. Arnaut, the "original" *miglior fabbro,* against almost all reason became a fixture of modernist poetry and letters because Ezra Pound found him the most charming and congenial of characters to play out, and because T. S. Eliot, who in turn thought himself a second Dante, thought Pound made the perfect Arnaut. The only little problem with this fairly standard and almost universally known story is that it leaves out the most critical element of any and all versions of literary histories: judgment, and especially veiled and damning judgments, faint praise.[2] But neither

2. As far as I can ascertain, only two critics have sensed the uneasiness of the Eliot-Pound relationship in the "miglior fabbro" line itself and as it is reflected in the appropriation of Dante and Dante-related masks to play out the difficulties at second-hand. Freccero 1986b, although he concentrates more on the Cavalcanti reflexes and on the Arnaldian, writes: "At the same time the appeal to Dante as literary ancestor in the work of Eliot may be interpreted as a claim to a poetic respectability not possessed by other poets, and especially not by Ezra Pound. Pound sensed in Dante something of the *bien pensant* and the conservative in comparison to the free-thinking daring of Guido Cavalcanti. It is difficult to resist pressing the analogy to apply to Eliot and Pound as well. At this level, the issue of Dante's 'influence' may well be a mask for contemporary rivalry: Eliot playing Dante to Pound's Guido, with attendant anxiety, as described by Bloom. To trace one's poetic lineage to Dante is tantamount to claiming the poet's laurels against all other contenders, at least in the case of Eliot" (3–4). Langbaum says the following of the differences between the poets after the publication of *The Waste Land:* "The very praise—the greatest living 'master of verse form'—implies a reservation that

Dante nor Eliot—nor Pound, for that matter—would imagine that one could construct a reasonable literary history without judgment, both open and veiled, and none of them, as poets and literary historians, shied away from the damning judgment.

The great peril of being a Truth-writer, of following the path taken by the Virgils and the Aeneases, is that one might misguidedly, perhaps even in good faith engage the wrong cause; one might use poetry to represent a Truth that was, in the end, not a Truth at all. This is perhaps the most acute problem with the belief in the Absolute and in poetry's obligation to be devoted to it absolutely: it is a merciless and pitiless enterprise, and there is little if any room for error. If it is poetry's obligation to speak Truth—because, ultimately, it shapes and defines Truth for others—then it is a grievous sin to use poetry and its powerful influence in any other way. This is the self-abnegation of wrenching oneself away from the very powerful temptations of a Dido or a Francesca, from the self-fulfilling lust of such poetry to a poetic enterprise that is of a different moral import altogether. There is considerable irony in noting that the poets that Dante judges deficient because they chose the wrong kind of poetry—all those who never see it as an enterprise that takes itself as Truth, the poets who never had the sort of revelation and transformation that Dante himself recounts in the *Vita nuova*, the innocents who worked with fiction and the aesthetic pleasures of art—these writers are left behind in Purgatory, expiating and working off a sin that is, after all, a redeemable one. Thus, although their creatures may whirl about with Dante's own, with a Francesca who proves just how effective

---

Eliot more or less maintains. Pound is the greatest living craftsman, but pointedly not the greatest living poet because of Eliot's doubts about Pound's content. The dedication of *The Waste Land* to Pound as 'il miglior fabbro' ('the best craftsman') *may* contain the same reservation" (171, emphasis mine). As the hesitation in Langbaum might indicate, the considerable discussions of the problems between Pound and Eliot and their poetic ideologies are invariably (and rather reverently) dated to the period *after* the publication of *The Waste Land*. This issue will be further discussed later in this chapter.

such creations can be, they themselves, the unconverted poets, do not suffer the harshest punishments. The damned poets are those whose sin was much graver: they did not merely write the wrong kind of poetry; they misread their own *libello,* they were blind to the inscribed meanings of the universe—and they thus revealed the wrong kind of truth. The trap, clearly, is that if one does choose to write about Truth there will also be falsehoods out there which may snare the engaged poet—and he, or they, are not as lucky, not as forgivable.

The Pound whose first infatuation was with the hermeticism and musicality of the Arnaut Dante would call—mysteriously, many have thought—*il miglior fabbro* (as Eliot would call Pound himself later on) had other favorite Dante poets as well, and a complex and often decidedly ambiguous relationship with Dante himself. Pound, in fact, serves as a remarkable guide to those we might call Dante's discarded poets: it is through Pound's efforts, arguably more so than those of any of the academic philologists that followed the career path he abandoned, that several of the poets cast out by Dante are rehabilitated, brought back from his Siberia. There is not only Arnaut, who is one of Pound's most enduring masks and voices, but other versions of himself, other voices: Bertran de Born, the focus of inspiration of three of Pound's major early poems, and Guido Cavalcanti, whose own poetry Pound translated even more indefatigably and more completely than he had Arnaut's.[3]

3. See chapter 1 for a brief discussion of Pound's translations of Arnaut. The translations themselves are available only in Pound 1985 (a limited edition not readily available; the quotes from the translation of "En cest sonet coind'e leri" cited here are from this edition, p. 43; it is a poem he translated circa 1917). Pound never completed, or at least was never able to have published, the full, separate edition of Arnaut's poetry he had intended. This and other aspects of Pound's relationship with Arnaut himself are discussed at length in the very thorough McDougal 1972: 102–20, where the author makes the very telling point that while Pound was very often interested in the personae of poets who fascinated him (including those of other Provençal poets—see discussion below of his poems with versions of Provençal poets such as Bertran de Born as characters), he was uncharacteristically not interested in Arnaut except through his *oeuvre.* Pound did,

Born is a haunting poetic figure in the *Inferno*, dealt with publicly: he is the first of the four Provençal poets to appear in the *Commedia* and he emerges as a poor reader, much like Francesca. Brave enough to write political verse, like his compatriot and fellow poet Sordello, he was ultimately on the wrong side, from Dante's rather strict vantage point, of a decisive political issue, a poet whose vision and poetry were indeed engaged, but wrongly and malevolently so.[4] But the Pound who professes to be mystified by Dante's damnation of that Provençal poet

---

of course, publish a separate and full edition of Cavalcanti, now available in the fine edition of Anderson 1983; see Anderson 1979 and 1985 for lucid and informative discussions of Pound's complex relationship with Cavalcanti. On this see also Wilhelm 1974, who also notes that Pound sensed the rivalry between Dante and Cavalcanti and tended to empathize with and favor the latter (332). For Pound and Bertran see McDougal 1972 and Shapiro 1974 and 1980, which, although focused on Dante's treatment of Bertran and the sestina, respectively, shed considerable light on Pound's perspective vis-à-vis both Born and Arnaut. Note that Pound's own *sestina* is discussed in the chapter on the Arnaldians (1980:48) and that the author is finely attuned to the fact that in Dante's universe Bertran's problem was, transparently, his fusion of art and "propaganda" (1974:115). I strongly disagree with the opinion that Dante by and large treats poets and poetry in a morally neutral fashion, and I believe the use of the word "propaganda" in this discussion may obscure the fact that what is at stake is propaganda in the wrong cause, but both studies are of extreme usefulness and interest. See also Picone for another study sensitive to the problem of the "treachery" involved in a misuse of poetry. An excellent primary source is Chaytor, which, although old, is still not outdated and provides an edition of the "troubadours of Dante." Finally, Pound's relations with Arnaut and Cavalcanti can be glimpsed in his own essays on these ancestral figures: that on Arnaut appears in the *Spirit of Romance* [1910] 1952:22–38), as does one of his several pieces on Dante, 118–65, and the essay on Cavalcanti can be found in *Literary Essays* (1954:149–200).

4. See Barolini 1984, 153–73, for a cogent and convincing reading of the close relationship between Sordello and Born, the only two "political" poets of the *Commedia*. She also sets aside and corrects the earlier canonical reading that eliminated Sordello as one of the Provençal poets, a reading that thus conveniently gave us three Provençal poets, rather than the four: Bertran, Sordello, Arnaut and Folquet. Although I will not deal with Sordello here, he, too, is one of Pound's masks and voices, particularly in *The Cantos;* see especially also Wilhelm 1977.

makes the striking Bertran the subject of two of his poems: *Near Perigord* and *Sestina: Altaforte,* both of which, not coincidentally, establish close links between Born and his compatriot Arnaut. Pound also rewrites Bertran's most famous poem, *Plan [Lament] for the Young English King,* for which Bertran is serving infinite time in the *Inferno.* Bertran thus emerges as the counterpart to the Provençal poet whose praises are exorbitantly sung in the *Paradiso,* Folquet, a poet not only dedicated to the right cause, having written fiercely against Albigensians, Moors and others worth battling against, but eventually converted away from poetry altogether and to the spiritual life. And, conspicuously, Pound adopts and plays with all of Dante's Provençal poets except Folquet.

Pound's interest in Bertran had its limitations and was largely played out in the poems he wrote of him; it certainly came nowhere close to the lavish attention reserved for Guido Cavalcanti, who is, in his excruciating silence, an equally fascinating and haunting absence in the *Commedia* itself.[5] Guido's poems are, in fact, a lifelong devotion for Pound, and his translations of Guido's remarkably difficult poems a major continuing effort. Pound thus chose as his most abiding hero Dante's great nemesis, that implacable other who is there and not there, everywhere, the *primo amico,* the best friend ignominiously abandoned in canto 10 of the *Inferno*

5. Discussions of the highly problematic Dante-Cavalcanti relationship abound: see the encyclopaedic Barolini 1984 for the full range of citations and allusions as well as extensive secondary bibliography. The most penetrating discussions, attuned to the delicacy of the rivalry, are the rich and subtle Durling 1983; Harrison, which is the most direct and unembarrassed of all studies of Dante's treatment of Guido; and Mazzotta 1986b and Freccero 1986b, each discussed and quoted above. Of unrivaled interest is Pound's own remarkably direct assessment in his essay on Cavalcanti, originally published in 1934; Pound frankly points out that Dante was far too conservative and strict to approve of the far more iconoclastic Guido, a Guido whose *Donna mi prega* is marvelously described in the following passage: "I mean that it shows traces of a tone of thought no longer considered dangerous, but that may have appeared about as soothing to the Florentine of A.D. 1290 as conversation about Tom Paine, Marx, Lenin and Bucharin would to-day in a Methodist bankers' board meeting in Memphis, Tenn." (Pound, ed. Eliot, 1954: 149).

in the spectacular scene when Dante meets not Guido himself, but rather his father, in Hell. As with Bertran, Guido is blamed not for the more elementary (and less grievous, it would appear) sin of choosing the wrong kind of poetry, but rather for having misused the enormous power of poetry, harnessed it to the wrong cause—and Guido, so spectacularly talented, was a master of misreadings: an Averroist, a disdainer of Virgil, a heretic who did not believe that love's images could be said.

Dante is a hard and relentless taskmaster and a merciless judge. Bertran and Guido are left behind to rot—at least until they become, through Pound's resuscitations, his rewritings and translations, very live and lively parts of the twentieth century and of the modernist tradition Pound played so important a role in creating. Pound's Dante is a treasure trove of new poetry and new voices, a magic land overflowing with masks and visions, and this Dante of his is his first and last love: the awesome teacher that inspires from the earliest days of apprentice poet to fellow exile of the solitary last years in Italy, other author of the other *cantos*.[6] For Pound, Dante is a giver of life, a poet who not only makes it new himself but fully writes, rewrites and prewrites several hundred years of lyric poetry, a major chunk of the history of lyric poetry, in fact—and Dante's poets, his Arnauts and his Cavalcantis, are brought into existence and into the tribe Pound will create through the *Commedia*. So if Dante is trying to write them out of literary history, Pound will simply write them right back in.[7] Dante would have been aghast and mortified, no doubt, to have seen this later revival, and the substantial

6. McDougal 1985 reveals Pound's earliest and significantly formative infatuation with Dante, traceable at least to unpublished notebooks from his student days, and goes on to explore the many ways in which Pound's Dante is a transcendental model for his own canon-forming poetic mission(s)—the "Maestro" of *The Spirit of Romance*.

7. In a rich and provocative article, McMahon explores the complex way in which Pound is able to embrace and substantially rewrite Dante at the same time, and the rewriting involves that "correction" of Dante's vision of Truth apparent in canto 26 of the *Inferno*, the canto of Ulysses, which is explicitly corrected in the first of the *Cantos*.

canonical influence as allies of Pound, of these variously imperfect poets he had laid to rest. But Pound's Dante did not rest easily, did not enjoy his univocal vision of literary history; this was a Pound, we must not forget, who thought Laurence Binyon's translation of the *Commedia*— one executed in "triple rhyme" and which seeks to achieve the poetic/musical impact of the original more than anything else, and thus is far too opaque and fragmentedly lyrical to capture the unified Truth of the original—was by far the best. Pound not only lavishly reviewed Binyon's *Inferno* when it first came out but remained in correspondence with him, aiding, abetting, and encouraging the translations of the other two *cantiche*.[8] And Pound's *Cantos,* in the end, speak far more to the virtues, poetic and epistemological, of lyricism and its unremittingly scattered voices than to the strong and stark and encyclopaedic unity that emerges as the voice of the namesake cantos of the *Commedia*.[9] Thus, it is in Pound's heroicizing of poets whose own voices are arrogated in the *Commedia*, in making new and influential and very loud the voices of poets with whom Dante himself had, at best, a problematic relationship that Pound registers his strongest rewriting of Dante. Born is transformed from sower of discord to hero of poetic harmony, and Pound's

8. The review, which indirectly provides some insights into Pound's ultimately great distance from Dante himself, was first published in 1934 and is entitled "Inferno." It is reprinted in Giamatti 1983: 175–86 and was included in the *Literary Essays* by Eliot. See the excellent and revealing Fitzgerald 1981, which laments (correctly, I believe) that the Binyon *Comedy* is so little known and almost never used—although it is indeed readily available in the Viking Portable Dante. For Pound's relatively distanced relationship see also Ellis, as well, again, as Pound's direct comments in the opening pages of the essay on Cavalcanti.

9. Kenner 1983 gives a charming and suggestive evocation of the genesis of Pound's *Cantos* at Penn—equal parts the Dante he was studying and that starkly fragmented and seemingly disjointed view of the universe that emerges from the idiosyncratic American collegiate curriculum—a course of studies which then, as now, sees no lack of unity in its lyricism. "By the time Ezra Pound had completed the freshman registration process what he had signed up for included the following: English composition; Public speaking; Algebra; German Grammar; American Colonial History; The Principles of Government in the United States; and Latin. And people have called the *Cantos* heterogeneous" (6).

Cavalcanti acquires the position of eminence and prominence among other poets that Dante's silence had sought to deny him. And most of all, at least symbolically, Pound himself will come to be known as the *miglior fabbro*. The epithet was bestowed on Pound by Eliot, and in this case, too, we shy away from the palpable disdain that lies not so far beneath the surface and that ever-so-polite tone. But in the context of Dante's poetic conversion, perceived and embraced by Eliot and trivialized by Pound, it is a crucial and telling line, fraught with great difficulty and delivering the sort of judgment that distances.

I I

Ieu suis Arnaut que plor e vau cantan

I am Arnaut who weeps and goes singing

Dante as Arnaut

It is in the ever-increasing clarity of the midpoint of the Pilgrim's journey, nearing the heights of Purgatory, that Dante finally confronts those poetic antecedents he wishes to acknowledge most directly—and where he sets out his critical difference from them most succinctly. It is here that he delivers his famous "miglior fabbro" epithet, one which initially surprised and baffled critics, who found Arnaut at best a peculiar choice, at worst a simply mistaken one, as the example of the "best" poet of the *parlar materno*. But critics got over those qualms soon enough, and because it was impossible to contradict Dante's seemingly simple and absolute sentence, have accepted Arnaut as Dante's exemplar of the "best" and found ways to account for it, to justify it, to explain it.[10]

10. There is a very extensive bibliography on the subject of Arnaut himself, a great deal of it provoked by and linked to the Dante citation although there is virtually no exploration of the possibility that there is irony or undercutting in Dante's "praise" or a tone of disdain in the words of the more directly disdained Guinizelli. Again, one can start with the meticulous philological discussion and thorough bibliography in Barolini 1984. Among many other studies to consult: Melli's near-classic article (1959), which provides an invaluable history of earlier

But it is in fact a very difficult choice to explain away at face value—particularly since it occurs at the climax of an extended replaying of his poetic conversion and transformations in the cantos of the poets. It is in cantos 21 through 26 of the *Purgatorio*—cantos that match up synchronistically with the key conversionary chapters of the *Vita nuova*—

---

thought—even then a substantial body of scholarship had dealt with the problem—on this critical appraisal on Dante's part that many critics found bizarre and/or unacceptable. Melli also traces Dante's shifting opinion of Arnaut (and with him Guinizelli) from the *De vulgari* to the *Purgatorio* and attempts to account for it, and although I strongly disagree with the double conclusion that Dante is sincere in the praise and that the root of it is his (Dante's) perception that Arnaut too is a poet who cultivates a unity of truth and poetry ("stretto accordo tra ispirazione ed espressione," 444) the study is an indispensable point of reference and departure; Smith, who maintains that Dante saw in Arnaut a universal archetype of troubadours; Hiscoe, whose review of earlier scholarship focuses intently on the problems of reconciling the poet, Arnaut, whom an earlier generation of scholars would have considered mediocre and obscurantist, with Dante's seemingly extravagant praise (Hiscoe's own solution is that there is parody at work and that there is a necessary secondary reference to the Biblical story of Daniel); Dragonetti 1977 is one of the more recent examples of many studies which (although this one is purportedly Lacanian) serve to justify Dante's apparent valorization through a study of Arnaut's remarkable technical dexterity; most recently, Shapiro 1982 suggests that Dante's relationship with Arnaut bears traces of a suppression of influence; and Yowell, in one of the most extreme positions of acceptance of the surface-level praise in *Purgatorio* 26, claims Arnaut is/was a model Poet for a Dante who is damning the excessive love ("trop amar") of both Francesca and some previous poets: "The distinction between *trop* and *ben amar* is, I believe, a necessary gloss on the lyric episode of Paolo and Francesca in *Inf.* 5 where we find condemned, not physical, erotic, or adulterous love, but excessive love (390)." Meanwhile, the "historical Arnaut," we are told, sensed a conflict between these two, the *trop* and the *ben,* and is redeemed because of "his struggle to forge a definition of measured love and his apparent irresolution" (393). Only McMahon, who is reading Pound's Dante, of course, senses the discrepancy between the types of judgements at hand: "He [Dante] pays grateful homage to Guinizelli and shows great respect for Arnaut. . . . Nevertheless, Dante's placing them in this circle reflects his moral judgment on their writings. . . . These two poets 'sinned' by writing amatory works that joined Hermes and Aphrodite, literary creation and that Dante sets out the *Commedia*'s rendition of that same transformation from one kind of poet to another. Here he replays out the process in a different and complementary fashion: he begins with his encounter with a Statius for whom he creates a Christian conversion, and finishes in canto 26 (one remembers here that in the *Vita nuova* the twenty-sixth chapter is the last to have *divisioni* following the poems, the last in the "old" poetic life before the revelation and transformations following from Beatrice's death—and the twenty-sixth cantos in the other two canticles of the *Commedia* are overtly keyed) with an equally fictitious convert, this time in terms of poetic style: Arnaut Daniel. And in the middle of it all, of course, is one of the most influential of all passages: the canon-forming exchange with Bonagiunta da Lucca, in the course of which Dante gives that enticingly but deceptively simple definition of the *dolce stil nuovo*.

This sequence of literally central cantos is well recognized as constituting the richest sustained discourse on Dante's part on the proper nature of poetry, and although no one has explored the strongly negative undertones of the "miglior fabbro" epithet, as I read it, the lavish amount of attention paid to these pivotal cantos does give us, at its most illuminating, the keys necessary to understand this "puzzling" praise.[11] It is here, to summarize a complex and compelling reading, that Dante's belief in the necessary moral rectitude and truth value of poetry are developed and set out, that Dante reflects and sets out his view that true

---

sexual desire, in an improper or 'unnatural' way. Dante, of course, implies that the *Commedia* embodies the divinely true, and therefore proper, union of Hermes and Aphrodite" (73).

11. The most compelling and sustained of the many studies is certainly that in Mazzotta 1979, see particularly chapters 5, "Literary History," and 6, "Allegory: Poetics of the Desert." DeBonfils Templer 1980 (undoubtedly written some years before the appearance of the Mazzotta book) gives a reasonable impression of earlier standard readings; more recently, Brownlee 1984 is a valuable addition to the observations in Mazzotta, extending the discussion from the *Purgatorio* chapters to the *Paradiso* and, as I have noted above, to the *Vita nuova;* again, Barolini 1984 serves as a comprehensive exploration of the citations of poets in this complex of cantos.

poetry and good literature have the power to engender a moral conversion—and thus we finally understand why poetry which has engendered some sort of false or immoral conversion is so vile. It is here, more than anywhere else in his writings, that Dante crystallizes his positive views on poetry, his belief that the world of poetic fiction must not be a solipsistic and self-enclosed entity, but rather that it is its duty to merge with personal and salvation history, to symbolize the intense coherence between literature and life, to be True (rather than factual)—in the language of the *Vita nuova,* not to need *divisioni.* Dante, to quote Mazzotta, "rejects that literature which is an intransitive aesthetic experience independent of the thought of God and believes, as the exchange with Bonagiunta exemplifies, that a literary text ought to be a vehicle to God, joining together the worlds of God and man" (Mazzotta 1979:223). Or, from a slightly different perspective, one quite consonant with that revealed in the *Vita nuova:* "The poem . . . is neither the imitation of God's way of writing nor a prodigious crystal, an idolatrous and self-referential construct; it occupies the ambiguous space between these two possibilities" (237).

But among his poetic ancestors there are many prodigious crystals, and certainly none could be more exemplary of the cultivation of writing as that idolatrous construct than Arnaut. What our readings of these cantos have *not* captured is that this profession of faith on Dante's part—any profession of faith, necessarily—*implies a rejection.* That rejection is that other side of the coin that is revealed when Dante has Guido Guinizelli call Arnaut Daniel "il miglior fabbro del parlar materno."[12] It is this line, in this context of a poetic conversion fully achieved and fully clarified, the poetic conversion first reflected in the *Vita nuova,* that has become canonized as an expression of essentially unmitigated praise, both in Dante and, half a millennium later, when T. S. Eliot uses it again to describe an Ezra Pound who had himself revived the long-dead cult of Arnaut as part of his new creation—so he and others understood it—of

12. For fuller considerations of the role played in these cantos by Guinizelli, and thus the impact of the line being uttered by him, see Barolini 1984 and especially Mazzotta 1979.

a long-dead lyricism. The reverentiality, that taking at face value vis-
à-vis Dante, is all too typical of the remarkable idolatry of Dante among
his scholars, one commented on in recent years by several critics.[13]
Something of the same clearly is at work in the almost universal
acceptance of Eliot's "praise" of Pound as the "best." And in both cases
there is a reluctance to face up to the harsh undercutting involved, the
apparent lack of generosity toward poets who had in both cases been
master-teachers—rather, I should say that in both cases critics have
preferred the warm glow and good feel of the apparent generosity in the
apparent praise.

But to accept the simple and straightforward judgment offered at the
surface level requires a set of odd assumptions and has led to the odd
canonization. For while in Dante's words of apparent praise there is, of
course, a gracious tribute to the poetic ancestry he has summoned up,
there can be little doubt that the entire point of the enterprise here is
one of distancing. And in neither the case of Dante nor that of his self-
styled successor is there any reason to assume that admiration is a simple
thing—or that praise cannot be coupled with disdain of major propor-
tions. Dante has acknowledged his indebtedness to the first writers of
the modern European vernaculars from whom he learned the funda-
mentals of writing in the *parlar materno,* the mother tongue, and Arnaut,
in that sense, is quite rightly viewed as symbolic and representative of an
entire tradition. But the emphasis in the canto itself is clearly on the fact
that he, Dante, is leaving them, has left them literally quite far behind.
And although their failure to see the right path, their failure to convert

13. See Valesio's comments in the preface to a new edition of Auerbach, which
include the following: "Contemporary Dantean criticism . . . has trouble becoming
Dantesque because it is still too bound to idolatry. I mean the idolatry of Dante"
(xvii); and, as part of the same extended discussion, "To be humble toward a
literary text is to make a mockery of humility" (xix). Harrison makes comparable
observations from a different perspective in his prefatory comments on the
"hermeneutic trap of Dantology. The trap is one that Dante himself set up by
embedding within his works the hermeneutic guidelines for interpreting them"
(ix).

was clearly a far less problematic failure than Cavalcanti's, they were not able to venture any further than the relatively dim light of Purgatory.

For Dante, unlike Arnaut and all his cohorts, has grown beyond the period of infancy and training and experimentation, beyond the period, in sum, of craftsmanship. Unlike his predecessor Arnaut, Dante realized the limitations of a poetry that dealt with a love whose only issue was the beauty, no matter how remarkable, of language itself, and of a suffering whose major, perhaps only value was to stimulate such poetry. The whole sequence of cantos that reaches its climax with the encounter with Arnaut—and ends with Arnaut himself speaking in the maternal Provençal—is crafted to expel the demons of the idolatry of pure self-referentiality, an idolatry of which Arnaut is clearly established as shaman. And that weeping Arnaut whom Dante meets in Purgatory, who comes out from behind the flames that hide him, should remind us, in his self-indulgence and tears, of the weepy young artist of the *Vita nuova*. Arnaut's sin, the one being expiated in Purgatory, is that of lust (love-related sins being conspicuously attached to poets, including Folquet in the *Paradiso*)—an excess of misdirected passion in love, Dante's reminder here, if any reminder was needed, of the intertwining of self-obsessed poetry with the pretense that it is about love. In this context, to call this Arnaut the "best craftsman of the mother tongue" is, at best, very faint praise indeed. (It behooves us, too, at this point to listen to the cadence of the line in Dante's language: "il miglior *fabbro* del parlar materno," the accent falling strongly and inevitably on *fabbro*— and not on the *miglior* that is normally focused on and as most of the readings of the line imply or suggest. In fact, the interpretative issue here is in some measure one of tone, since meaning is as contingent on tone as on any other linguistic parameter.[14]) Arnaut, then, is first and

---

14. I am indebted to Barbara Smith for noting that with verbal delivery alone one can completely modify apparent meaning, and even "the best" can mean quite the opposite. One also recalls that the entire plot of the movie *The Conversation* hinges on a misinterpretation of one "simple" line—"he would kill us if he could"—which with one pattern of accentuation is a statement of fear and with a different one justifies a planned murder.

foremost a *fabbro,* a craftsman, and he is paying here the price of the conceit and the lustful enamorment with his own craft, with language itself, in Purgatory.

More striking still, perhaps, is the fact that Dante's Arnaut has made it even this far by repenting of that very sin, this infatuation. Much has always been made of the fact that Arnaut and Arnaut alone speaks in "his own" language, but this is a trap.[15] He is now an Arnaut who no longer revels in his hermeticism, who no longer speaks obscure and recondite and beautiful magic but instead a clear and contrite Provençal of Dante's own making. In a number of ways the transformation wrought on Arnaut's language is such that it is far more foreign—to its speaker, certainly—than many of the other languages spoken in the *Commedia.* The Arnaut whose most famous tornada is "Ieu suis Arnauts, qu'aimas l'aura E chatz la lebbre ab lo bou E nadi contra suberna" (I am Arnaut who hoards the wind and chases the rabbit with the ox and swims against the swelling tide) has been chastened into an Arnaut who in Dante's *langue d'oc* says "Ieu suis Arnaut que plor e vau cantan" (I am Arnaut who weeps and goes singing). Dante's Arnaut describes his own past, his poetic past, clearly enough, as "la pasada folor" (my past folly). It verges on the gratuitous, in fact, that poor old Arnaut, he who reveled in the arcana of chasing the wind, now damned and disposed of and having delivered up his recantation in language so far from his precious *trobar clus,* is seen, in the last line of the canto, turning back into the fire which purifies him: "Poi s'ascose nel foco che li affina."

III

London Bridge is falling down falling down falling down

Poi s'ascose nel fuoco che gli affina . . .

15. "And it was Cavalcanti's friend Dante who so commemorated the great troubadours, permitting the greatest, Daniel, to speak his own Provençal, whereas even Odysseus must speak Italian" (Kenner 1971:342) is, except stylistically, typical.

We are in the closing lines of Eliot's *The Waste Land,* a poem of spectacular canonical force and one that reveals the probably unrivaled canonical power of its editor, its *fabbro,* Ezra Pound. The rediscovery of the original manuscript reveals that the poem received its definitive form at the hands of an Ezra Pound who mercilessly blue-pencilled and edited the original Eliot gave him in 1921, an original from which he deleted, among other things, a lengthy section which reworked *Inferno* 26, the canto of Ulysses, counterpart to the Arnaut canto of the *Purgatorio,* remembrance of the conversion of the *Vita nuova* and subtext for his own rewriting in the opening of his own *Cantos.*[16] It is a moment at which Pound is at the height of his career as patron and mentor of the modernist movement—he has gone from young philologist, precocious and eccentric reader of the foundations of modern literature, to creator of a new modern literature himself—and this is particularly the moment of his most remarkable help to Eliot, an Eliot who at that point owed him almost all of his public exposure and thus his success as a poet. It is still some years before the ruptures that were to openly separate the two poets. Most of all, and in light of the discovery of the manuscript that lays bare the astonishingly powerful and pivotal role Pound had in crafting Eliot's breakthrough work, it is the moment of Eliot's greatest debt to Pound and the climax of Pound's beneficence and paternity. It is thus apparently fitting that *The Waste Land,* beginning with the first reprint of 1923, carries the dedication, "For Ezra Pound, il miglior fabbro," which in the first edition Eliot had written by hand into Pound's own copy. It sounds like marvelous praise—and unstinting praise and gratitude would certainly have been the order of the day— and thus it has been taken by Eliot and Pound scholars who have either read the Italian epithet itself at face value or have relied on the interpretations of the line in the *Commedia* by Dante scholars—an

16. The manuscript with Pound's annotations, a fascinating document to peruse, was published by Valerie Eliot in 1971, approximately two years after its existence was brought to her attention. It can be consulted with much profit, providing full details of the complex and remarkable history of Pound's editorial work on *The Waste Land* and much other valuable information.

evaluation, as I have just noted, almost exclusively dedicated to justifying and "understanding" the cause of Dante's "praise."[17]

But if Pound had been cultivating his affinities with Dante the collector of many voices, with the *trobar clus* and with Dante's other poetic bêtes noires,[18] Eliot had much less ambiguously, certainly far more reverentially, embraced the postconversionary Dante himself. Eliot will come to embrace fully the Poet of Truth and his views about the proper nature and role of poetry as his model, and in the end it will be difficult to construe his use of Dante's verses in *The Waste Land* as innocent.[19] It is an almost impossible task to set out the numberless

17. It is well known that, for a number of different reasons, Dante was of enormous importance (and arguably still is) in the development of American literature, to a limited extent in the nineteenth century and to the remarkable extent in the twentieth that the Pound-Eliot crux discussed here reveals. See the many essays (only a handful of which I am discussing here) in McDougal, ed. 1986, which includes studies of Dante as a subtext for many of the most canonical of American poets. See also the fascinating Reynolds, a major study of Joyce's relationship with Dante, which inevitably yields insights on the relationships we are more directly concerned with here. For something of an overview, of the overall presence of Dante in American letters, see Cambon 1969: 119–45 (although Cambon tends to treat appropriations and other forms of intertextuality in a perfectly straightforward fashion). The Giamatti collection of essays includes belletristic as well as scholarly "appreciations" (many, of course, from a period when the distinction was negligible) and provide a full historical perspective of "Dante in America." Both Pound and, especially, Eliot figure prominently in all these studies.

18. I add here that Pound's first collection of poetry, published in 1908 in Venice, is *A Lume Spento,* a line of Dante spoken in Purgatory by the troublesome Manfred (Frederick II's illegitimate son) lamenting the injustices of the world. While the straightforward—and altogether appropriate—interpretation of the allusion is, of course, that it is Pound lamenting the injustices of the world he has recently abandoned and, like Manfred, looking forward to the better things to come in this new (Old) world, it is nonetheless appropriate to note that, here too, Pound is associating himself with a Dante character who is problematic in the *Commedia,* Manfred all the more so because of his father, who—can this be by chance?—is damned with Cavalcanti the father in the *Inferno.*

19. The bibliography on Eliot in general is, of course, vast. Particularly helpful

ways in which Dante was Eliot's truest mentor, a mentor who did not have to be overcome, without reducing the complex and extremely productive relationship to an inventory of borrowings and citations. But Dante's presence is in fact palpable everywhere in Eliot, from the outset of his poetic career, with the *Figlia che piange*. And it only increases as he matures as a poet, ranging from the "mere" quotation to an intimate involvement and, ultimately, fraternal sympathy of not only Christian ideology but, which is perhaps less readily visible, of poetic ideology.[20]

---

general, largely canonical, overviews include Moody, ed., and Headings 1982 (the Twayne Eliot, recently revised). Review essays of some of the most recent studies in the centenary explosion of 1988 include Updike's review of Ackroyd 1984, of special, implicit interest because of Mr. Updike's own explicit melding of the poet/critic roles, and Jenkins, Sherry, and Haughton. The work that covers, or at least in some measure delves into, Eliot's relationship with Dante is also daunting and quite often overlaps with considerations of Eliot's relationship with Pound. See the 1958 study by Mario Praz, who reminds us that despite his Harvard education (and Harvard's strong tradition of Dante studies; see Giamatti), Eliot really became apprenticed to Dante thanks to Pound, who, characteristically, was able to present Dante as a living part of the poetic continuum and divorce him from any academic mustiness. Praz also sketches out the relationship between Eliot's evolving theoretical postures and his study of Dante—exactly the sort of examination Brombert had finished in 1949 in a little-known study (see note below). See also the lucid McDougal 1985 (in McDougal, ed. 1985), which includes a fuller reading of the relevant *Purgatorio* 26 than is normally the case in Eliot/Pound studies (and one notes that McDougal opens his 1972 book on Pound by recalling his own training in Romance philology at the University of Pennsylvania) and explores the use Eliot makes of Arnaldian allusion throughout his *oeuvre*. McDougal also affirms Praz's judgment that Pound served explicitly as Eliot's teacher of Dante. Soldo's study of Eliot's markings of his edition of the *Commedia* is helpful. Gaskell serves, more recently, as a comparable catalogue of aspects of the poetic relationship; see also Freccero 1986b, Langbaum, and McMahon, discussed in n.2 above.

20. See Eliot's own varied and seemingly endless writings reflecting more or less directly on Dante. Eliot's major critical pieces on Dante include the early (1929) essay simply entitled "Dante" (which is reprinted in the *Selected Essays*), and, at some twenty years remove, the talk entitled "What Dante Means to Me" he delivered in 1950, reprinted in Giamatti as "A Talk on Dante." It is worth examining closely. The observation that a poet-critic reflects most clearly on

The range is telling: entitling his collection of poems published in England in 1920 *Ara vos prec* (part of Arnaut's little speech in the *Purgatorio*); the epigraph of *Prufrock;* the well-known clear allusions and citations in *The Waste Land* (to be discussed further, below); the "commentary" on *Purgatorio* 16 that is the poem *Animula,* which begins with a

---

himself when writing about poetry or about another poet is tacitly, almost consciously acknowledged in the disarming opening line, "May I explain first why I have chosen, not to deliver a lecture about Dante, but to talk informally about his influence upon myself?" (219, all citations from the Giamatti reprint). The brief and in some ways uninspired piece, which has the considerable value, from our perspective, of being a "mature" evaluation on the part of the poet, confirms throughout two of the postures that are critical for this reading of the "miglior fabbro": Firstly, Dante's "influence" is a comfortable and unambiguous one, unthreatening because it is a necessary part of the background noise, a constant and ever-increasing presence which can grow with the aging and the maturing of a sure poet—a sacred text, in other words, which, at least in Eliot's tradition, does not need to be cleared away. Eliot embraces Dante the way he embraces the English language itself, the way he embraces Shakespeare: they are necessary tools, the rudiments of one's education as a writer. Secondly, Dante is the ultimate influence (he does not say the ultimate model, but that is clearly what is at stake) because of the *Commedia*'s successful attempt to speak transcendent Truth: "It [the *Commedia*] is therefore a constant reminder to the poet, of the obligation to explore, to find words for the inarticulate, to capture those feelings which people can hardly even feel, because they have no words for them. . . . The task of the poet, in making people comprehend the incomprehensible, demands immense resources of language; and in developing the language, enriching the meaning of words and showing how much words can do, he is making possible a much greater range of emotion and perception for other men, because he gives them the speech in which more can be expressed" (226–27). This is at once a superb reading, verging on a retelling, of the ideology of writing and its relationship with truth developed in the *Vita nuova* and a succinct statement of Eliot's own view of his own poetic enterprise. The great poet is never merely a craftsman; Dante is never called a "miglior fabbro" here, significantly; he must say the unsayable—not, of course, in the poetry of those who believe that the words themselves will create a meaning, but in the limpid clarity of a poetry that will yield a meaning that has been read from the universe. How else will the reader understand such Truths? And that the poet, again, the great poet, is obliged at least to endeavor to "say the unsayable" is "quote" from the Dantean text: "Issues from the hand of God, the simple soul"; and *Sovegna vos,* once again Arnaut's words from the *Purgatorio,* which originally appear in an early version of *The Waste Land,*[21] only to be excised and then reappear in *Ash Wednesday.*

While Eliot's relationship with Dante—a Dante he would not know without his other maestro, Pound—is thus broad and complex, there appears to be a special interest in Dante's Arnaut. Arnaut, in turn, comes doubly introduced to Eliot by each of his two most influential teachers, Dante and Pound. This is an Arnaut whose uncharacteristic Provençal verses keep reappearing in his poetry, an Arnaut who becomes almost embarrassingly identifiable, in a number of ways, with his translator, his modern voice and mask, Pound the philologist of living poetry. Even without the dedication one might have surmised the connection and made something rather different of it, since the Arnaut figure, in his speech in the *Commedia,* Dante's Arnaut, is a pathetic, expurgated poet, repentant, "purified" of all that which, presumably, made him "il miglior fabbro" in the first place. And the lines quoted elsewhere by Eliot are the most touching and pathetic, the "Ara vos prec. . . . Sovegna vos a temps de ma dolor" (And now I pray you. . . . remember me in my time of pain). This is the prayer, indeed, of one poet being left behind by another. "Remember me. . . ." The kind of relationship that implies, then, would perhaps have been more apparent were it not for the line, the quote, the dedication, that seals the Pound-Arnaut identification— and almost completely conceals its black side.

Eliot had begun his career as a critic with the belief, elaborated in his

---

implicit in the conviction that poetry has moral power, has the ability to mold what and how others perceive and feel; it cannot be innocent. The mature Eliot is stating more plainly, then, what he has suggested in *The Waste Land* and what we saw in the story of the *Vita nuova.* Eliot and Dante both recognize, with varying degrees of equanimity, how necessary for the craft those models are. And both believe themselves to have taken the next step, to have wrested the god of language from its pedestal and replaced it with another god, one is tempted to say a stranger god.

21. See page 101 of Valerie Eliot, noting that Pound (unclear) has written in by hand the line "Consiros vei la pasada dolor" only to have it crossed out.

famous essay *Tradition and the Individual Talent,* that poetry was an
"impersonal" phenomenon and needed to be met on those terms. This
acceptance of poetry as something that best exists as an aesthetic
phenomenon and outside belief systems was one he eventually rejected
and soundly repudiated, and it is highly significant that his conversion
from those earlier views—views with which he clearly associated his
mentor Pound—appears to have taken place, or at least to have been
fully articulated, at the time he became an intensive reader of Dante. In a
little-known and rarely cited but immensely useful essay, Victor Brom-
bert meticulously traces the development of Eliot's critical thought on
the nature of poetry and his conversion from a belief in the indepen-
dence of poetry from the belief system of the poet to an ambiguous
middle-of-the-road posture to, finally, a full rejection of his earlier,
clearly embarrassing (for him) stance, which had made aesthetic values
something separate from all other values.[22] It is in reading Dante, more
than any other poet, that Eliot finally cannot avoid confronting the
problem of belief in poetry and its ultimate irreconcilability with his
earlier "impersonal" theory. And it is in *writing* his 1929 essay on Dante
that Eliot literally writes out his conversion, and reminds us poignantly,
in his young and painful uncertainties and doubts, of the young author
who is the ambiguous hero of the *Vita nuova.* He finishes his essay on
Dante with a statement as rash, from some perspectives, as the *Vita
nuova*'s own: "It would appear that 'literary appreciation' is an abstrac-
tion, and pure poetry a phantom; and that both in creation and enjoy-
ment much always enters which is, from the point of view of 'Art,'
irrelevant."[23]

22. Brombert 1949 was written as the author's senior essay at Yale and
published as the selection for the Undergraduate Prize Essay. It is thus not overly
surprising that it is not better known, although it would be of considerable use to
authors who have worked on the subject extensively since then (Praz, cited
previously, and most recently Ellman 1987, who has written an entire book on the
subject). Both the documentation and the insights of the Brombert essay remain of
great value (including especially the meticulous primary bibliography on the
subject), and this little-known piece constitutes an unusually clear guide to Eliot's
many and dispersed writings on literature and on criticism.

23. Cited in Brombert 1949, p. 27; see also Eliot [1929] 1950: 199–237.

Much like Dante, Eliot eventually fully repudiates his earlier views, and in the preface he wrote to a late edition of *The Use of Poetry and the Use of Criticism,* he calls his earlier, more famous essay a juvenile effort, "dating from a period when I was somewhat under the influence of Ezra Pound's enthusiasm for Remy de Gourmont . . . the product of immaturity."[24] This is hardly a surprising disclaimer for a poet-critic who had written, in his 1935 essay *Religion and Literature,* the following: "The 'greatness' of literature cannot be determined solely by literary standards. . . . If we, as readers, keep our religious and moral convictions in one compartment, and take our reading merely for entertainment, or, on a higher plane, for aesthetic pleasure, I would point out that the author, whatever his conscious intentions in writing, in practice recognizes no such distinctions." This is, as Brombert points out, an espousal of what he had strenuously denounced in *Tradition and the Individual Talent,* and it is thus only to be expected that in later years he would plead that anthologists of the future choose the later essays, with their postconversionary perspective, rather than the earlier ones he clearly thought were so immensely misguided. His singling out of Pound's influence on his "juvenile" and "immature" thoughts—once again, the foolishly immature figure of the misguided young poet of the *Vita nuova* comes to mind—is one of many indications of the line he had drawn long before between himself and the stepfather of *The Waste Land.* For, as I have noted, if his relationship with Pound was fraught with anxiety and rebellion and, ultimately, characterized by that seemingly indispensable rejection, that with Dante could afford to be a much more straightfor-

---

Brombert himself is left somewhat aghast by the radicalness of the position and comments that it is "regrettable" that Eliot should have gone so far out on a limb, "from one extreme to another." But Brombert himself goes on to explore and cite, in concrete and undeniable detail, that other extreme—the pole at the other end of the conversionary experience—which Eliot did in fact reach and articulate.

24. These quotes are from the preface to the 1964 edition, written by Eliot in 1963. It appears in the Harvard University Press reprinting (although note that the copyright dates for the book in question remain 1933 and 1961). As anyone who has done any work on Eliot knows full well, the copyright issues are complex and difficult.

ward one of role model and adulation, something evident in everything from his extravagant talk, where he tells us Dante was "the most persistent and deepest influence upon my own verse," to his loving and largely reverential rewriting of Dante in his own poetry—including those verses, such as the Ulysses canto, exorcised by Pound. Dante would even provide the masks and the lines—the very terms—that Eliot would use to leave Pound behind, burning in the purifying flames. "Poi s'ascose nel foco che li affina."

I V

I have tried to write Paradise

Do not move
  Let the wind speak
          that is paradise.
(Ezra Pound, canto 120:803)

Eliot's abiding concern in poetry and criticism alike—and the focus of his distinctive and Dante-like conversion—is clearly the issue of belief and Truth and how these may or may not be separable from poetry. For lyric poetry this is an issue closely linked to musicality, and Eliot had in fact discussed the issue of the "musicality" of poetry and language and the potential for incoherence therein in, not surprisingly, his essay on Pound (Eliot 1918). It is unclear to what extent these really are separable issues: Eliot claims, at least in 1918, that words must be (and are) used to express both "beauty of sound" and meaning, and that meaning as such is a different thing from belief. And yet, his ultimate conversion, which entails, as did Dante's, a rejection of poetry as something that can be divorced from a belief system, entails just as clearly a rejection of the distinction between "meaning" and "belief"— where there can be a meaning that can exist outside of some sort of belief system. What Eliot sees in Pound, a Pound tied to an unreconstructed Arnaut, what Dante saw in Arnaut himself before he reconstructed him, is a belief in poetry that ties the language of poetry to the rationally inarticulable meanings of music, to a poetry where the sounds themselves create the meanings, are the meanings, are, in sum, the overriding belief. A prodigious crystal.

Pound's essay on Arnaut, "Il miglior fabbro" (one of the chapters of *The Spirit of Romance*), is everywhere concerned with the rhythms and sound evocations of the master craftsman rather than with any conventional "meaning" in the way the later Eliot and Dante would have understood it. But Dante is Pound's great maestro as well and at pains, when it is necessary, to make him behave: he will confront, for example, the fact that Dante's apparent praise of Arnaut is not, on the surface of it, self-explanatory, and says that critics are unable to appreciate Dante's high esteem because they know nothing about Arnaut's poetry.[25] Pound's Dante has singled out Arnaut "not so much [due] to obscurities of style, or to such as are caused by the constraints of complicated form, and exigency of scarce rimes, but mainly [due] to his refusal to use 'journalese' of his day, and to his aversion from an obvious familiar vocabulary. He [Arnaut] is not content with conventional phrase, or with words which do not convey his exact meaning." In fact, the "exact meaning" of the high lyricism of Arnaut and his translator and champion Pound is a very different "exact meaning" from that Eliot and his Dante would conceive. The Dante who reaches the clarity of vision of the *Paradiso* does not let the wind speak.

A careful reading of Pound's essay reveals, aside from the radically problematic statement dealing with Dante's assessment, an acute sensitivity to the hermetic musicality of Arnaut's verses and an early version of his own aesthetics. He defines Arnaut's onomatopoeia, for example, as "making the sound follow the sense of the word," speaks repeatedly of the "sound echoes" of natural phenomena Arnaut is "describing," notes that the "excellence of its [a poem's] construction may, I think, be understood by anyone who will sing the given stanza aloud," talks about

25. This statement is made at a moment in Dante scholarship when critics merely puzzled, or were somewhat incredulous, at Dante's singular praise and before the subsequent campaign to "justify" or "validate" Dante's judgment taken at face value.

"metaphor by sympathy," by which he clearly means the sound evocation of a given state, revels in the imitations of the sounds of the seasons and of "bird notes," speaks of Arnaut's having perfected work with rhyme, of "jazzy" lyric measures, of stanza answering stanza. It is not at all clear, then, whether Pound's assertions of belief in the sincerity of Dante's "il miglior fabbro" epithet are playfully disingenuous or a reconstruction, a reading of Dante that is in considerable measure wishful thinking: Pound's Dante, the Dante who whispers to him to make the cantos new and gives him the languages to do it, the voices of Sordello and Cavalcanti and Born and Arnaut—that Dante would never abandon his multiple other selves to forge a single true voice.

One of the compelling aspects of Pound's and Eliot's fascination with the Arnaut conundrum is that it reveals in considerable nakedness the extent to which a poet writing as a critic is speaking about himself, and, just as nakedly, the intertwining of issues that scholarship has tended to prefer to separate into categories clearly marked as separate or separable. These might be called the "critical" versus the "literary," and whether it is found in Frye's renunciation of the evaluative activity in criticism or in more recent reactions to deconstruction which recoil at the notion that the several categories of writing are "equal," the tendency to maintain these as distinct categories has been and continues to be a strong one. In this case, however, when we deal with writers such as Pound and Eliot—and especially, perhaps, Dante—we must reckon with the fact that these writers themselves saw little validity in such distinctions, except perhaps insofar as they might be theoretical or hypothetical. In Dante's "literature" we find what are arguably his finest critical statements about other poets and poetry in general; in Eliot's and in Pound's acts of criticism we find reflections, direct and indirect, of their own art and of concerns which are both critical and literary, and which in the end cannot be fruitfully isolated from each other. In fact, the vicissitudes of what I have been calling poetic ideology correlate remarkably—although not necessarily precisely in time and space—

with vicissitudes in critical ideology. The two sides of the coin are, not surprisingly, often indistinguishable from each other.

It seems to me necessary, meanwhile, to emphasize the great extent to which Pound is a deft reader of Arnaut, because he is in several crucial ways the same kind of poet; he shares the fundamentals of a poetic ideology which is rooted in the primacy of lyricism and language—and fears neither hermeticism nor self-idolatry. In his direct comments about Arnaut and in the quality of translations he did of Arnaut's verses, we read compelling evidence everywhere that he saw Arnaut as that kind of poet; but in fact Pound almost everywhere exalts in the musicality and the hermeticism of other poets. Once again, as with Eliot's pride in Dante, it is impoverishing to resort to lists, but to get a taste one can leaf through almost any of Pound's writings, critical or poetic, to hear the champion of the poet as creator, rather than revealer, of Truth speaking: the Chinese ideograms become Western poetry, certainly a celebration of the power of the sign—whether acoustical or not is no longer the issue—to create meaning; the interview in the early sixties where he says of his poetic/linguistic difference with Eliot that "I should think the divergence was first a difference in subject matter. He has undoubtedly got a natural language. In the language in the plays, he seems to me to have made a very great contribution. *And in being able to make contact with an extant milieu, and an extant state of comprehension*" (Hall 1962:37, emphasis mine); his composition of operas (Villon and Cavalcanti) based on the poetry of poets, an act of returning lyrics to their proper and original role as one that is an acting out of the belief articulated more directly elsewhere that "poets not interested in music are bad poets"; and, with very direct respect to Eliot, "In any case let us lament the psychosis / Of all those who abandon Muses for Moses."[26]

Perhaps at the beginning of this list, at the head of these evocations

26. For these and numerous other anecdotal and scattered quotes, see the extremely informative Gallup 1970, written in the wake of the recovery of the manuscript Pound edited of *The Waste Land*.

and suggestions and statements of a distinct ideology, belong his obser-
vations about Dante, refracted through his comments on Binyon's
marvelously sound-accurate *terza rima,* which remains, however, an
opaque version of a text that seeks precisely to repudiate opacity in
poetry. It is a "review" itself so transparently a piece of Pound literature,
so openly and aggressively defiant of all the rules of critical idiom and
convention, that it is dangerous to cite as one would a more "direct"
exposition of views. Nevertheless, the Binyon and the Dante that Pound
praises to high heaven in this remarkable piece are finally freed from the
shackles of "the abominable dogbiscuit of Milton's rhetoric" and are no
longer "pre-Raphaelite," Dante emerging here "with all the faults of his
original"; but most of all, the Binyon Dante is Pound's great delight
because it has got the sound of the original ("whether or no he invent a
'system' or theory for explaining that sound"), a revelation that, for
good measure, is followed by a disdainful recounting of Yeats's not being
particularly impressed, apparently, by a recitation by Pound at Siracusa
of some Greek verse in Greek.[27] It is clear that Pound's disdain has
nothing whatever to do with whether Yeats or anyone else could
understand Greek; one is tempted to say, quite the contrary, that what
Pound is embracing at every step is the power of what eludes linear,
positivist, discursive understanding. Clearly, in his poetic practice—and
the *Cantos* are the climax—Pound is far from being a simple worshipper
of sound, an American Mallarmé. But he has turned upside down the
Romance philology from which he was a refugee—a philology that is
radically positivist as a new science, a philology that mimics, in its dim
understanding of it, the clarity of Dante and Eliot and that sets itself up

27. The passage is worth citing more fully: "I remember Yeats wanting me to
speak some verse aloud in the old out-of-door greek theatre at Siracusa, and being
annoyed when I bellowed the ποιχιλόθρον ἀθάνατ' Ἀφροδίτα and refused to
spout English poesy. I don't know how far I succeeded in convincing him that
English verse wasn't CUT. Yeats himself in his early work produced marvellous
rhythmic effects: 'legato' verse, that is, very fine to murmur and that may be
understood if whispered in a drawing-room, even though the better readers may
gradually pull the words out of shape (by excessive lengthening of the vowel
sounds)" (Giamatti, ed.: 179).

as a simple reader of an already inscribed text.[28] But Pound sees himself as a Maker rather than as a simple reader beholden to the superior text he must explicate, and in all his writing he runs with Arnaut, Arnaut who runs with the wind and incants his powerful magic. In the universe that believes that poets and critics, each in their own way, are mere decipherers and retellers of other texts, they who make the uncanny canny for the rest of us, it is madness and heresy to believe that the poet and the critic make the text—and thus the Truth.

His relationship with Dante, then, cannot but be problematic and ambiguous: he is appreciative of the magic, often as incantational as his own, that permeates the poem and makes its language glitter at every turn, and it is this that makes Binyon's translation so powerful and good for him. But he resists, for the same reasons, reading and acknowledging the Dante who is Eliot's ally, whose goal as a writer is to make the magic into the servant of Truths that can be said, to bring union and unity and coherence out of the whirlwind that others see as poetry, to forge that hybrid of poetry and Truth. Pound rebels at the very notion that such a unity can be achieved, and the *Cantos* may perhaps be read as an open defiance, a vigorously and consciously destructive reading of the master cantos of the *Commedia,* an extended correction.[29] Pound's *Cantos* are very much like Pound's standing on a fragment of a pillar at Siracusa and

28. Pound's truncated studies in Romance philology at the University of Pennsylvania are often mentioned but little analyzed, although it seems to me clear that his *Spirit of Romance* is, perhaps quite unconsciously, his radical rewriting of the premises of the philological enterprise and its linear and rationalist understanding of literary history. Oddly enough—appropriately, in many ways—Penn rejected the request made in 1920 that the *Spirit of Romance* be accepted as the dissertation for the Ph.D. (in lieu of the projected study of Lope de Vega that went by the wayside when Pound left Penn with an M.A. and all the course work for the Ph.D. completed in 1907). See Wallace for an informative narration of Pound's academic career at Penn and the appendices of Hoffman, ed. for further useful primary documentation; additionally, William Roach, longtime chairman of the Department of Romance Languages, compiled a list of Ph.D. dissertations in the department from 1896 until 1975 (personal collection).

29. As McMahon has noted, the first *Canto* is a correction of *Inferno* 26, see n.7 above.

reciting Greek—or it could have been Chinese or Old Provençal for that matter, any or all blended in evocations of a language we do "understand."[30] This, clearly, is a stunning counterpoint to the cantos that culminate in "ma già volgeva il mio disio e 'l velle / sì come rota ch'igualmente è mossa, / l'amor che move il sole e l'altre stelle" (but

30. Perhaps the only reading of the Pound *Cantos,* in fact, that would be accepted with any consistency is that they are immensely difficult, if not altogether unreadable in any linear sense of the word (although certainly their poetry and hermeticism can be discussed and are, from a different perspective, very productive of other poetic reactions). What the *Cantos* evade altogether is any possibility of global explanation or an interpretation that would yield what "it means"— again, quite the reverse, intentionally, I would say, of the poem they thus mock, for if nothing else Dante's *Commedia* (like *The Waste Land,* of course, and even more so Eliot's later work) begs to be interpreted and to be made into meaning. For the most provocative and resonant readings of the *Cantos* see the indispensable and free-ranging Kenner 1971; Bernstein 1980, which explores the *Cantos* as a modern epic and overflows with insights about the difficult relationship with Dante's text as does Wilhelm 1974b and 1977; and, more recently, Ellman and Kenny. It is telling to compare the general differences even in something so elementary as quantity between Eliot and Pound criticism. The former is rich and appropriately dedicated to the task that the poet himself seems clearly to have planted, that of determining meaning, that task exhorted in *The Waste Land* and in so many other writings: to use literature to make sense from meaninglessness, to grasp and rework the literary tradition to give "a shape and a significance to the immense panorama of futility and anarchy which is contemporary history" (Eliot on Joyce's *Ulysses,* in *Selected Essays*). The writings on Pound, on the other hand, particularly on the *Cantos,* are not only fewer but, as one of those critics has put it recently, faced with avoiding the contagion of unreadability (Ellman: 138). Eliot himself, of course, rendered the judgment from the outset, even while he was praising Pound's "craftsmanship" in the *Cantos:* "In the *Cantos* there is an increasing defect of communication" ("Ezra Pound" in Russell, ed. :33). See also Kenny's assessment of the current state of affairs in *Canto* criticism: "haunted, embarrassed, by its [antirationalism's, the *Cantos'*] dislocating power. . . . With its critical derangements and irrational intuitions, the defiantly arcane scholarship on Pound has continued to filter through the very sound as well as terminology of its master's voice" (18). For reflections on the *Cantos* as a version of the *Commedia* see Cambon, who dwells on the relatively superficial similarities (such as a full range of social interests) and Wilhelm 1974b, with insights into both similarities and critical and

already my desire and my will were revolved, like a wheel that is evenly moved, by the Love which moves the sun and the other stars [*Paradiso* 33:143–45]), only to be able to begin with the darkness again of the "mezzo del camin."

Pound does not want to accept Dante's rejection of the poets that taught them both how to write, poets often much like himself, poets who exist because Dante captured them for posterity. But perhaps it is precisely because Pound does understand that the maestro repudiated them and abandoned them that he so relentlessly gives them voices and renews their presences and life in letters and in the making of a new tradition. In this, modernism is built on the stark terrain of *langue d'oc*. In *Near Perigord*, Pound, rewriting the *Commedia*, gives us one of his different versions of the Provençal poets in Dante:

>   And in the quietest space
> They probe old scandals, say de Born is dead;
> And we've the gossip (skipped six hundred years).
> Richard shall die to-morrow—leave him there
> Talking of trobar clus with Daniel.
> And the "best craftsman" sings out his friend's song,
> Envies its vigour . . . and deplores the technique,
> Dispraises his skill?—That's as you will.

This is not "only" poetry, of course, but poetry like Dante's in the sense that it is vigorous and biting literary criticism at the same time, and we should not be surprised, finally, that such a poet is such a superb critic-reader-translator-rewriter of the master of the *trobar clus*. But beneath the politeness, it is clear that some *do* dispraise the skills of those

---

telling differences; and especially the always rich Kenner 1985, who reflects on the failure of the *Cantos* to be like the *Commedia* (or *The Waste Land* or *Ulysses*, for that matter) in achieving the kind of crystalline unity that might have seemed desirable. He concludes, commenting on the verses from canto 91 quoted above, "It is not a secure achievement; no vision lasts. . . . He is not in Paradise, he has only mastered the knack of occasionally glimpsing Paradise, in moments when he can calm his perturbing spirit whose perturbations he knows more bitterly than any critic" (55).

who believe themselves Makers of magic rather than mere readers and reflectors of a far larger text and Truth. We come full circle, in fact, when we realize that the "differences" with Pound that Eliot would later mention publicly are precisely those that separate Dante from Arnaut.

In 1921, as *The Waste Land* was going to press, Eliot revealed much in a review he published on Joyce's *Ulysses,* where he asserted the very Dantesque belief that literature must be what he calls "classical," i.e., writing that brings out order and continuity from chaos, and that is distinguishable from a "false" classicism, which involves merely "selecting mummified stuff from a museum" (176–77).[31] Though Eliot politely declined to name names, it is hardly audacious to assume that not far from his mind was the Pound who had been publishing rewrites of Arnaut (and Guido Cavalcanti and Bertran de Born—further and further into Dante's dark pit). The only little inconvenience in noting all of these links—and their markedly negative undertones—is that it makes Eliot seem like such an ingrate. It might even cast him as a hypocrite—and perhaps, ultimately, it is a similar reverence that has led Dante critics, in their turn, not to see the knife sticking in Arnaut's back as he is dismissed as the "miglior fabbro." But it seems to me that it is not hypocrisy in either case, at least not in the banal social sense of the word, but the more complex, and certainly more common need to difference and distance oneself as a poet from a powerful antecedent (or antecedents, since one can admit that Arnaut is himself exemplary of the prepossessing Provençal tradition). The relationship is further complicated by the problem of indebtedness, a problem of which Eliot is fully consciously aware, and which he attempts to deal with straightforwardly and honestly by acknowledging it, although the acknowledgement does not in this case (perhaps in any case) exorcise the ghost and pay the debt.[32]

31. The review, entitled (tellingly) "Ulysses, Order, and Myth," appeared in *The Dial* in November 1923. It is reprinted in Kermode, ed. 1975.

32. The most important document in this is undoubtedly Eliot's essay on Pound, first written in 1946 (and including a brief postscript from 1950, when it

It is also attributable to a genuine and in some ways dramatic difference in ideology among poets which in both of these cases is tempered and immensely complicated by the great dependence of one on the other. Eliot, in his late evaluative essay on Pound, deftly summarizes that Pound's greatest contribution to poetry was his insistence that poetry was an Art, and elaborating on some of the ways in which Pound was obsessed with the language in and of itself—although Eliot, in what is clearly meant to be a charitable and praising essay, is also avoiding the issue of what one does with the language. There is little reason to doubt the sincerity of the praise as such, but what is left unspoken in 1946— and there is much left unspoken—is the critical difference which in Dante's more explicit system was the purging of Purgatory, the damning of such faint praise. Both the praise and the damnation, in other words, may be sincere.

V

"I wished at that moment to honour the technical mastery and critical ability manifest in [Pound's] . . . own work, which had also

was first reprinted). It begins with a long accounting of Eliot's personal debt: "It is as well, in writing at the present moment about Pound, to acknowledge one's greatest personal debt at once" (25). The setting out of the degree of debt, however, reveals at least some of the severe problems that plagued the relationship, principally the extent to which Pound is an oppressive and overwhelming benefactor and ultimately a stifling figure: "Indeed, he was ready to lay out the whole of life for anyone in whose work he was interested. . . . Yet, though the object of his beneficence might come to chafe against it, only a man of the meanest spirit could have come to resent it" (27). There are further revealing comments in this piece, including one in which he says that he would "like to think" that the blue-pencilled manuscript of *The Waste Land* had disappeared, but on the other hand, he should wish it to remain as "irrefutable evidence" of Pound's "critical genius." Overall, in fact, the Pound that emerges from Eliot's praise is the Pound, familiar to all of us since Eliot's view here has largely become canonical, who is the ultimate—and ultimately oppressive—father figure, the ultimate creator of opportunities for other poets, the teacher, the critic, the maker of poets. For a more recent and scathing perspective on this, see Ruthven.

done so much to turn *The Waste Land* from a jumble of good and bad passages into a poem." (Eliot, on the *miglior fabbro* dedication, quoted by Gallup: 58)

We turn back to *The Waste Land,* a poem whose final form is so critically that given it by Pound that it is literally best seen to be believed.[33] But while Pound did a good bit of the crafting of the poem, Eliot's vision is far from obscured. We get a poetic glimpse of Eliot's monumental attachment to Dante's poetic ideology, we begin to get a taste of what will be considerably clearer in Eliot's later work, that belief that poetry must indeed be a moral enterprise beyond the "merely" aesthetic or musical, beyond the hermeticism, the meaninglessness, of what is in fact "the waste land." It would be an impossible task to give any kind of "resumé" of critical views of that poem; they are not only copious but very wide ranging. But, in meaningful parallel with the spectacularly large corpus of readings of Dante, some aspects of *The Waste Land* and its powerful relationship with Dante emerge clearly.[34] It will be seen, in the end, that the most critical of the attachments that exist between Dante and Eliot is one that certainly transcends allusion and quotation; it is to

33. It is essential to look at Valerie Eliot's edition of the facsimile to begin to appreciate the radical nature of the "editorial" work done by Pound. It is difficult, in fact, to come away from seeing that text and ever again imagine *The Waste Land* as Eliot's "own."

34. It is telling to look at recent criticism of *The Waste Land* by an important critic: In a compelling essay on Pynchon and Eliot, Wendy Steiner concludes by describing *The Waste Land* as follows: "Without the historical sense, the centrifugal otherness of allusions, we are locked within the wasteland solipsism the poem deplores . . . full meaning enters the text for Eliot only when history does, and the modern wasteland is redeemed only when people again read literature, value the tradition, and themselves create the syntheses that actively remake the past into a historical present" (Steiner:334, 338). Although Steiner says this is a radical reading within the canonical tradition of Eliot exegesis, it constitutes a precise description of the Dantean subtext, and in fact, Steiner's conclusions, those cited here and others, fully resonate with some of the best Dante criticism of recent years, particularly that which has mapped out the key cantos of the *Purgatorio,* discussed above.

be found in Eliot's compelling interpretation of the import of Dante's poem, a poem which he will "imitate" in the sense that he will himself, in a landscape that is different and yet astonishingly the same, write poetry that is committed to saying Truth, to the sayability of a Truth that far transcends "facts."

The Waste Land sits at the brink of Eliot's own conversion, uncannily like Dante's own in its external manifestations: the turning towards a "classicism" (as he defines it, the recovery of the meaning of belief), a conservatism, and a Christianity that will consternate many of his contemporaries—and *The Waste Land* is followed by the credos that are *Ash Wednesday* and the explicitly Catholic *After Strange Gods*. Once again, however, conversion, that turning definitively toward something, necessarily implies—requires—a rejection and a turning away. In later years, in fact, Eliot would make statements where his differences with Pound are impossible to ignore; but what is critical to grasp is that the criticism is the same as—and is best manifest in—the far earlier and, by certain lights, conspicuously inappropriate "miglior fabbro" allusion. Eliot's "criticism" of his former patron and mentor, in lines such as "I confess that I am seldom interested in what Pound is saying but only in the way he is saying it" (Gallup:59), could in fact be taken as perceptive literary-critical fact—with which, incidentally, the modern Arnaut would no doubt scarcely have quibbled. Elsewhere Eliot noted—this time in a clearly judgmental tone—that "the greatest poets have been concerned with moral values"; but once again, a Pound (or an Arnaut, or a critic with the ideology of the latter two rather than the former) might well state the opposite as a conviction, which is all it can amount to—a belief, a judgment. What is critical is that the judgment will be strongly biased, if not altogether predetermined, most conspicuously when the critic is a poet-critic, by the beliefs the critic holds about his own work, by the value system that he brings to bear on his own writing.[35]

---

35. See von Halberg for a helpful discussion of American poet-critics in this century; although the focus is on the postwar period, von Hallberg not only discusses Pound and Eliot in these roles directly, but much of what he has to say about the poet-critic's evaluative function, particularly in contrast with the schol-

In defending the Pisan *Cantos,* for example, Eliot tempers his judg-
ment—again, although he, Eliot, considers it adverse, Pound would not
have thought it to be so—that the poetry is much too obscure to be
understood by saying, "But the craftsman up to this moment—and I
have in mind certain recent and unpublished cantos—has never failed"
(Eliot [1946] 1973: 34).[36] That craftsman. The craftsman who shaped

---

ar's avoidance of such a task, is of direct relevance. Von Hallberg traces the changes
in the entire critical-poetical-professorial complex that have divorced criticism
(now largely the domain of professors) from poetry (written by those who do not
as often also write criticism, and when they do so, von Hallberg maintains, it is
never of the range that antecedents such as Pound and Eliot did). And whether this
change is lamentable or not it does make it considerably more difficult to fully
imagine and understand the intimacy and interchangeability of the poet-critic
relationship, and of the concomitant cross-fertilization and ideological intimacy
between critical and poetic writing that existed not only when Pound and Eliot
wrote but when Dante did as well (unless, of course, we are familiar with the Latin
American tradition within which the poet/critic is as vigorous as always, witness
Octavio Paz, most prominently, and certainly not exceptionally). It may well be
perceived as ironic that it is the "conservatives" of what is now the vast bulk of the
critical profession—the professoriat—that recoil from the poststructural insights
and ideologies that in fact seek to reestablish (rather than create, *ex nihilo* or in any
sort of revolutionary sense) the intricate intimacy where critical and poetic writing
are not neatly distinguishable. One wonders; for example, what most current
academic readers of Pound's review c f Binyon would make of it did it not have the
name "Ezra Pound" attached to it; one could safely bet that with another name it
would not have a prayer of making it into any of the standard academic journals in
the field.

36. Again, Eliot's essay on Pound is remarkably telling. As noted there, his
evaluation of Pound's accomplishments are that he was a great maker of other
poets and of language itself. In fact, the part of this canonical evaluation regarding
Pound as a great patron of poets has recently come under severe attack; see
Ruthven, who claims that the principal benefactor of Pound's generous patronage
was himself, and that of others was "evidence of a desire to dominate, a will-to-
power," which is most clearly shown in the Pound-Eliot relationship. "Other
writers were construed invariably as disciples to Pound, apprentices in the
presence of a master craftsman." I note that Ruthven cites the "miglior fabbro"
dedication as open evidence of a subservience in Eliot which Ruthven goes on to

Eliot's language far more directly, far more literally than Arnaut did
Dante's. The craftsman who, so many years (and so many worlds)
earlier, was the "miglior fabbro" of his own *Waste Land*. Does it really
matter how conscious Eliot might or might not have been of his
immensely significant repetition of the same word? Is it perhaps not
even more poignant to imagine that Eliot is not able to be fully conscious
of the depth of distance, perhaps fear, involved when he dedicates the
poem to the craftsman who had made it possible, quite literally—or
how ungracious and ungenerous such a dismissal might seem, if fully
understood? And what of Pound, who had better reason than almost
anyone else to know just how ambivalent such praise was? In the back
room, perhaps, both the good doctor and his creature are all too aware
of the break at hand, and the inscription talks about the future as much
as about the past. Like the Dante he reveres, Eliot is without a doubt
genuinely grateful, he genuinely loves the father figure from whom he
learned the craft that he will use to write his soul—but, no less than
Dante, he feels himself and his poetry to be a step removed from and a
step beyond "mere" craftsmanship, feels that craftsmen enamored of the
craft itself—and its beauty and its products (a beauty and a product that
itself is true and meaningful)—are not the "greatest poets." It is not
clear, even, whether Eliot—or Dante, for that matter—consciously
turned away from the embarrassing and frightening heresy lurking
about: that rash notion that the poet as Maker creates rather than reads
texts. Eliot's Arnaut too, is left, at the end as well as at the beginning of
the poem, to be burned up and purified, purged of scandalous conceits,

---

say was in fact probably ironic—but the irony is seen only as manifest in privately
made statements (1300). The difficulty in all of this is that it is impossible to
delineate neatly—not just in Pound's case but in many others, perhaps all others,
including, most obviously, parental relationships—just where kindness and gen-
uinely "selfless" patronage (if there is such a thing) leave off and are replaced by
manipulation, shaping, and power and control. It is most likely they are the two
faces of the same coin and cannot, perhaps, exist one without the other, although
there may certainly be a question of degree. There is no question here, however,
that Pound was immensely helpful to Eliot and that Eliot felt some degree of
largely repressed chafing at the obligation that entailed.

his hermetic and lovely and magic poetry left behind for the more momentous, if straightforward, pursuits and the one true faith—faith, in this case, in both cases, in the ability to make language convincingly say the Truth to others.

V I

It is no coincidence that the vagaries of ideology in literary criticism—how a text is read, interpreted for others—can be seen to dovetail and intersect with the most fundamental ideological constructs writers themselves forge about their writing. In part, as I have discussed above, this is attributable to the personal overlap between critics and poets that, until relatively recent times, was the seemingly natural state of affairs. In such a universe, it is to be expected that the concerns and beliefs of both readers and writers should share salient features, although, of course, the stated ideologies that may be articulated in criticism may exist, if at all, in far less perfect practice in poetic writing. The latter is likely to be far less unambiguous and thus far more open to a variety of possible interpretations, including those which might legitimately appear to be in contradiction to theoretical postures found elsewhere. But the overlaps, of course, are often if not always revealed and perhaps caused by the greater subtlety of literature itself, which is so often an act of literary criticism, however obliquely. In the case of the authors we are dealing with here, Dante, Eliot, Pound, the metaliterary and literary-critical aspects of their most "creative" work is never far from the surface; in some cases, as with Boccaccio, the criticism inscribed in the literature is stronger and more compelling than that which stands by itself, which must adhere, at least to some extent, to the rules of straightforward criticism and may thus lack a certain subtlety and vision, a darker side, perhaps, to which the poetry can give full vent.[37]

37. The exception, of course, is Pound himself, who writes most of his criticism with a poetic verve and unconventional (in terms of criticism) lyricism that is outside the normal range of critical writing, even for poets. Note the contrast, for

It is also not unreasonable to assume that there are constraints and inhibitions built into a critical genre that is openly—and presumably transparently—evaluative, but that these constraints melt away when the greater subtleties of poetry are the guiding hand, or (and it is perhaps the same thing) that the criticism can say only what is acceptable consciously, but poetry, like dreams, allows the often more monstrous truths of the unconscious to rear their heads. Given the clearly problematic relationships that exist among many poets, particularly when there are relationships of paternity and debt and inheritance at stake, it is not surprising to detect major critical stances forged in the more difficult arena of their poetry. And this, finally, is what accounts for apparent differences of evaluation, discrepancies, for example, in Dante's evaluation of certain key poets in the *De vulgari* as opposed to that discernable in the *Commedia*—and for the same reason it is simplistic and treacherous to project from one to the other. Meanwhile, conversely, the critical writings may reflect more—certainly as much—on the poet himself than on the others he discusses in such an apparently straightforward fashion. Eliot's famous (and later repudiated) critical essay *Tradition and the Individual Talent* appears to discuss, first and foremost, the proper stance of the reader/critic vis-à-vis the text, but it is clear from the outset that the critical stance is inseparable from the assumptions held about the nature of the text itself. Thus, the judgments rendered and the postures criticized about reading are reflections of views not only on what a literary text is but on what it ought to be, thus reflecting back ultimately on the ideology of the poet.

The types of direct overlaps are various and entangled: writing that is, on its surface, literary criticism about other authors is at once reflective of the stances and literature of the "critical" author himself; Pound's remarks on Binyon's translation and Eliot's *What Dante Means to Me* are exemplary. Critical writing concerning what literary criticism and reading ought to be reflects, either explicitly or by implication, views on what literature itself ought to be, since the legitimacy of a given critical

example, between his critical writings and Eliot's. Boccaccio's different readings of Dante will be discussed below in the epilogue.

posture is necessarily dependent on a specific concept of the nature of the literary text—here, Eliot's *Tradition and the Individual Talent* is a transparent example. Literary texts themselves may, in whole or in part, constitute intricate acts of historical literary criticism and/or expositions of essential ideological postures vis-à-vis the reading and writing of literary texts: both the *Vita nuova* and the *Divine Comedy*, especially *Purgatorio* 21–26, are essential and fairly explicit examples, as is *The Waste Land*.

At the same time, it is impossible to resist observing comparable cycles and dialectics in literary and critical styles and ideologies that may or may not be intimately related but are not necessarily correlated at a given moment: a vogue of hermeticism in lyric poetry will have a counterpoint in a conspicuous movement towards a secular mimeticism, for example; the rigorous formalism of structuralism unleashes a diversity of critical stances intent on localizing texts in a variety of social contexts. The clichéd and too often banal cycles, never neat, of course, of literary histories can be reread, *grosso modo,* in a history of literary critical thought, particularly of the speeded-up twentieth century. What is intriguing is the extent to which writers themselves (and not just the often superficial histories of "Romanticism coming from the Enlightenment" recitations of graduate students and textbooks) take refuge in extreme and neat positions in their statements of principles, whether they are inscribed in their poety or in their theoretical expositions. A subtler critic still operates within those temporal boundaries and the diachronic mode, although he or she will use the well-delineated positions to expose the subtleties of the individual writer within a school or a period; the subtler writer presumably has access to the various registers he may otherwise depict as being inimical to each other. The writer, too, in many cases, is motivated in the delineation of clear-cut stances by complex needs, anxieties about both past and future.

What we see in the drawing of the line in the sand that is that the "miglior fabbro" epithet is a constellation of issues and postures, variously critical and poetic, that are, if not universal, ones we can glimpse recurrently at a number of important junctures in the histories of literature and—when it is viewed as a separate discourse—criticism:

the delicate, at times impossible problem of balancing out great debt to a writer or a tradition with the perceived need to surpass them and redefine their terms; the Platonic confrontation between the "primitive" (and thus powerfully dangerous) in writing (music, the poetry of music and unreason, shamanism, vision) and the more difficult but ultimately reasonable philosophy (and thus the kind of poetry that serves philosophy); hermeticism and formalism, on the one hand, with their emphases on the ontological independence of the text, and an engaged secularism which does not tolerate an erasure of history, on the other; and so forth. All of these struggles are acted out in the *Purgatorio,* with the ancestor figure emerging from the fire, praised and yet damned, only to return again, now revealed as eaten up and spat out again by Dante as a remarkably different Arnaut—and once again, in a further act of literary-historical interpretation, as a dedication that inscribes not only the unavoidable public debt that has been incurred, but the momentary escape from the unconscious of the murderous poet who sees the fatal limitations of the teacher. And *The Waste Land,* like the *Commedia* it can marry with impunity, is no less concerned with the issues of generations and the extreme dangers of alienation, sterility and barrenness. And once again, in the great and painful turmoil of the process of conversion, the poem that is left behind, like the *Vita nuova,* now is a tribute to what is being abandoned, to a poetry that created a poetry incomparable, finally, to the lasting and transcendent value of literature that simply reads and then tells the Truth.

IV

Blindness:

Alephs and Lovers

Era inevitable: el olor de las almendras amargas le recordaba siempre el destino de los amores contrariados.

It was inevitable: the scent of bitter almonds always reminded him of the fate of unrequited love.

"Y hasta cuándo cree usted que podemos seguir en este ir y venir del carajo?" le preguntó.

Florentino Ariza tenía la respuesta preparada desde hacía cincuenta y tres años, siete meses y once días con sus noches.

"Toda la vida" dijo.

"And how long do you think we can keep up this goddamn coming and going?" he asked.

Florentino Ariza had kept his answer ready for fifty-three years, seven months, and eleven days and nights.

"Forever," he said.

—Gabriel García Márquez, *El amor en los tiempos del cólera*, translated by Edith Grossman

I

$\mathcal{J}$orge Luis Borges begins the last of his nine essays on Dante with the arresting line "Mi propósito es comentar los versos más patéticos que la literatura ha alcanzado" (155) (My purpose is to comment on the most moving and plaintive lines in literature).[1] The pathos that has left Borges so clearly affected—and that in some ways in Borges's recounting is far more passionate than we are used to reading in Dante himself—is not only that Dante's mortal, earthly, "real" love was unrequited and tragic, but that even in fiction, a monumental fiction constructed precisely so that he could meet the vanished Beatrice once again, Dante could not fully falsify matters, could not be glaringly untrue to the earthly truth that had so scarred and shaped him. Thus, his argument goes (here and in the previous essay, also devoted to the figure, the persona, of Beatrice), Dante could not quite make her nice, could not so transfigure a transcendent truth, the transcendent truth that she had never loved him, and make her do all those things that in his heart of hearts he no doubt wanted—most of all, of course, to have her love him as he had her. Dante has been trapped and tricked by his own belief in Truth.

1. Borges wrote widely and in a number of different genres about Dante, but his overtly critical views seem to find fairly definitive expression in the collection of nine essays entitled *Nueve ensayos dantescos* (Borges 1982). I have also used the single essay entitled "La divina comedia" included in the collection *Siete noches* (Borges 1980), which almost without exception includes the same views and focuses on the same cantos and the same cast of characters (Francesca, Ugolino, Ulysses, Beatrice), except that the nine essays range somewhat more widely and less predictably. Translations of citations from both these critical texts are my own. Finally, although Borges's allusions to Dante in his fiction are also numerous and very widely spread—see Thiem 1988 for a comprehensive recent compilation—I have focused primarily on the most direct and most famous of Borges's stories "about" Dante, "The Aleph," first published in 1945; the cited translation is by di Giovanni, in collaboration with the author (Borges 1970).

It is not surprising that this same Dante, Borges's Dante, would damn the most marvelous of his creatures, Francesca, a Francesca who flaunts a wildly passionate, requited love in the poor Pilgrim's face, a Francesca who cannot help but rub it in by using the *noi* form, who does not, cannot, of course, regret her love because it is what she is. Borges is quick to point out that after her first narration all Dante really wants to know from her is how and when they, the lovers, knew that they were, in fact, in love with each other, mortal and mortally dangerous love, and it is precisely that question that provokes the second part of Francesca's lovely recounting of the book and the kiss. This Dante is not impervious to envy, at least a slight tremor of it, and while Borges is at pains to point out, to say out loud, that Dante does not (mis)use his powers to condemn and save for petty or personal reasons, one is left, in the aftermath, with a slightly bad taste in one's mouth: could he really have resented passionately requited love, the fulfilling embrace, so much? His Beatrice seems everywhere, alive or dead, incapable of such passion, seems, indeed, to be the serenity that comes outside such passion, only in its wake or absence, and in Dante's terms it is a true love that transcends—and ultimately negates, explicitly—the kind of passion that the whirling dervish Francesca embodies.

But after the simplicity, that simple lovingness and sentimentality of Borges's reading settles in, after we realize that this, after all, is why his Beatriz is but a portrait hanging on a wall (not that she would be a dead woman—that much we understood—but a portrait that smells of dust and cold), after all this there remains the simple but compelling question: why did he have to make her that way? Why can Dante, in his remarkable literary prowess and in the midst of a monument erected precisely so he could meet up with her once more, not make Beatrice cherish and love him, even, if he so wished and willed it, be passionately and madly in love with him? Borges's answer to his own implicit question is at first glance either lame or disingenuous: because he had to remain true to the historical truth. Coming from a writer dedicated to dismantling the epistemological divisions between literary truth and other truths—and written about the author of a magic text such as the

Vita nuova—it is an argument that on the face of it seems to melt away when you pour water on it.

Or perhaps it is simply Borges's way of signalling and repeating a very "Dantesque" lesson about the reading of texts: that the Truth is there, in the text, but only if we are able to believe in it. Borges's momentary play at the pseudonaive reader—clearly a role he cherishes—lets us see the more important truth uncovered by his apparently simple reading: that, because History and Truth and Text coincide, Beatrice must be precisely what she is. What Dante knows, and only momentarily regrets in that second circle of Hell, is precisely what he traced out in the *Vita nuova:* that writing passionate love is, like physical passion itself, only a temporary and evanescent revelation, whereas even the pain in writing a love like Beatrice is transcendently powerful, True. Borges the reader, who talks about the "truth" of historical events and who sheds tears at the pathos of Beatrice's last smile, is speaking as one who doesn't quite believe in the truth of the matter. He knows too well that the *Commedia* is a text that cultivates total vision and total engagement with the Truth—and that Dante's notion of the Truth is infinitely beyond the more banal one of personal history. But, writing passionately as the innocent reader, Borges doesn't quite buy it. What better criticism, finally, of Dante's logology—celebrated elsewhere by Borges the admirer of Dante[2]—than Borges's suggestion that in the end, at the

---

2. The logology as a reflection of the universe and all its truths is explicitly recognized by Borges at the outset of his *Nueve ensayos:* "Imaginemos, en una biblioteca oriental, una lámina pintada hace muchos siglos. . . . Declina el día, se fatiga la luz y a medida que nos internamos en el grabado, comprendemos que no hay cosa en la tierra que no esté ahí. Lo que fue, lo que es y lo que será, la historia del pasado y la del futuro, las cosas que he tenido y las que tendré, todo ello nos espera en algún lugar de ese laberinto tranquilo. . . . He fantaseado una obra mágica, una lámina que también fuera un microcosmo; el poema de Dante es esa lámina de ámbito universal"(85) (Let us imagine, in an oriental library, an illustration painted centuries ago. . . . Day is done, the light dims and as we become a part of the engraving we realize that there is nothing on earth that is not there. What was, what is, what will be, the history of the past and of the future, the things I have had and that I will have, all of this awaits us somewhere in this peaceful

summit of Dante's creation, literally, she had to be as distant as she had been in life, because Dante could not break from the mold, could not invent something richer. Beatriz is the dead woman, a dusty portrait hanging in darkened, chilly rooms that are going to be demolished. Truth is the Aleph, the magic shown to the faintly ridiculous Daneri, who doesn't really know the true magic of poetry.

Before Borges, only Petrarch managed an equally coy and devastating reading. And as in the case of Borges (or for that matter, in the case of Dante himself, with respect to Arnaut), it is the sort of love-hate relationship that throws off sparks of resentment as easily as it does the flattery of imitation, the reverence of certain kinds of acknowledgment. And what Borges never said was whether the different pictures of Beatriz vanished in the same dust as the demolished house—and the Aleph in the basement—or was dragged off to a new home by a Daneri who by then had used the Aleph for what it was worth to him, to win his literary prize. The portrait, at any rate, is never seen again.

I I

Chi è questa che vèn, ch'ogn'om la mira,
e fa tremar di chiaritate l'are,
e mena seco Amor, sì che parlare
null'omo pote, ma ciascun sospira?

O Deo che sembra quando li occhi gira
dical'Amor, chi'i' nol savria contare:
cotanto d'umiltà donna mi pare
che ogn'altra inver' di lei la chiam'ira

Non si porìa contar la sua piagenza,
ch'a le' s'inchin' ogni gentil vertute,

---

labyrinth. . . . I have imagined a magic object, an engraving that would also be a microcosm; *Dante's poem is that picture of universal scope* [emphasis mine]). One of the many things striking about this passage is the extent to which the description of such a universal text is like that of the Aleph, seen by the character Borges in Daneri's cellar and then "written" by the innocent Daneri himself.

e la beltate per sua dea la mostra.
Non fu sì alta già la mente nostra,
e non si pose in noi tanta salute,
che propriamente n'avrian canoscenza.

Who is she who comes, that everyone looks at her,
Who makes the air tremble with clarity
And brings Love with her, so that no one
Can speak, though everyone sighs?

O God, what she looks like when she turns her eyes
Let Love say, for I could not describe it.
To me she seems so much a lady of good will
That any other, in comparison to her, I call vexation.

One could not describe her gracefulness,
for every noble virtue inclines towards her
And beauty displays her as its goddess.

Our mind was never so lofty
And never was such beatitude granted us
That we could really have knowledge of her.

(*The Poetry of Guido Cavalcanti,* trans. Lowry Nelson, Jr., 6–7)

No poet can have had a relationship with Dante at once so painfully and nakedly neurotic and, in terms of the posterity that obsessed the later poet, so successful as Petrarch. Petrarch is a Borgesian reader: as with Borges's famous observations, most succinctly enunciated in his essay on Kafka, Petrarch deftly creates his own precursors, writes anew for us his literary ancestry, from the Augustan poets to, most conspicuously, Dante himself. The *Rime sparse*[3] achieves among other things

3. Petrarch's collection has had a number of names as well as a number of shapes throughout its history; I have relied on and quote Robert Durling's excellent edition and translations, and I prefer the title (also used by Durling) of *Rime sparse,* "Scattered Rhymes," as opposed to *Canzoniere,* rather too simply "Song book," or the more cumbersome Latin *Rerum vulgarium fragmenta,* although all three have been and continue to be used with such regularity—and with differing

precisely what Borges suggests the successful epigone will manage: to make us read the "original," the precursors, in a different way. A recent study rather neatly points out that in this scheme of things Borges has deftly inverted the usual order of poetic obligation, for now the precursor owes a debt to the epigone, for the latter has caused the former to be read anew.[4]

But this presumes innocence, of course, of which there can be precious little in literary relations: if nothing else, already inscribed within Borges's reading itself, and within virtually any theory of reading beyond the most naive, there can be no "innocent" reading, far less any pure or "faithful" rewriting, even when that is the apparent, perhaps even conscious intent. But most precursors would have little to be grateful for in the inventions, the readings and writings, of their epigones, particularly those most richly talented, most frequently read (and thus, presumably, with the greatest press). For it is not the malformation of the new poet, in the Bloomian frame of analysis, that is at stake and to be feared. Rather, understanding the radically adiachronic nature of literary history, it is the interpretation of the earlier poet, potentially supreme in its influence, by those unborn, by the unknowable future,

philological justifications—that it has through usage become more a matter of preference than of any bona fide authenticity.

4. Thiem 1988 is a remarkably useful article, providing not only considerable insights into Borges's relations with Dante but a comprehensive inventory of these relations and a thorough and very helpful bibliography for those of us who are also reversing the expected order of readership: medievalists and Dantisti reading Borges. Stefanini, on the other hand, can be perused as a more typical example of the study that concludes that Borges's treatment is parodic. Among Italianists this is the all too predictable conclusion, since it can scarcely be imagined that serious mockery of Dante—i.e., reservations about his value—could be written by someone like Borges. This is part and parcel of the kind of reverential criticism which has also prevented critics from seeing the ungracious cuts to Arnaut and Pound, and no doubt it is also a part of the post-Frye perception we maintain that when one is writing "criticism" that is the straight stuff, to be taken at face value, like scientific writing. Thus, since Borges's "straight" writing on Dante is almost embarrassingly adoring, he must be "playing" in "The Aleph."

that critically affects and effectively writes the course of literary history. And it is a literary history, as I have discussed in the previous chapter, that until relatively recently was not written by the "professional" literary historians but by the critical readings, either direct or inscribed in their own poetry, of later generations of poets. In these terms Borges and Petrarch are allies and contemporaries, part of the same chapter in a synchronistic history: they would have us read Dante in very much the same way. And, inevitably, their reading of the precursor that the one cannot name and the other names and names and names into a kind of banality tells us at least as much, probably more about themselves. And that, of course, is exactly as things are supposed to turn out.

Petrarch's rather tortuous relationship with a Dante who, already in Petrarch's lifetime, was casting a long and seemingly impenetrable shadow over all poetry has been dealt with at some length and from a number of perspectives, although, as in other related matters, the strength of Petrarch's own dicta on the subject have had a surprisingly powerful effect.[5] And Petrarch's stated position on the subject, neatly

5. Among the most useful I note: Foscolo's 1823 study, interesting and important for obvious historical reasons but also because of his focus on the issue of vernacular as a focal point of both congruence and difference between Dante and Petrarch, and because he is an early critic in the tradition of those who will see the clear antithesis between Beatrice and Laura (a critical tradition which will encompass Freccero 1975 and Vickers 1981); Freccero's now classic and indispensable 1975 "The Fig Tree and the Laurel" and the superb introduction to Durling's edition and translation are in a number of ways critical breakthroughs in dealing with the clearly literary relationship between the Petrarcan corpus and the Dantesque predecessors; Mazzotta 1978 is the study I have found most helpful, with emphasis both on Dante's concept of allegory as Petrarch understood it and on Petrarch's cultivation of a belief in the necessary ambiguity of language; Vickers 1981 emphasizes Petrarch's ability to manipulate two different and potentially contradictory traditions in order to carve out a third and unique place for himself within it; Waller 1980 has a number of insights on the relationship, although she begins with this highly puzzling statement: "Thus we need not deny that Petrarch's poetic originality often takes the shape of a struggle with his precursor Dante, but we need not see his poetry solely in terms of that struggle either" (12). Given how relatively little attention it has been paid, and how diffuse that attention tends to

set out to Boccaccio (the one other individual from whom Petrarch logically enough assumed he would have sufficient empathy and sympathy to fully understand) was that he, Petrarch, had never read Dante, precisely in order to avoid the kind of "influence" future readers would certainly seek and find.[6] Petrarch, at least, knows he must struggle to

---

be, this is peculiar. But she often makes telling statements on the relationship, most notably: "Where for Dante error would be more a matter of the reader than of the text, for Petrarch error and its concomitant problems for reading and readability become located in the text itself" (38); see also the incisive and original Shapiro 1980, as well as the more typical, straightforward Sturm-Maddox 1985, who devotes two chapters of her book on Petrarch to the "subtexts" of Dante and provides a detailed and thorough accounting of "Dante in Petrarch"—although she seems scarcely concerned that all of this takes place within a context of specific and insistent denial.

    6. The letter itself, *Familiares* XXI, 15, is worth reading in its entirety, as virtually every line of its six or so printed pages is as revealing as an exaggeratedly staged analytic session could be, beginning with the staggering fact that Dante's name is never even mentioned. The Bernardo 1985 translation is an excellent resource (202–207). There are two detailed studies that do focus on the letter and its implications: the early Bernardo 1955 and Paparelli 1979. The latter, in classic philological fashion, traces out both the history behind the exchange of letters between Boccaccio and Petrarch and the critical reactions to and evaluations of Petrarch's remarkable epistle over the years, from Foscolo's "fascio di contra-dizzioni, d'ambiguità e d'indirette difese di sé" to Contini's more decorous "ambiguità psicologica." His own assessment is that it is a "masterpiece of hypocrisy" (*capolavoro di ipocrisia,* 77) although his reading of the letter itself more often identifies irony than hypocrisy as such. Paparelli conspicuously does not cite the earlier study by Bernardo (which had appeared in *PMLA*), which, despite the critical naiveté of the moment, is by far the most thorough and, ultimately, most incisive study. It includes considerations of the various possible explanations for Petrarch's stance with respect to Dante, as well as a detailed reading of a different Petrarchan letter, one written to his brother Gherardo, who has entered a monastery, on the difference between the active and the contemplative life (this letter has more recently been analyzed in Mazzotta 1988, who comes to compara-ble conclusions about it). Bernardo concludes that "for poetry to be great there was really no need to 'dismiss the hypothesis of the active life by reaccepting the contemplative ideal as a superior one' as Dante had done" (499), and that Petrarch

write not only the poetry but that poetry's own future history. Crucially, he knows he has the power to write another poet's history, without ever even naming him.

Multiple ironies abound, none more significant, perhaps, than that the poets whose "influence" Petrarch not only acknowledges but cultivates are far from the center of his attention, that center where Dante, or more precisely a refutation of Dante, resides. And it is no less ironic, perhaps, that in this way Petrarch's stated view is accurate even if it is false: the kind of "influence" that Dante has on him cannot be measured in the same terms as any or all of the other "precursors" openly inscribed in his works. With Dante, read but indeed not read and studied like the others at all, the relationship is paradigmatically Borgesian: he will give us a reading of this "precursor" that we will not be able to fully escape, he will write some of the parameters of literary history for us—and he will do it all with scarcely a whisper of the other's name. That is the price of earlier fame and the vulgarity and popularity Petrarch both criticizes and envies in Dante and covets and fears for himself: the *Commedia* is public property and public knowledge, and Petrarch can come along and, in the utter discretion needed to salvage dignity and propriety and obscure all indications of envy, tell us just what is wrong with it—and why the *Rime sparse* are, ultimately, better poetry. Borges can have only pretended that these ancestral relationships were even remotely innocent; it is the same pretense one can hear on Petrarch's lips in that famous letter to Boccaccio, it is the pretense we hear on every page of "The Aleph," where Borges himself, in full "innocence," gives a version of Dante, an ancestor he elsewhere reveres, that is powerfully unreverential.

I make no attempt at a comprehensive view of either epigone's relationship with the Dante he battles on so many pages, nor am I interested in those relationships for the light—the "influence"—possibly shed on the later poet. These are other subjects, and they are treated, at least in part, by other critics. The far more restricted subject of my

---

believes it is possible to have a vernacular poem which is Christian and yet remain poetry without becoming theology.

attention is the one Borges and Petrarch cry out to have examined: the influence they have on Dante, how they have cajoled and coerced and poeticized us into reading him, how they shape him. And why the blind Argentine and the probably insufferable, wandering half-Avignonais, half-Florentine should have so closely shared a vision of their elder is the delicious question that emerges forcefully, and is probably doomed to lie, at best, half-answered.

III

Lasso me, ch'i' non so in qual parte pieghi
la speme ch'è tradita omai più volte!
Che se non è chi con pietà m'ascolte,
perché sparger al ciel sì spessi preghi?
Ma s'egli aven ch'ancor non mi si nieghi
finir anzi 'l mio fine
queste voci meschine,
non gravi al mio signor perch'io il ripreghi
di dir libero un dì tra l'erba e i fiori:
"drez et rayson es qu'ieu ciant em demori."

Alas I do not know where to turn the hope that has been by now betrayed many times! For if there is no one who will listen to me with pity, why scatter prayers to the heavens so thickly? But if it happens that I am not denied the ending of these pitiful sounds before my death, let it not displease my lord that I beg him again to let me say freely one day among the grass and flowers: "It is right and just that I sing and be joyful." (This and subsequent citations from Petrarca, *Petrarch's Lyric Poems,* trans. Robert M. Durling, 150–51)

Arnaut Daniel has come back to life. He has beaten his way back from those purifying flames that made him spout that crystal-clear Provençal, doing, no, saying penance for so much poetic sin in his past. And he has come back not only to take back that repentance but to beg for the chance to do it again, to beg to be allowed to be free merely to sing, as he once did, before being locked up in a Purgatory that asked of him much more than mere happiness and singing. Arnaut is back with a vengeance here: his is not only the last line but the general structure of the entire poem, canzone 80, technically readable as a *sestina*—that seductively difficult form whose invention made Arnaut (in)famous.[7] Even more: in this tour de force of poetic imitation and commentary, with each stanza recasting the poetics of a different predecessor and finishing with a direct quotation from that poet, Petrarch does homage to Arnaut even in the Dante stanza. After Petrarch has given voices to Arnaut and to Guido Cavalcanti (another poet with whom the reprimanded Arnaut might have felt some kinship, another of Dante's "victims"), Dante's stanza is a recasting of one of the *petrose,* those spectacular odes to the virtuosity and hermeticism of Arnaut that Dante had once written but, of course, repented of.

Petrarch's Arnaut of that first stanza, which opens with a "Lasso me" that ties him to the most conventional of the love plaints of the Provençal lyric—and, equally, is the first of many hints that this Arnaut knows his fate lies with Dante—is engaged in a stark defense of his own poetics. Like the converted Arnaut created by Dante, he has forsaken the striking hermeticism that made his name. Here, however, it is to do battle, a battle over his own poetics, with that other Arnaut of the *Purgatorio.* He has almost given up, he has almost yielded to the (once again Borgesian) fate of having Dante rewrite and seal his poetics for posterity, and give him a place in literary history that is false. But hope is momentarily restored, a new epigone and historian comes along, and it would appear that he will not be "denied these pitiful sounds before my death." Petrarch's choice of verse in Provençal to have his reinvented

7. The incipit that Petrarch uses here is in fact now believed to not have been composed by Arnaut, but it is clear that that was once the attribution and that Petrarch would have thought it Arnaut's. The *sestina* is a *canso* (the Provençal for *canzone*) with an undivided stanza and a number of remarkably challenging rhyme schemes. Detailed discussion of the form, its invention and difficulties can be found in Wilhelm 1982. The one in this *canzone* of Petrarch's is among the least pyrotechnical: a *canso a coblas dissolutas,* where the same rhymes are not used throughout the entire poem. For further details on the different rhyme and metrical schemes used by Petrarch see Durling's introduction.

and revivified Arnaut recite is a curious case of a false attribution contextually working as well as or even better than any "authentic" verse of Arnaut's might have: again, a limpid style stands in place of that Pound-like difficulty that was the real Arnaut's. In this particular poetic instance—Petrarch's battle with Dante over the validity and merits of the poetics of the *trobar clus*—the arrow-straight statement of the "simple" joys of "carefree" verse serves the rhetorical purpose best. The falsely attributed verse, ironically, expresses that most fundamental aspect of the value of lyrical language as well as many of Arnaut's own, and better (certainly more directly) than most of his more famous verses. And the Petrarchan verses that introduce Arnaut—an Arnaut whose soul speaks Italian before he sings in the Provençal of his youth— carefully construct an impeccably simple scene for that reprisal of that much-desired singing itself, "tra l'erba e i fiori" (among the grass and flowers). The simple joys of song are "just and right" in and of themselves, as "meaningful" (or not) as the grass and flowers themselves.

The rehabilitation of Arnaut is given a broader frame of reference than the single, particular poet: Petrarch knows full well that what is at stake is more than Arnaut Daniel pure and simple, both for Dante and, in reprising the battle, for himself. The abundance of allusions to a discarded past for which the poet yearns ("omai piú volte," "ancor . . . anzi 'l mio fine," "perch'io il ripieghi . . . un dí . . .") dovetails perfectly with the extensive and often diffuse thematics of memory that permeate, for some even dominate, the *Rime sparse*.[8] But in this particular case, at least,

8. Barolini's recent study (1989) explores this issue extensively and sees the structure itself of the collection, as well as internal thematics, as serving Petrarch's major preoccupation, that of the irrevocable passing of time and coming of death. (The preoccupation with the many different kinds of time and of memory is also crucial in Thomas Greene's rich and powerful reading.) In a discussion of *canzone* 70, Barolini signals that Petrarch's use of other poets' incipits as the final verses of each of the stanzas of this poem is one of Petrarch's many strategies to subvert clear closure. In addition, "most striking is that Petrarch's use of the first verse of his own collection's first canzone, 'Nel dolce tempo de la prima etade,' as the last verse of canzone 70; thus not only have beginnings become endings, but endings

where the metaliterary and the metaliterary-historical issues are so unambiguously at the surface, that past is at the same time the very specific poetic past that precedes Dante himself, and Dante's rewriting of it. For if Petrarch is engaged in this Borgesian creation of a literary history, he is doing so in silent but unmistakable response to the literary historian who precedes him—Dante. Dante, in turn, like Petrarch himself, is a historian aware that what is at stake is the future and its readings. And we see here a characteristic example of Petrarch's most fundamental strategy, that "genius" that will allow him to battle Dante most effectively: he makes unmistakable reference to the rival ideology but never graces it with much beyond the necessary allusion, is never trapped into the obeisance and reverence and acquiescence of more extensive imitation. Petrarch is battling for the supremacy of lyric, and he will wage his battle in its fragmented and allusive and ambiguous tones: the Arnaut of a half-canto, the Arnaut of three full *terzine* in Provençal, is here come and gone with one stanza where he is half himself and half Petrarch, a purposefully ambiguous "I" that suggests the merger of advocacy of a good trial lawyer—and one fleeting verse in Provençal. Petrarch is taunting Dante with the spareness of his lyric and, a bit more disingenuously, with the innocence and purity and unencumbered value of song itself. Just as Petrarch is pleading not only his own case but Arnaut's, Arnaut/Petrarch is pleading the case of lyric poetry before Dante and Dante's revisions to literary history, and, most crucially, lyric poetry after Dante. In this version of the story, a version set to stand as a rival to that of the *Vita nuova* and the cantos of the *Commedia* that pursue and fill out the argument, the creative freedom from the external ideology and its manifold constraints of the love lyric is the response to Dante's charge of solipsism: the poet otherwise constrained is gagged, muted, infertile. And value? The lyric, the song, the sounds that may or may not make sense—sense being an ideological construct, after all—are themselves and in and of themselves meaningful, as much as their setting, "tra l'erba e i fiori."

into beginnings, since the canzone's end finds him at the beginning of his own story, at the 'prima etade' "(24).

Ragion á ben ch'alcuna volta io canti
però ch' ò sospirato sì gran tempo
che mai non incomincio assai per tempo
per adequar col riso i dolor tanti.
Et s'io potesse far ch'agli occhi santi
porgesse alcun diletto
qualche dolce mio detto,
o me beato sopra gli amanti!
Ma più quand'io dirò senza mentire:
"Donna mi priega, per ch'io voglio dire."

It is just that at some time I sing, since I have sighed for so long a time that I shall never begin soon enough to make my smiling equal so many sorrows. And if I could make some sweet saying of mine give some delight to those holy eyes, oh me blessed above other lovers! But most when I can say without lying: "A lady begs me; therefore I wish to speak."

The second rehabilitation and rewriting: the most conspicuous ghost of the *Commedia* makes a stand. The almost shockingly strong and unexpected "Ragion" opens the second stanza, and when we know for sure, with that infinitely famous "Donna mi prega" as the final line, that we have been listening to the now-faint voice of Guido Cavalcanti, we smile, remembering that first "Ragion"—we know now it is a sly pun, Petrarch playing, syntactically, with the allusion to a "reason" with which, in veiled and hushed tones, Dante has banished him from literary history altogether. But this beginning of the Cavalcantian stanza is thus also intimately tied to the stanzaic chapter on Arnaut: the echo, the resounding argument is that it is right and just and fitting. Again, too, Petrarch's own most familiar voice(s) melt with, weave in and out of those he is resuscitating: here, Petrarch's lament about the difficulties of beginnings, of writing, of achievement, all melt into the pleas to be heard from the conspicuously silenced Guido of *Inferno* 9. And again, the quarrel over the judgment of history, the history they are writing in their poetries, is with Dante, with Guido but the spoils, the exemplar.

Petrarch's defense of the obliquely but surely damned Guido is as elegant and lyrical as that of Arnaut, single biting jabs, traces of irony: he asks for the chance to please, to caress with his love verses that one with the "occhi santi," and Petrarch's Laura melts momentarily and the one whom Guido is accused of slighting emerges.[9] Guido's miraculously sweet love poetry is heard at a distance; perhaps it is the incomparable "Chi è questa," a lovemaking that, had she been allowed to hear it, would certainly have given those blessed eyes the greatest of delights. The otherwise banal and predictable result, the poet blessed above all others, is now no slap at the hubris of the other's version of the damned and the blessed in literary history. And it is Guido, in Petrarch's pointed revision, who will come out on top ("e me beato sopra gli altri amanti!") because of his great poem of reason, written in truth and for truth and because it was necessary to say, because the lady asked for it, in truth: "Ma più quand'io dirò senza mentire." Guido did not stray from the right path, Guido did not lie, Guido was on his right path; his Lady asked him to talk about such things.

> Vaghi pensier che così passo passo
> scorto m'avete a ragionar tant'alto:
> vedete che Madonna à 'l cor di smalto
> sì forte ch'io per me dentro nol passo.
> Ella non degna di mirar sì basso
> che di nostre parole
> curi, ché 'l ciel non vole,
> al qual pur contrastando i' son già lasso;
> onde come nel cor m'induro e 'naspro,
> "Così nel mio parlar voglio esser aspro."

> Yearning thoughts, which thus step by step have led me to such high speech: you see that my lady has a heart of such hard stone

9. One of the longest-standing exegetical disputes is who the "disdained" one is in *Inferno* 10, the two likeliest being Beatrice or Virgil. Although Freccero makes a convincing case that it is in fact Virgil, I would sustain here that Beatrice echoes no less strongly in Petrarch's reading—a reading, of course, that can readily conflate both.

that I cannot by myself pass within it. She does not deign to look so low as to care about our words; for the heavens do not wish it, and resisting them I am already weary; therefore as in my heart I become hard and bitter: "So in my speech I wish to be harsh."

This is the centerpiece, the summit: in the middle of the poem, in the third of the five stanzas, Petrarch reproaches Dante with yet a third ghost, one with which Dante himself deals repeatedly in the *Commedia,* one whose guts are spilled out in the first half of the *Vita nuova*—Dante before his conversion. But this is Petrarch's younger and more vulnerable Dante, a different voice is talking, and it is the same younger Dante we glimpse in Borges's essays on Francesca and on Beatrice, a Dante whose heart will, indeed, turn to stone in the very cold shadows of a love whose greatest mercy and passion is a ghost of a smile. The conceit of the troubadours was wrong, was reversed hyperbole—the single weak smile does not sustain the fainthearted poet and lover. At the apex, then, of Petrarch's counterhistory are Dante's brilliant, sparkling, tough *petrose,* a poetry abandoned by Dante just as Guido and Arnaut were. Once again, the erratic and partial touches, those touchstones of the lyric both revive a past and banish the memory of the canto after canto of sustained arguments, of the well-ordered history of a neat and well-ordered universe: Dante's powerfully lyric voice of the *rime petrose* appears and takes charge, and it tells us that it is this, finally, this bitterness and impenetrability of *Madonna,* that has created the later, tougher Dante. Petrarch whispers the same dark and scurrilous thought that Borges suggests through the rhetorical ploy of the unsought but fervent denial: that Dante is embittered and envious, and in his hardness the lover turns away from love and damns it. Francesca is an object of envy and vengeance; Borges plants the seed, tries to deny, falls back.

Infinitamente existió Beatriz para Dante. Dante, muy poco, tal vez nada, para Beatriz; todos nosotros propendemos por piedad, por veneración, a olvidar esta lastimosa discordia inolvidable para Dante. . . . Pienso en Francesca y en Paolo, unidos para siempre en su Infierno. "Questi, che mai da me non fia diviso. . . ." Con espantoso amor, con ansiedad, con admiración, con envidia. (Borges, *Nueve ensayos*, 152–53)

For Dante, Beatrice existed forever. But Dante scarcely existed for Beatrice—perhaps not at all. Because we feel sorry for him and because we venerate him, we all try to forget this terrible discrepancy that was unforgettable for Dante.... I recall Paolo and Francesca, together, forever, in their Hell. "This one, who will never be separated from me...." With a frightening love, with anxiety, with admiration, with envy.

Paolo y Francesca están en el Infierno, él [Dante] se salvará, pero ellos se han querido y él no ha logrado el amor de la mujer que ama, de Beatriz.... Quienes no comprenden la Comedia dicen que Dante la escribió para vengarse de sus enemigos y premiar a sus amigos. Nada más falso. Nietzsche dijo falsísimamente que Dante es la hiena que versifica entre las tumbas. La hiena que versifica es una contradicción.... (Borges, *Siete noches*, 24–25)

Paolo and Francesca are in Hell, he [Dante] will be saved, but they have loved each other and he has not had the love of the woman he loves, Beatrice.... Those who do not understand the Comedy say that Dante wrote it to take revenge on his enemies and reward his friends. Nothing could be more false. Nietzsche said, ever so falsely, that Dante is the hyena who writes poetry among the tombs. A hyena who writes poetry is a contradiction....

Petrarch's melting of voices with this Dante is confusing, dizzying; in "vaghi pensier" (yearning thoughts) we drift from one poet to the other without boundaries, confused even by "nostre parole" (our words), as if the two were indeed one. But if the *petrose* themselves were as hermetic, many of them, as their title (and clear inspiration in the *trobar clus*) implies, Petrarch once again, as with Arnaut, makes limpid verse appear, opens Dante's heart of stone for him: You see what and how I have come to, you see she is impenetrable (the striking "Madonna à 'l cor di smalto..." [My lady has a heart of stone...]), you see that up in the heavens she is too high to look down and grant favor and listen to *our* poetry . . . and I grow weary of this and "in my heart I become hard and bitter" and write hard and bitter verse. . . . Petrarch attacks the extant version of history head-on: the earlier Dante, he, I, we—for that he is now part of me—loved the crystals of lyric love, but his heart hardened and wearied, he gave up, he couldn't make it, he abandoned the magic of such poetry. And then we hear Borges, his voice now overlapping too, tell the rest of the same story, as he talks about the last encounter with Beatrice:

> Ausente para siempre de Beatriz, solo y quizá humillado, imaginó la escena para imaginar que estaba con ella. Desdichadamente para él, felizmente para los siglos que lo leerían, la conciencia de que el encuentro era imaginario deformó la visión. De ahí las circunstancias atroces, tanto más infernales, claro está, por ocurrir en el empíreo: la desaparición de Beatriz, el anciano que toma su lugar, su brusca elevación a la Rosa, la fugacidad de la sonrisa y la mirada, el desvío eterno del rostro. . . . (*Nueve ensayos,* 161)

> Separated forever from Beatrice, alone, humiliated perhaps, he imagined the scene to imagine he was with her. Unfortunately for him, and happily for his readers for centuries, his awareness of the fiction of the encounter deformed the vision. From that fact come the atrocious circumstances [of their meeting]—so much more infernal, of course, because it takes place in the empyrean: the disappearance of Beatrice, the old man who takes her place, her rude elevation to the Rose, the fleetingness of the smile and the look, the eternal turning away of her face. . . .

And in the crescendo of different voices, melding voices, that are accumulating in the *canzone,* the hint is that the harshness of the "parlar" is no longer that more or less innocent game of reinventing that earlier lyric tradition, paying homage to predecessors like Arnaut. No, the harshness in this new version of history—and Petrarch shows the cruel ironies and creative possibilities of histories by thus recasting Dante's own verses—is the harshness of his dealings with the Arnauts and the

Guidos, the harshness of his unblinking and uncompromising vision of Great and True Poetry.[10]

> Che parlo, o dove sono, et chi m'inganna
> altri chi'io stesso e 'l desiar soverchio?
> Già s'i' trascorro il ciel di cerchio in cerchio
> nessun pianeta a pianger mi condanna;
> se mortal velo il mio veder appana
> che colpa è de le stelle
> o de le cose belle?
> Meco si sta chi dì et notte m'affanna
> poi che del suo piacer mi fe' gir grave
> "La dolce vista e 'l bel guardo soave."

What am I saying? or where am I? and who deceives me but myself and my excessive desire? Nay, if I run through the sky from sphere to sphere, no planet condemns me to weeping. If a mortal veil dulls my sight, what fault is it of the stars or of beautiful things? With me dwells one who night and day troubles me since she made me go heavy with the pleasure of "The sweet sight of her and her lovely soft glance."

Perhaps it is the multiplicity of voices that is confusing. Who knows how many of these poets are saying the same thing, went through the

---

10. Mazzotta 1978, focused somewhat differently on the "language of the self," provides a number of readings of Petrarch's poetics as reflected in the *Canzoniere,* and particularly as they correspond or not to Dante, that enrich my own reading here. The Petrarch that emerges here, in his struggle with the problem(s) of self, is one whose poetics are those of fragmentation, and for whom and in whom thematic criticism is insufficient (274). Of particular interest and relevance is certainly Mazzotta's reading of another *canzone,* 125, which also directly inter-weaves the voice of the Dante of the *rime petrose,* a poem, finally, also indicting Dante's poetics, although in this case because they mistake the thrust of the Augustinian theory of language. Once again, the impact of Petrarch's "rebuttal" is that he, Petrarch, is far more astute a literary historian and critic, that he got Augustinian poetics right—he, and not the Dante who claimed, in so many ways, to follow Augustine's teachings and paths.

same crises: "What poetry do I write, what punishment exists beyond my own insatiable Desire?" Petrarch speaks here, pointedly, not only for himself, and not even only for the other three whose shadows and echoes pop in and out of this song, but for all poets, for the Poet that struggles with voices, with postures, with ideas. Once again, an almost cruelly simple opening has struck us at heart, given us the terms of engagement: "Che parlo?"—"What am I saying?"

And in the struggle with the response we sense the presence, still, again, of the most important interlocutor, Dante, of course, a Dante now beyond the stark lyric of stony rhymes, a Dante whose bitterness the more innocent voice of Petrarch reproaches: it is not written in the circles of the heavens that one must weep, that one must turn to sights beyond simple beauties. The inherent but often incomprehensible preciousness of the lyric, already captured by Arnaut, sitting in his field singing, reappears here, and certainly nowhere more so than in the starkly simple and sweet couplet "che colpa è delle stelle / o de le cose belle?"

The value of poetry is inherent and in its reflections of other inherent beauties. The poet here is laden down, night and day, with that beauty and that sweetness and that simplicity, "the sweet sight of her and her lovely soft glance." Hearing Cino da Pistoia's voice at the end of this stanza, we confirm what we intuited: that the voices resounding here are those that played back and forth in *Purgatorio* 24, that this is Petrarch's visit to and engagement with the *dolce stil nuovo*. Again, Dante is reproached for abandonment of an earlier version of himself, one shared, in poetic moments of far simpler bliss and harmony, with Guido and Lapo and Cino himself. But the reproach is losing its edgy tone, for the voice of Petrarch here is hinting that it is Dante being left behind, running from one sphere to the next.

> Tutte le cose di che 'l mondo è adorno
> uscir buone de man del maestro eterno,
> ma me che così a dentro non discerno
> abbaglia il bel che mi si mostra intorno;
> et s'al vero splendor giamai ritorno

l'occhio non po star fermo,
così l' à fatto infermo
pur la sua propria colpa, et non quel giorno
ch' i' volsi in ver l'angelica beltade
"Nel dolce tempo de la prima etade."

All things with which the world is beauteous came forth good from the hands of the eternal Workman: but I, who do not discern so far within, am dazzled by the beauty that I see about me, and if I ever return to the true splendor, my eye cannot stay still, it is so weakened by its very own fault, and not by that day when I turned toward her angelic beauty: "In the sweet time of my first age."

All the shadows and ghosts of Dante were, indeed, being left behind, and now, having rehearsed all the arguments, having listened to the voices, learned from the voices of all those poets and poetries, Petrarch emerges triumphant: the lyric poet in the First Age after lyric poetry has been cast aside and condemned and abandoned. Petrarch will prove that history, that judgment, premature—or rather, he will prove the greater power, for history, of the future over the past. He brings us back to himself: the himself of the earliest stage, the "prima etade," first *canzone* of the same work in which this *canzone* is embedded, the *Rime sparse*. But it is more, of course, than the cleverness of the structural arrangement: 23 is a different version of the Poet's coming of age, as might well be surmised by its incipit. The one hundred and sixty-nine verses of the poem—indeed, structurally, the first long poem and thus a pointed hiatus and retrospective (the second of the collection, if one counts as first, as one must, the opening sonnet)—trace and recall, in flashes and suggestions, the genesis of poetry for a Petrarch struggling with and dwelling on just what he is, what he can be: "Lasso, che son? che fui?"(30). Echoes here, throughout this poem, where the struggle is more with Ovidian voices and with what Laura shall be, of 70.

And in 70, in this last stanza of the *canzone,* there is still one last jab at the nemesis who tried to write him, Petrarch, out of poetic history before he had even had a chance to write himself in. "I, who do not discern so far within"—you who imagine you can know the workings, the whys and the reasons of the *maestro eterno*, are clearly deceived. I am simply dazzled by the simple beauty, my eye, my poetry, my soul will write that—and that, of course, is the truest reflection of the eternal "workman," to shine back out into his universe its simplest and most dazzling beauties, in the simple dazzle of their incomprehensibility, in the confusing simplicity of a lyric voice. I am Maker, you are mere Reader.

One is struck that Durling, whose translations hew closely, although never pedantically or unlyrically, to Petrarch's text, chooses to translate *maestro* here as "workman." The translation is justifiable philologically, and the precise context of "uscir buone de man," with a palpable sense of the simple manual labor involved in such creation, adds to the conviction. (And is that Eliot's echo we hear in the background, "Issues from the hand of God, the simple soul . . ." his bittersweet reflections on Dante in *Animula?*) Most of all, to summon the "maestro" here is to throw us back, once more and with a vengeance now, to the central cantos of *Purgatorio* where Cino's *dolce stil nuovo* and Arnaut converge and where Dante, finally, laments their limitations. Petrarch too says out loud what the mad and heretic Pound will rant and rave about: God himself is the *fabbro* that Dante has disdained; he makes simple and good things with his hands, he issues them into the world. You cannot disdain me. It is I, that "simple" lyric poet, echoing and repeating His work, His kind of near-blind creation and issue, who am closest to the Maker himself. I run with the wind who speaks Paradise.

I V

Existe ese Aleph en lo íntimo de una piedra? Lo he visto cuando vi todas las cosas y lo he olvidado? Nuestra mente es porosa para el olvido; yo mismo estoy falseando y perdiendo, bajo la trágica erosión de los años, los rasgos de Beatriz. (Borges, "El Aleph," *El Aleph*)

Does this Aleph exist in the heart of a stone? Did I see it there in the cellar when I saw all things, and have I now forgotten it? Our minds are porous and forgetfulness seeps in; I myself am distorting and losing, under the wearing away of the years, the face of Beatriz.

The name of Beatrice is the last on Borges's lips in "The Aleph," the vanishing Beatriz fading away, inevitably, with time, treacherous and false time that erodes what once seemed clear and crystalline and unforgettable. We are astonishingly close to a Petrarchan poetics here, and this rude and sad ending throws us back to the beginning of the story, of course, for we are forced to realize that the entire narration, which hardly seemed so at first, was from that final perspective of sand escaping inexorably through the fingers—and created, no less obviously, in the bittersweet, half-successful, half-failed effort to retrieve, to halt and turn back that erosion. So we return, as we must, to the beginning, to the opening sentence of "The Aleph"—and the signs are all there, embarrassingly obvious now:

> La candente mañana de febrero en que Beatriz Viterbo murió, después de una imperiosa agonía que no se rebajó un solo instante ni al sentimentalismo ni al miedo, noté que las carteleras de fierro de la Plaza Constitución habían renovado no se qué aviso de cigarrillos rubios; el hecho me dolió, pues comprendí que el incesante y vasto universo ya se apartaba de ella y que ese cambio era el primero de una serie infinita.

> On the burning February morning Beatriz Viterbo died, after braving an agony that never for a single moment gave way to self-pity or fear, I noticed that the sidewalk billboards around Constitution Plaza were advertising some new brand or other of American cigarettes. The fact pained me, for I realized that the wide and ceaseless universe was already slipping away from her and that this slight change was the first in an endless series.

Death and memory and the apparent vanity of doing much about either: death comes and memory, just as inexorably, slips away—except, of course (although this we cannot, we need not, be told too directly), through the magical powers of poetry, of writing. Borges has tricked us, with too-obvious names and story lines, into thinking we are in Dante's universe; but we are, far more so, in Petrarch's universe, that universe of belief in the great and powerful magic of poetry—that lyricism that alone can stand up to the erosions of time and deaths and changing universes. The story's second sentence, following hard on that "this slight change was the first in an endless series," begins, "Cambiará el universo, pero yo no, pensé con melancólica vanidad . . ." (The universe may change but not me, I thought with a certain sad vanity . . .). Few phrases could have summoned Petrarch as poignantly and empathetically as that *melancólica vanidad:* the last stanza of that remarkable opening sonnet reverberates vividly—"et del mio vaneggiar vergogna è 'l frutto . . ." (and of my raving, shame is the fruit . . .).

The Poet, Borges like Petrarch before him, sits in melancholy contemplation of that wasteland of memory and of the follies of youth, but he, they, are no less struck with the new life that has come from those ruins, the vital poetry, the song, the story, that, in an unsayably different way captures—or does it really create?—both ruin and a fleetingly glorious past. While a Virgil or a Dante or an Eliot might see in such a wasteland the destruction from which a new empire or greater, wholer Truth is waiting to be crafted, these poets harbor an ambition both more and less astonishing: to play back, to reinvent, the magic and the beauties of imperfections, dispersals. The loss is irretrievable but a new magic is brought forth. The *rime* are *sparse,* scattered, because that is the shape of the universe and the human condition. The lyric form—and Borges's short stories, particularly in that necessary context of the omnivorous and overweening novel, are as strikingly lyrical as the Petrarchan sonnet—refracts that liminality and ambiguity back at both poet and audience and revels in their bittersweet beauty. Such language both cannot really say what can be said directly and says far more than that.[11] And this, of course, is the heart of their opposition to Dante's

11. De Man [1964] is an especially helpful reader of Borges in terms of a general "placement": "The least inadequate literary analogy would be with the eighteenth-century *conte philosophique* . . . he differs, however, from his eighteenth-century antecedents in that the subject of the stories is the creation of style itself. . . . His main characters are prototypes for the writer, and his worlds are prototypes for a

logology.[12] The second sentence continues: "Alguna vez, lo sé, mi vana devoción la había exasperado; muerta, yo podía consagrarme a su memoria, sin esperanza, pero también sin humillación" (I knew that at times my fruitless devotion had annoyed her; now that she was dead I could devote myself to her memory, without hope, but also without humiliation). Voices come and go, poets fade in and out; the Dante that is being constructed here is that same one we find venerated, but frankly pitied, in the Borgesian essays, humiliated by a hard and unrelenting Beatrice, a lover whose heart has turned to stone, whose poetry turned beyond love. Even in death, in the invention of literature, that is, there is no hope: Dante will not be happy with crumbs, with imperfection.

The multiple voices of "The Aleph" continue to tell this story of a Petrarchan Dante, a story told in the first person by an Argentinian who calls himself Borges. The Borges liberated from humiliation by the death of Beatriz celebrates her birthday, the thirtieth of April, every year after her death with a visit to her house, a house lived in by her father (a very fleeting presence) and a first cousin with a name overwrought with meanings, Carlos Argentino Daneri.[13] Borges comes to look at her

---

highly stylized kind of poetry or fiction. . . . His stories are about the style in which they are written"(23). DeMan also emphasizes that Borges is enveloped in the notion that poetic invention and the creative act begin and are rooted in duplicity, and that the appearance of God will signal the end of poetry. How far from Dante!

12. Again Mazzotta provides a similar and supportive reading, even when the focus is somewhat different: "For Petrarch, language is the allegory of desire, a veil, not because it hides a moral meaning but because it always says something else" (291); "To his faith in the mimetic possibilities of language, Petrarch opposes the notion of a radical inadequacy of language. If allegory for Dante (as Petrarch read him) is the envelope of hidden truth and an instrument of knowledge, for Petrarch it is constitutive of language and marks the distance between desire and its signs"(292).

13. The Daneri, as pointed out long ago by Monegal, is a rather conspicuous conflation of Dante Alighieri; see Thiem for a full bibliography and greater detail on the intricacies of Dante allusions. I note also in passing that "first cousin" in Spanish is the far more poetic and less remote *primo hermano*—noteworthy given the intimacy between Daneri and Beatriz that the pathetically jealous Borges vaguely suspects.

pictures. The birthday visits become pilgrimages, anniversaries, for years, then decades during which, through accident as well as calculation on Borges's part, the visits have become more intimate and Borges gets to know the peculiar Daneri, fatuous, pompous, useless. "Su actividad mental es continua, apasionada, versátil y del todo insignificante" (His mental activity was continuous, deeply felt, far-ranging, and—all in all—meaningless). It turns out, finally, that he is a writer of literature:

> Tan ineptas me parecieron esas ideas [Daneri had just held forth on how modern man had made himself complete, autonomous] tan pomposa y tan vasta su exposición, que las relacioné inmediatamente con la literatura; le dije que por qué no las escribía. Previsiblemente respondió que ya lo había hecho. . . .

> So foolish did his ideas seem to me, so pompous and so drawn out his exposition, that I linked them at once to literature and asked him why he didn't write them down. As might be foreseen, he answered that he had already done so. . . .

For years, in fact, Daneri has been writing a work that will express a total vision of the universe that comprehends all previous authors, all matters; he is writing the globe itself in verse, inch by inch. Borges becomes Daneri's listener, reader—no longer merely the yearly visitor on the occasion of Beatrice's birthday. Borges humors him—and he is again referred to as "el primo hermano aquel de Beatriz"—clearly because it is a tie to her, it allows him to say her name. But then, as an open manifestation of how inexorably time and change runs over so many things, Daneri's ancestral home, which for Borges is the last material tie to Beatriz, is threatened with demolition. Because of the tie to the dead woman, Borges is more than alarmed, but Daneri is virtually hysterical, because, he confesses, he needs the house in order to finish his book, his poem of the universe, "pues en un ángulo del sótano había un Aleph. Aclaró que un Aleph es uno de los puntos del espacio que contienen todos los puntos" (because down in the cellar there was an Aleph. He explained that an Aleph is one of the points in space that contains all other points). The rest of the story spins out in a tone that fluctuates between the comic-ironic (hilarious and absurd conversations between Daneri and Borges, Borges deciding in one instant that Daneri is mad, that for that matter Beatriz was as well, and then snatching a moment alone in the living room to talk to her portrait) and a cutting seriousness. One scarcely knows whether Borges is smiling or not as he goes down the cellar stairs: Daneri allows Borges himself to descend to see the precious Aleph, and it turns out it does exist, after all, and it does contain the universe. It is Borges, then, at that moment, who is faced head-on with the great problem Daneri has already tackled, and whose inadequacy at the task was condescendingly disdained—how to describe that whole, universal vision: "Arribo, ahora, el inefable centro de mi relato; empieza, aquí, mi desesperación de escritor. . . . Cómo transmitir a los otros el infinito Aleph, que mi temerosa memoria apenas abarca? . . . Por lo demás, el problema central es irresoluble: la enumeración, siquiera parcial, de unconjunto infinito" (I arrive now at the ineffable core of my story. And here begins my despair as a writer. . . . How, then, can I translate into words the limitless Aleph, which my floundering mind can scarcely encompass? . . . Really, what I want to do is impossible, for any listing of an endless series is doomed to be infinitesimal). Borges is stuck, and yet he does decide to try it, and gives an obviously partial and scattered list of events, places, and all manner of things, the two pages or so are, finally, high lyric, poetry far removed from the presumptuous narrative with the difficult form Daneri had adopted. And while Daneri and his epic poem seem never to flinch at the possibility of recounting and making diachronic a vision that has no time, Borges's lyric is rooted in its own insufficiencies and ends.

Vi la reliquia atroz de lo que deliciosamente había sido Beatriz Viterbo, vi la circulación de mi oscura sangre, vi el engranaje del amor y la modificación de la muerte, vi el Aleph, desde todos los puntos, vi en el Aleph la tierra, y en la tierra otra vez el Aleph y en el Aleph la tierra, vi mi cara y mis vísceras, vi tu cara, y sentí vértigo y lloré, *porque mis ojos habían visto ese objeto secreto y conjetural, cuyo nombre usurpan los hombres, pero que ningún hombre ha mirado: el inconcebible universo.*

Sentí infinita veneración, infinita lástima.

I saw the rotted dust and bones that had once deliciously been Beatriz Viterbo; I saw the circulation of my own dark blood; I saw the coupling of love and the modification of death; I saw the Aleph from every point and angle, and in the Aleph I saw the earth and in the earth the Aleph and in the Aleph the earth; I saw my own face and my own bowels; I saw your face; and I felt dizzy and wept, *for my eyes had seen that secret and conjectured object whose name is common to all men but which no man has looked upon—the unimaginable universe.*

I felt infinite wonder, infinite pity.

But Borges and even the ridiculous Daneri *have* seen the "inconceivable universe"—and Borges, the author now, rather than the narrator, has succeeded once again in mystifying us, in giving us a tone, above all, that is at once derisive and admiring, credulous and incredulous. This is that same Borges, indeed, who writes about Dante Alighieri with both veneration and pity, who tells us on every page of his Dante criticism that what Dante did could scarcely be done and is thus the greatest literary achievement ever; but one never gets away from that tone of pity, that hint that that is all, somehow, something other than poetry. The most coherent and comprehensive recent study of Borges and Dante, focusing on the Aleph, concludes, roughly, that this is far from a somewhat simple Dante parody (the conventional line of criticism) but rather an assertion of the importance of a method of significant omission for the modern poetics of total vision, as opposed to the encyclopaedic or epic method of total enumeration (Thiem:108).

But Thiem believes that Borges's (positive) model really *is* Dante, particularly the *Paradiso,* and thus falls into the critical trap that author-predecessors are either venerated or not—or that the options here are either veneration or parody. But Borges himself gave the most direct statement: *I felt infinite veneration and infinite pity.* Close readings of Borges's direct readings of Dante, of the *Paradiso* particularly, reveal ample quantities of that same paradox, which is perhaps more closely linked to the much-abused Petrarchan oxymoron than one might have thought. And Borges, the narrator now, closes the book on the Aleph after that conspicuously brief prose-poem about it: he refuses to discuss it with Daneri, he leaves the house forever, the house is demolished, he starts to forget it. . . . The Aleph, in his poetics, becomes nothing more and nothing less than other experiences and memory traces, imperfectly crystallized in a poem. It is only Daneri who believes it is writable, who finishes his book and wins a prize for it. The story itself ends, as we have already seen, with that throwback to its beginning, that infinitely moving and surprising statement that he is beginning to forget even Beatriz.

Borges's Beatriz, especially in conjunction with his essays on Beatrice in the *Purgatorio* and *Paradiso,* is a fulcrum of images and meanings, the stark emblem of why pity and sadness and disappointments haunt all those pages; and it is through her that we sense most clearly those great misgivings Borges has about Dante. For the pity exists not because she is dead but because the author never knew how to recover her, even in death, and because her cruelty, her absences, finally made him turn away. It should be clear from the necessarily fragmented recounting of "The Aleph" I have given that there is a cacophony of poetic voices in the story—and that they are attached to more than one character: the Dante created here is as much the Borges as the Daneri. (In great measure, of course, this is what prevents its being a simple parody.) For Dante as Daneri, Beatriz is a necessary but unspoken attachment, a cousin whose pictures are still scattered throughout his house, and he is a man who welcomes a stranger to his house to commemorate her birthday, years after her death. But her name never passes his lips—it is never even clear he understood what that Borges was doing in his house every thirtieth of April—and it is eventually evident that his great attachment is, of course, the Aleph, his inspiration, his source, his magic touchstone.

At first Daneri himself has no importance for Borges except as the cousin to the dead Beatriz—a Beatriz, one is compelled to note, who is never described as alive except at the instant Borges comes to the conclusion that Daneri is mad, and decides that she probably was as well.

> Beatriz (yo mismo suelo repetirlo) era una mujer, una niña, de una clarividencia casi implacable, pero había en ella negligencias, distracciones, desdenes, verdaderas crueldades, que tal vez reclamaban una explicación patológica.

> Beatriz (I myself often say it) was a woman, a child, with almost uncanny powers of clairvoyance, but forgetfulness, distractions, contempt, and a streak of cruelty were also in her, and perhaps these called for a pathological explanation.

The beloved, then, was infinitely unworthy, that same Beatrice who is created cruel even in the *Purgatorio* and *Paradiso*. And then, slowly, Daneri becomes much more, and Borges's remaining attachments to her are merely incantational, like the habit of a prayer, and a vulgar one at that. Daneri, finally, is the link not to his cousin but to the Aleph itself, and thus, for Borges, Beatriz herself is but the first step to the grand vision, to that moment of clairvoyance and ineffability in the basement of her ancestral home. This, in the end, was all she really gave him, although it would seem it was perhaps a great deal, because she appears to have been otherwise unable to be fulfilling at all. Borges, like Petrarch, is a stunning and magical historian and in a handful of lines can lay bare the ambition and the hurt—each in their own way part of the obsession with truth—that are two sides of the same coin:

> Carlos Argentino observó, con admiración rencorosa, que no creía errar en el epiteto al calificar de sólido el prestigio logrado en todos los círculos por Alvaro Melián Lafinur, hombre de letras . . . yo tenía que hacerme portavoz de dos méritos inconclusos: la perfección formal y el rigor científico, "porque ese dilatado jardín de tropos, de figuras, de galanuras, no tolera un solo detalle que no confirme la severa verdad." Agregó que Beatriz siempre se había distraído con Alvaro.

> Carlos Argentino [Daneri] remarked, with admiration and envy,

that surely he could not be far wrong in qualifying with the epithet "solid" the prestige enjoyed in every circle by Alvaro Melián Lafinur, a man of letters . . . he [Daneri] suggested I make myself spokesman for two of the book's undeniable virtues—formal perfection and scientific rigor—"inasmuch as this wide garden of metaphors, of figures of speech, of elegances, is inhospitable to the least detail not strictly upholding of truth." He added that Beatriz had always been taken with Alvaro.[14]

Hurt and ambition. Little wonder, given such a reading of the *Vita nuova* and the *Commedia,* that Borges prefaces his remarks to the encounter with Beatrice in the *Paradiso* with that arresting "I want to comment on the most moving [literally, full of pathos] verses literature has ever produced." But there is more than even that, implicitly, that is pathetic, pitiable, for Borges the writer and the consumer and inventor of writers is not so irreducibly romantic that even the most irremediable of romantic attachments would in and of itself provoke such great pathos in him. Clearly, it is the result, at least in this case, as he sees it, of that failure in love: the abandonment of even the possibility of love poetry for the Aleph in the basement, for that clairvoyance, that universal and epic vision. For the sight of what others might call empire, or grandeur, or God.

Se Virgilio et Omero avessin visto
quel sole il qual vegg'io con gli occhi miei,
tutte lor forze in dar fama a costei
avrian posto et l'un stil coll'altro misto;

di che sarebbe Enea turbato, et tristo
Achille, Ulisse et gli altri semidei,
et quel che resse anni cinquantasei
si bene il mondo, et quel ch'ancise Egisto. . . .

If Virgil and Homer had seen that sun which I see with my eyes,

14. I think this translation of the crucial "Beatriz se había distraído con Alvaro" obscures the strong implication in the Spanish that there was an active relationship involved, that Beatriz had *amused* herself with Alvaro.

they would have exerted all their powers to give her fame and would have mixed together the two styles:

For which Aeneas would be angry; and Achilles, Ulysses, and the other demigods, and he who ruled the world so well for fifty-six years, and he whom Aegisthus killed, would all be sad. . . . (Petrarch, *Rime sparse,* Poem 186, first two stanzas of sonnet)

V

THE ALEPH

What eternity is to time, the Aleph is to space. In eternity, all time—past, present, and future—coexists simultaneously. In the Aleph, the sum total of the spatial universe is to be found in a tiny shining sphere barely over an inch across. When I wrote my story, I recalled Wells's dictum that in a tale of the fantastic, if the story is to be acceptable to the mind of the reader, only one fantastic element should be allowed at a time. For example, though Wells wrote a book about the invasion of Earth by Martians, and another book about a single invisible man in England, he was far too wise to attempt a novel about an invasion of our planet by an army of invisible men. Thinking of the Aleph as a thing of wonder, I placed it in as drab a setting as I could imagine—a small cellar in a nondescript house in an unfashionable quarter of Buenos Aires. In the world of the *Arabian Nights,* such things as magic lamps and rings are left lying about and nobody cares; in our skeptical world, we have to tidy up any alarming or out-of-the-way element. Thus, at the end of "The Aleph," the house has to be pulled down and the shining sphere destroyed with it.

Once, in Madrid, a journalist asked me whether Buenos Aires actually possessed an Aleph. I nearly yielded to temptation and said yes, but a friend broke in and pointed out that were such an object to exist it would not only be the most famous thing in the world but would renew our whole conception of time, astronomy, mathematics, and space. "Ah," said the journalist, "so the entire thing is your invention. I thought it was true because you gave the name of the street." I did not dare tell him that the naming of streets is not much of a feat.

My chief problem in writing the story lay in what Walt Whitman had very successfully achieved—the setting down of a limited catalog of endless things. The task, as is evident, is impossible, for such chaotic enumeration can only be simulated, and every apparently haphazard element has to be linked to its neighbor either by secret association or by contrast.

"The Aleph" has been praised by readers for its variety of elements: the fantastic, the satiric, the autobiographical, and the pathetic. I wonder whether our modern worship of complexity is not wrong, however. I wonder whether a short story should be so ambitious. Critics, going even further, have detected Beatrice Portinari in Beatriz Viterbo, Dante in Daneri, and the descent into hell in the descent into the cellar. I am, of course, duly grateful for these unlooked-for gifts.

Beatriz Viterbo really existed and I was very much and hopelessly in love with her. I wrote my story after her death. Carlos Argentino Daneri is a friend of mine, still living, who to this day has never suspected he is in the story. The verses are a parody of his verse. Daneri's speech on the other hand is not an exaggeration but a fair rendering. The Argentine Academy of Letters is the habitat of such specimens. (Borges, "Commentaries," in *The Aleph and Other Stories*, 263–64)

It is one of the most recent and generally felicitous commonplaces of Petrarch criticism that Petrarch's struggles with defining himself and his poetry are at the very heart of the *Rime sparse*. It is also understood now that Petrarch's disavowal of Dante, both direct and through conspicuous silences, is itself to be dismissed, for Dante's presence is, finally, as conspicuous (if not more so) in Petrarch's vernacular poetry as that of any other of his poetic ancestors, those he chooses not to deny. But it is far less well understood how closely these two issues are interwoven; and a critical tradition that once accepted the Dante exclusion, as it did the literal truths of a Laura and her anniversaries, now largely feels it is sufficient to merely note the conspicuous falsehood of the denial of Dante while it acknowledges his many presences in the *Rime sparse*. Such denial is assumed to be either a normal thing to do and thus not worth dwelling on—or perhaps it is that the implications are far too banal, shallow, and embarrassing to be worth much space and time, particularly since we now know it to be a false denial and it no longer prevents us from finally seeing the Dante allusions, calques, "influence."

But I would argue that in fact the particular textual uses Petrarch makes of Dante are colored and shaped by that search for definitions of self and poetry, and that a necessary part of that search is bound up with the most difficult of ancestral relations for him, that with Dante. In other words, given the critical context that Petrarch at one level overtly and unambiguously absents Dante from the *Rime sparse,* it seems problematic to deal with the presences one then does detect—the structural affinity, the verbal echo, the allusion—as if that denial simply had not been uttered, or were a slip of some sort caused by an unrelated and simple personal jealousy or some other flaw that was somehow irrelevant to the poetry itself. We are hardly dealing with banal or pseudo-psychological analysis here, but rather with a remarkably powerful and meaningful juxtaposition that is potentially of central importance to at least one possible reading of the *Rime sparse.*

It is instructive to note that Borges scholars have been puzzled by the fact that Borges plays Petrarch in this way as well: he does not, first of all, actually name Dante in "El Aleph," a story which includes direct acknowledgements of a number of other authors. Most of all, the "history" of this little story has been largely written by Borges himself— once again in a stunning lyricism, in that commentary on "The Aleph" that speaks powerfully on the issue of literary history and its makings. In the middle of this combination of explicit self-analysis and Borgesized literary criticism, he says it right there in black and white, in a sharp evocation of the positivism and linearity of the dominant critical mode, for all to see: my story is a simple thing, not ambitious, and to see Beatrice in Beatriz and Dante in Daneri is part of the obsessive historicizing of literary critics. Not only that: the truth is there really was a

Beatriz Viterbo and I really did adore her and there really was a Daneri
and he really is my friend. . . .

The numerous interpretations of this curiosity are not unlike those in
the equally curious case of Petrarch: one notes it and goes on, or calls it
an instance of "Bloomian anxiety" and goes on, no less blithely, as if the
problem of a complex relationship has been dealt with by the simple
incantation of Bloom. Again, the fundamental critical problem that
emerges is that overt references in a context in which the very pos-
sibility of such references being made has been excluded are very
specially marked. And in both cases, one must begin with the most
innocent of observations, namely that the denials of "influence" from
Dante are transparently—intentionally—false and ludicrous, *first and
foremost to their authors.* Certainly one cannot read Borges's paragraph
denying Dante's presence with any less of a smile than the paragraph
where he tells us about the "journalist"—another species of critic, no
doubt—who asks whether there really is an Aleph . . . and who believed
it had to be all "true" or all "false." Again, the issue is settled in the last
paragraph, after the denial of Dante's Beatrice and the assertion of the
true love of his own Beatriz: Borges the Maker is showing us he can play
any game, including the I-write-the-Truth game. Meanwhile, no less
importantly, in the denial of the undeniable, what is also taking place is
the establishment of a parallel universe. For both Borges and Petrarch,
Dante is explicitly made what he was and is, historically and personally
to one, canonically for the other, as for ourselves: the very parameters of
a universe, a fundamental guideline so obviously present that it is
precisely the strong interpretations within the text, those transforma-
tions and remarkable interpretations, that constitute the real rejection.
It is not the silence or the denial in Petrarch or Borges that excludes
Dante; quite the contrary: the very conspicuousness of the gesture is
what asserts the inevitability of Dante's presence. And, concomitantly
and conversely, it is within such an inevitable presence, it is the citations,
the game of reenactment, that are used to deny; for denial means a
tampering with the future for poets of this magnitude, it means that
brand of historical revision that powerfully recasts and rewrites a
predecessor.

And at the very beginning is the denial of that diachronic concept of history, a concept that is strongly bound to the epic, to the Daneris, to the literary historians who see "influence" in such positivistic ways. Such linearity is inimical to the "simpler" project at hand, to the synchronic moment of lyricism that shuffles time around and rearranges it, that tells us that metaphysics is that simple and atemporal list of the universe. "What eternity is to time, the Aleph is to space. In eternity, all time—past, present, and future—coexist simultaneously." The irony, then, lies simply in the fact that although the Aleph does exist, it vanishes the instant we try and tell it rather than suggest it. This is a step not so very different from Dante's own faint praise; this is veneration and pity, a reverence that distances, or perhaps that recognizes and emphasizes the great distances that are already there. The irony, if irony there can be in what is at least in part a natural cycle, is that Dante is left behind in the historiography created by the later lyricists precisely because he turns away, in their visions (and to a great extent in his own as we see in his treatment of Arnaut), from simple love song to universal poet. Here, in this telling of it, Dante's heart did turn to stone, and he lost his youthful ability to transform love, an inherently inadequate and transitory phenomenon, into a poetry of perpetual desire: his Beatrice was never alive enough, powerful enough—like Virgil and Homer, he did not have a sun resplendent enough. And both writer-historians, Borges and Petrarch, understand intimately—and with this the subject of their analysis would scarcely disagree—that at the heart of Dante's conversion is that same issue of the nature of poetry and what it can and should do and be. Not, Does the Aleph exist, does Beatrice exist—only those who cannot conceive literature at all would ask such a question— but, *How* and *where* do they exist: have I made them or have I revealed them?

In their recreation of Dante, both Borges and Petrarch are, of course, exercising the same powerful prerogative of shaping and fashioning an ancestry that Dante himself used incomparably, and that most if not all writers do to some extent, as Borges himself has pointed out. Once again, time is of the essence and literary history is a great deal like the Aleph, "a tiny shining sphere barely over an inch across." In fact, if we go back to the beginning once again, we understand the frankly subversive historical project that is "The Aleph." The story begins with two epigraphs, in English and from a purposefully scattered past, a past that sheds light on the future. From *Hamlet:* "O God! I could be bounded in a nutshell, and count myself a King of infinite space"; and from *Leviathan:* "But they will teach us that Eternity is the Standing still of the Present Time, a *Nunc-stans* (as the Schools call it); which neither they, nor any else understand, no more than they would a *Hic-stans* for an infinite greatness of Place." And while Dante casts the whole enterprise in absolute moral terms that seek to fix future time in its grasp, the kabbalists and magicians who follow in his wake will mock that reading of time; only the young and foolish think one can master time and be the King of infinite space. Crucially, these are the poets of a different kind of Belief, and they insist on a different kind of moral hierarchy: they believe in what is sayable, in the superb *voice* that tells us about how much he really loved Beatriz. In these terms, one finds it easier to understand the curious structure of the *Rime sparse,* in which the opening sonnet appears to undercut the love poetry that will follow, but at closer inspection in fact denies the "conversion" that will supposedly take place.[15] In these terms both Borges and Daneri in "The Aleph" are highly privileged— but probably unique. Both Petrarch and Borges look Vision, and the possibilities of writing transcendent Truths, in the face and turn away— perhaps, finally, because it could only be done by Dante, it had been done by Dante and thus could not possibly be redone. Perhaps because they thought it other, far inferior to, the magic lyricism of which they

15. See the recent psychoanalytical study by Braden (which includes an excellent analysis of Petrarch's dialogue with Augustine in the *Secretum*), who arrives, through a quite different mode of analysis, at conclusions about the *Rime sparse* complementary to those of Mazzotta, quote above: "It is a story in which utterance fails systematically of its ostensible external goal, to double back on its originator"(147). Crucially, Braden outlines the multiple failures of the purported conversion, a conversion for which Petrarch keeps waiting, at least half-heartedly, but that simply will not come; and the fact the greatest poetic effect is that the ultimate external object of desire does not exist except in our imagination (154).

were both masters and fervent believers. There is the reverence and veneration, there, in the silences of denials, the most charming and sincere of acknowledgements: Dante was and is the unique visionary and universal and inimitable Poet. Of course, now we see that it is not Dante we should see in Daneri, for Dante is the Aleph itself. And he cannot be retold without grotesque parody.[16]

But it is precisely in the inimitability of his now sacred text, in its wake, that any sort of literary history can follow, and that, of course, is the center of Petrarch's struggle with his notions of self and of his art, a struggle that was as voracious, and ultimately as successful, as it was precisely for the reason that it took place because of Dante and with Dante and against Dante. One can only begin to imagine the extraordinary and oppressive power, personal and literary (and for Petrarch this distinction would have been minor, if it existed at all), of living and working in the close-cropped shadow of Dante's *Commedia,* of Dante's recognition, of the suspicion that the text had now been written, that the love lyric was dead, that any budding poets after him may as well lay down and die—all suspicions inscribed by Dante himself within the *Commedia* and easily decipherable by as formidable a reader as Pe-

16. In his most recent meditation on poetry, *Ruin the Sacred Truths,* the always provocative Bloom offers a reading of Dante that in texture resonates more strongly of Borges as a kind of answer to his reading than of the conventional academic readings of recent years: Dante, a preternaturally strong poet, is both prophetic and very much the creator of his own universe, and his Beatrice is "at the center of an idiosyncratic gnosis" (47). In this universe, a universe in which the commonplace distinctions between sacred and secular in textuality are spurious, Dante is also an Aleph, but, crucially, an Aleph that is nakedly magical: one poet's construct and thus personal revelation. Oddly enough, Bloom too sees fit to close his own meditations on the *Divine Comedy* with the image of Beatrice's smile (a Beatrice who is the final and singular guide because she is so explicitly his own creation): "Freud . . . lamented his failure to cure those who would not accept the cure . . . Dante too would not owe any man anything, not even if the man were Virgil, his poetic father. . . . The cure was accepted by Dante from his physician, Beatrice, but she was his own creation, the personal myth that centered his poem. In smiling and looking at him as they part, she confirms the cure"(50).

trarch.[17] We can hear in the background the noise of fame, treacherous fame, and even more treacherous popularity, both bones of contention, thorns intricately bound up with the omnipotent one of language, the *volgare*. Dante has taken more than his fair share; and even in Borges's universe, the flaw of Daneri the writer of the Aleph is that of a kind of voraciousness, that belief that language can be so infinitely expanded and recalibrated and manipulated that it will be able to say the Aleph.

Petrarch grappled painfully, at times ironically, with what the *volgare*, the vernacular, was, and whether he could possibly be a poet of a language that would then be taken over by those, the *volgo*, who had been given access to it—and Dante's own fame and success could in some ways be sneered at because it had slipped away from him, it had been appropriated by an infinitely unworthy public.[18] Petrarch would even come to claim, in the all-revealing letter to Boccaccio, that he had given up "his [Dante's] style of composition to which I devoted myself as a young man, for I feared for my writings . . ."—feared that his poetry too would come to be changed as a vernacular language itself is, sung and resung until it was something else altogether, eroded and altered by time itself.[19] The difficulty in interpreting these comments of Petrarch's—and our assumption that he was being hypocritical (or worse, since we know he was very far from abandoning poetry in the vernacu-

17. Petrarch's letter to Boccaccio, after several preliminary sentences, gets to the matter at hand as follows: "In the first place, you ask pardon, somewhat heatedly, for seeming to praise unduly a fellow countryman of ours who is popular for his poetic style but doubtless noble for his theme; and you beg pardon for this as though I believe that praises for him or for anyone else would detract from my personal glory" (Bernardo, ed and trans. 1985:202). For a discussion of the vexing problem of Dante's very long shadow in the context of the history of later Italian literature see chapter 2 above.

18. ". . . these silly admirers who never know why they praise or censure, who so mispronounce and mangle his verses that they could do no greater injury to a poet . . ." (Bernardo 1985:204–5).

19. Tanturli believes that Petrarch was the first in several hundred years of Italians—Renaissance Humanists—to disdain Dante because of their disdain for the *volgare* itself.

lar)—is due to two kinds of interference: First, our own knowledge of the history that would follow, i.e., that Petrarch's vernacular poetry would become so substantial and integral a part of the subsequent poetic tradition. Second, our assumption that to say "the vernacular" is to have said one thing, that all styles within the vernacular, in other words, are like each other. But Petrarch was in fact making the crucial distinction between two possible vernacular styles exemplified in crystalline fashion in "The Aleph": the infinite, expansive, and universal style that Daneri tries, a Daneri who in his own muddled way believes that his writing must mirror, must tell and narrate, the infinite Truths of the Aleph; and the elliptical and allusive style, radically incomplete, that is what Borges, the narrator, comes up with, scarcely more than a suggestion—that incandescent suggestion that the sparkle is more powerful than the Vision.

Or, perhaps, it is that the gloss is more powerful, more magically subversive, than the master text. For perhaps part of what is taking place here, and what so intimately links together Petrarch and Borges, is the kind of marginality, or looming, potential marginality, with which both are burdened by Dante. In the case of Borges, the argument has been marvelously made by González Echevarría that Borges's Derridian affinities—that starkly kabbalistic attribution of primacy to writing and texts themselves—is rooted in the Latin American writer's inherently marginal position vis-à-vis the European tradition: "The relationship may be understood in the sense suggested by Derrida's epigraphs, as a supplement that repeats the original tradition, by taking its place, by rewriting it from within, but always as if it were from without" (González Echevarría [1983] 1986b:231). In the end, this is a remarkably precise meditation on what Borges is doing with the *Divine Comedy,* venerated but hegemonistic, in his "Aleph"—and, in quite different but congruent historical circumstances, what Petrarch and his *Rime sparse* are doing. While in the distant twentieth century Borges would have to create the space for an absence of Dante achieved by the overwhelming and almost caricatured references (to the point of it all seeming to many to be a parody), that overwhelming and probably also caricatured presence was, no doubt, an oppressive reality for Petrarch, a Petrarch whose kindred souls in a number of ways may turn out to be the Latin American writers who have always shared with him that need to work from a "strategic marginality," as González Echevarría has put it.[20]

Thus the genius of Petrarch's defense—self-defense may be more like it—was to use that universality of presence for his own purposes, to write a *Rime sparse* that not only is a parallel universe but a text and a poetry that distinguish themselves clearly, in the apparently silent interstices, from that text that is the bearer of a shockingly powerful new tradition. Petrarch must strike back at the challenge to the future, for the threat of Dante is precisely that, a threat to drown out his voice before it was even raised. Poor Petrarch, a Latin Americanist might be tempted to say. So far from God, so close to Dante. But the Petrarchan voice that emerges under such conditions is one that revels in its powerful fragmentariness and succeeds precisely through proclaiming the superiority of that momentary, perhaps vanishing, but certainly magical glimmer that has characterized other writers who have seen the power inherent in a "commentator's" role, writers like Garcilaso the Inca and Carpentier—and of course Borges. And coyly, craftily, Petrarch will craft for himself the kind of subversive centrality that Dante has, in the end, denied himself: imitability. For, we should notice now all the more clearly, Petrarch's lament about Dante was not that he was imitated (of course not—how could Petrarch, the classicist, lament any such fate?)[21] but rather that he was mistreated by "the rabble," who "mispronounce and mangle his verses." That is the problem with becoming an Aleph: only the Daneris—perhaps from time to time a pitiful Pellico—will be a part of your tradition. To hear Borges tell it,

20. Petrarch's multiple and variegated affinities with Latin America are beginning to surface as a subject of critical interest: Professor Roland Greene of Harvard, for example, is currently engaged in a project exploring the relations between Petrarchan discourse and the colonial enterprise, particularly how the ethics of Petrarchism operate as a crucial language in the earliest colonial texts. I am grateful to the author for sharing his work-in-progress thoughts with me.

21. See Petrie's lucid discussion of Petrarch's belief in the importance of imitation, particularly of the Augustan poets, as well as her comments on the related problem of the acquisition of fame.

Dante made himself inimitable, and left only to the unwise and untalented the vain hope of a mangled and pompous copying. But there can be no greater fame than the kind of utter imitability inspired by the finely hewn and starkly limited *Canzoniere*.

By going outside (and, we will grant, he says, beyond) the normal human condition, the normal boundaries of writing, Dante made himself unique, the *Commedia* a sacred text; but what he garnered for both in literary history was, inevitably, a place in certain key ways also outside and beyond and above. Petrarch's place, in part because the *Rime sparse* is set up in deliberate and inescapable counterpoint and revision, is paradoxically back within that history, at its center, as a new beginning that is the opposite of the dead end Dante saw as a new life. Petrarch becomes the most vitally imitated poet in the history of poetry. The *Commedia* may not exactly sit on the shelves gathering dust, but like most sacred texts, it is read primarily by the devout and the already converted. More importantly, the *Commedia,* in its inimitable vastness and astonishing ambition, may serve as an absolutely necessary part of one's literary education—as Pound says, "Anyone who don't know the *Commedia* is thereby ignoramus"—but it cannot, as a whole, be held long enough to be the kind of "influential" text that will generate bona fide children rather than fragmented commentary. The failed attempts at following such an overweening model run the gamut from Pellico's *Prigioni* to Pound's *Cantos.* As Freccero notes: "While almost all modern poets can trace the Dantesque ancestry of some of their verses, none can claim him as a model. To speak of Dante's influence, then, is to speak of the ways in which fragments of a no longer vital tradition have been used, often ironically, in order to shape totally different individual talents" (Freccero 1986b:3).[22] Borges tells us, in fact, that the Aleph cannot be rewritten successfully, that it can only convert away from

22. This necessary clarification—and limitation—of what can possibly be called Dante's "influence" appears in the first essay of a collection devoted to "Dante Among the Moderns" (McDougal, ed. 1986) and is especially welcome given the tendency, very much apparent in the introduction to that volume, to see Dante as a highly "influential" poet in the conventional sense of the word.

literature, that the Truth project is far too inimical to the literary one. Some days Dante is the Aleph and others he is Daneri.

But how different from Daneri's or Pound's is Petrarch's fate, how different the fame he achieved for himself. Although his name is far less known and his text's name virtually unknown (except among the cognoscenti), his love poetry has reverberated, often quite precisely, in virtually every poet in his wake, with the great love one has of what is imitable. Eschewing a universal *volgare,* he has in most ways escaped the rabble: they do not mispronounce his name or mangle his text, as indeed they do Dante's. But, in a different order altogether, the many different features of the *Rime sparse* are the perpetual and inescapable conceits of the lyric, its rhythms and its fragmented sparkles, the magic incantation whose exact origins are lost in time; and time is irrelevant now. Most of all, there is infinite imitability, even when it is unconscious, in the uncertainties and ambiguities and belief in unknowable and inexpressible magic that are in the Poet Petrarch constructed. Thus, even in the late twentieth century, when lyric has become rock (not, clearly, the *petrose* of Dante), Petrarch's presence is heard and seen everywhere by those who know—even, of course, among those who are consciously oblivious of his existence, or of who the "real" Laura might be, the one constructed in the *Rime sparse.*[23] She has been so vastly influential, we do not even remember her name anymore. We don't need to.

At the end, I return to that vision that Borges has of Dante's pathetic last look at Beatrice, and to Borges's sense of sadness that, as a love story, it had to end that way. In his *Essay* Borges does not quite say—whether by choice or inability is neither clear nor determinable—what "The Aleph" ever so clearly reveals: that such a sad end is (from the point of view of poets like him and like Petrarch, those who have not abandoned a belief in their own powers, their almost limitless shamanism) the just

---

23. Nancy Vickers has been doing extraordinary work in the last several years on the dispersal—the inevitable process of illegitimization—of Petrarch in contemporary music, a dispersal due in great measure to the fact that Petrarchism spread far beyond the "high" cultural content within which it is normally studied (Vickers 1988).

deserts of a poet like Dante who has cast his lot with Truth. That
Beatrice, like the Beatriz in Borges's story, can never be anything more
than what she was in life; she is trapped in dusty photographs of specific
days and accountable hours, chained to realities that were often not so
beautiful. How much better, how much simpler, how much more
human and poetic, to yield to the temptations of duplicity, to believe in
language, to incant and create a lover, to understand that if I say,
"Beatriz Viterbo really existed and I was very much and hopelessly in
love with her," it is a truth no one can ever deny, and to recognize that
"the poet is of the devil's party," as de Man put it. Pellico's great failure
in prison comes back to haunt: he yields to virtue and rejects the good
story—and then we remember that in so doing he was executing an
excellent reading of Dante, a Dante for whom Francesca could be a
spectacularly good story, but not, finally, Beatrice. Love should not be
blind, just the poet; for in blindness creation may thrive, whereas vision,
finally, yields but Truth. And there is poor Dante, he tells us, vast, great,
inimitable achievement in hand, such a gift as no man has ever made for
a woman; and he has come such a long way, constructed such a
monumental edifice, all to get to her again, to try once again. But the
Truth is still, of course, the same: she turns her back, she walks away.

Epilogue

Liberation:

Galeotto and Doubt

Of course the men didn't dig the two imitation white boys come in on their leisure. And when I spoke someone wd turn and stare, or laugh, and point me out. The quick new jersey speech, full of italian idiom, and the invention of the jews. Quick to describe. Quicker to condemn.
—LeRoi Jones, *The System of Dante's Hell*

Lolita, light of my life, fire of my loins. My sin, my soul. Lo-lee-ta: the tip of the tongue taking a trip of three steps down the palate to tap, at three, on the teeth. Lo. Lee. Ta.

She was Lo, plain Lo, in the morning, standing four feet ten in one sock. She was Lola in slacks. She was Dolly at school. She was Dolores on the dotted line. But in my arms she was always Lolita.

Did she have a precursor? She did, indeed she did. In point of fact, there might have been no Lolita at all had I not loved, one summer, a certain initial girl-child. In a princedom by the sea. Oh when? About as many years before Lolita was born as my age was that summer. You can always count on a murderer for a fancy prose style.

Ladies and gentlemen of the jury, exhibit number one is what the seraphs, the misinformed, simple, noble-winged seraphs, envied. Look at this tangle of thorns.
—Vladimir Nabokov, *Lolita,* chapter 1

I

Comincia il libro chiamato Decameron, Cognominato Prencipe
Galeotto. . . .

Here begins the book called Decameron, otherwise known as
Prince Galahalt. . . .[1]

*J*t is with these straightforward first eight words that Boccaccio, in
the marked incipit of the *Decameron,* sets out the parameters of his
reading of Dante and starts to nudge us in the direction he will push,
more or less relentlessly, for the rest of his enormous and enormously
challenging text. And if for him, as for so many others, Dante is a true
believer in the revelation of the text—and the concomitant obligations
of the author—Boccaccio is fascinated with the other side of the coin:
the reader, his interpretation(s), and their difficulties. As we can so
quickly, and apparently simply, read, the convergence of Boccaccio the
reader of Dante and Boccaccio the spinner of tales that tease a reader's
interpretive bent is plainly exposed from the outset of the work he
subtitles *Galeotto.* Fittingly, the "Galeotto" epithet or *cognome*[2] has

1. All quotations from the *Decameron* are from the edition of Cesare Segre and
all translations from that of G. H. McWilliam.
2. Surname, literally. The full title of the work is presented as *Comincia il libro
chiamato Decameron, Cognominato Prencipe Galeotto, nel quale si contengono cento novelle,
in dieci di dette da sette donne e da tre giovani uomini.* The McWilliam translation, like
most of those into English, disguises the explicit morphological relationship
("Here begins the book *called* Decameron, *otherwise known* as Prince Galahalt,
wherein are contained a hundred stories . . . , where the "chiamato . . . cog-
nominato" (named . . . surnamed) is both repetitive and genetically inseparable. In
Italian the sequence framing the two names emphasizes the relationship of one
name (*Decameron*) as the given or "first" name to the other (Prencipe Galeotto) as
the family or "last" name. The relatively simple taxonomy here is critical: the
Decameron is one member (specimen) of the family (class) of Galeotto texts.

always been an interpretative conundrum, for, like much else in the *Decameron,* the "logical" or "obvious" meaning or interpretation is one that places the reader in an untenable situation.

I I

Masetto, at the end of 3.1, having sexually satiated himself and a bevy of nuns (initially through the ruse of pretending to be a deaf-mute but eventually as part of an openly and flagrantly corrupt arrangement among intimates at the convent), delivers his interpretation of why he has had such a long and prosperous life, blessed with many children and multiple and plentiful satisfactions:

> Cosí adunque Masetto vecchio, padre e ricco, senza aver fatica di nutricar figliuoli o spesa di quegli, per lo suo avvedimento avendo saputo la sua giovinezza bene adoperare, donde con una scure in collo partito s'era se ne tornó, *affermando che cosí trattava Cristo che gli poneva le corna sopra 'l cappello.*

> Thus it was that Masetto, now an elderly and prosperous father who was spared the bother of feeding his children and the expense of their upbringing, returned to the place from which he had set out with an axe on his shoulder, having had the sense to employ his youth to good advantage. *And this, he maintained, was the way he treated anybody who placed a pair of horns upon His crown.* (emphasis mine)

Masetto's perfectly logical and in some ways irrefutable conclusion is that the good life—his good life, at any rate—was his because it was thus that Christ treated him who cuckolded him, him who had slept with his brides, the nuns. It is an interpretation rooted equally in the belief in a cause-and-effect principle operative in life and in stories alike, and in the concomitant belief in the very possibility of a clear and clean-cut, definitive interpretation of a sequence of events, a story (this latter being sometimes, but not necessarily, referred to as the "moral" of a story; thus the morals of many of Boccaccio's stories present the distinct problem of being immoral by virtually any standards. Masetto is guilty not only of deception and of fornication; no less grievously, he is spectacularly guilty of obvious and logical but thus facile and poor interpretation—and in this latter he is little different from many of the readers of (and in) the *Decameron*. The reader of the *Decameron*—and certainly not just a hypothetical devout medieval reader—knows immediately that Masetto's interpretation of his life and its rewards (rather than condemnation and punishment) is blasphemously wrong. But that reader and critic is in most cases trapped by the same impulse that drove Masetto: to extract and articulate a sure and identifiable (and articulable) meaning. And the very absurdity (in "moral" or interpretative terms) of the dénouement of this story, as well as of countless others in the *Decameron*, has driven many critics to assume that Boccaccio was thus writing "moralless" stories and, from a moral or Christian perspective, a work that was "meaningless" at best, the way that modern literature supposedly is. Thus, one of the dominant readings of the *Decameron*, and the one which has dictated the terms of many discussions and conditioned other readings, is that it was a celebration of the end of the moralizing of the Middle Ages, a liberation from the constraints to be both chaste and to make reasonable, moral sense of difficult stories. The dominant response to this reading is no different epistemologically but arrives at the opposite conclusion: the stories, and the *Decameron* as a whole, do have a meaning, but this medieval text is so highly encoded that its moral is not readily available to later readers, largely deprived of the keys to the reading that does make sense.[3] Both postures, in the end, remind us of Masetto himself and make us much like him as readers: our story is utterly without moral until and unless the lost or hidden key is

3. Branca is the earliest thorough exponent of the "global and serious meaning" view, as his title might suggest; Hollander's various studies constitute a major body of work in establishing the *Decameron* as a meaningfully Christian text, and are especially useful here in that he has explicitly focused on Boccaccio's relationship with Dante. Kirkham, too, argues that an orthodox Christian morality is decodable even in the most radically subversive of stories: In the notorious and much excised story of Alibech putting the devil into hell, the appropriate and rather elaborate keys provide the real moral reading, that "illicit love leads to perdition" (93).

recovered, and then the underlying true and Christian meaning is revealed.

I I I

"Quando leggemo il disïato riso
  esser basciato da cotanto amante,
  questi, che mai da me non fia diviso,
la bocca mi basciò tutto tremante.
  Galeotto fu il libro e chi lo scrisse:
  quel giorno più non vi leggemo avante."

"When we read how the longed-for smile was kissed by so great a lover, this one, who never shall be parted from me, kissed my mouth all trembling. A Gallehault was the book and he wrote it; that day we read no farther in it." (Dante, *Inferno* 5, 133–38)

In such a context the straightforward and largely canonical interpretation of the Galeotto surname—that Boccaccio is repeating Francesca's famous line, itself taken at face value, and calling his own book, as well as himself ("chi lo scrisse"), a potential pander—is not altogether surprising, although it cannot help but leave at least some readers either puzzled or appalled, much as Masetto's interpretation of his fate must leave some of us open-mouthed, at least if we were to do as Masetto suggests, which is to take it all at face value.[4] With the single word "Galeotto," Boccaccio has not only evoked a slightly dizzying series of textual references but sent us scurrying backwards to a number of

4. Durling 1983 finishes a key article, which will be discussed more extensively below, by noting that the very subtitle of the *Decameron* is still not well understood: "Perhaps the pun *Guido:guida,* with its clear roots in Dante, is one of the keys to another puzzling allusion, the subtitle of the *Decameron, Prencipe Galeotto.* Like Cepparello and Dido, the book itself has two names, and the second cries out for interpretation. And the parallels between Boccaccio and his character Guido include the question of whether the author of the *Decameron* is quite the worldling (Epicurean) that he delights to claim to be . . ." (291–92).

books, books all within books, in this vexing entitling. We are forced, before ascribing any meaning to the Galeotto that is the *Decameron*'s other name, to ponder closely Boccaccio's attitudes towards texts, and especially their interpretation. At the center lies Boccaccio's own most crucial interpretative act, the reading of Dante in general and of canto 5 especially, a reading transparently presupposed in Boccaccio's most fundamental introduction to his own work. And it seems difficult to dispute that in the entitling of the work, more keenly even than in the Proem, the frame and a number of startlingly metaliterary tales, Boccaccio is confronting the reader with the dual and inseparable problems of the nature of the text and the nature of its interpretation.

He could scarcely have picked a more pointed and stunning evocation of the thorny issue: the seductive Francesca's transference of deadly guilt to the book she was reading stands, in virtually whatever fashion it is interpreted, as an unrivaled portrait of the intricacy of a reader's relationship to a text. Boccaccio's choice of name for his own book betrays his extreme concern for the issue of interpretation. And this book's meanings are from the outset explicitly grounded in the problem of interpretation itself, clearly evoked at the outset by the summoning of his complex relationship with Dante, as his reader, and his no less difficult relationship with his own readers. It is in the preface to Day 4, as well as in many—arguably all—stories, that we realize how critical and difficult Boccaccio rightly judges his relationship with his readers to be. And in the Galeotto citation, as well as in a number of key tales, we perceive that Boccaccio realized it was bound to be a relationship conditioned by the same readers' relationship(s) to Dante. The *Commedia,* even then, was an inescapable text on whose heels, and potentially in whose shadow, Boccaccio was writing. With one "simple" evocation at the outset, then, this work, which is characteristically read as a liberation from the heaviness of medieval Meaning (itself a problematic caricature in many ways), binds itself openly to the dominant other text of the moment. And in doing so, in making a specific statement about the relationship between his text and Dante's, he has also tied himself inextricably to a panoply of the most difficult interpretative problems, ancient and modern—most fundamentally, perhaps, the philosophical and philological issue of definitive text and definitive interpretation. In this, in some basic ways, the Boccaccio of the *Decameron* sits in a different kind of chair: he urges us, most of all, to dwell on ourselves, readers, critics, interpreters. The search for Truth appears to have turned away, for the instant, from both poet and text, and is glancing, perhaps nervously, at the reader, Contingency itself.

The initial difficulty of the Galeotto conundrum in Boccaccio's text is that the first answer to the riddle is another riddle: what does it "mean" in the *Commedia*'s fifth canto? The second riddle is, if not more difficult, more complex, and it is not fortuitous that Boccaccio's evocation of the Francesca episode is the earliest of innumerable ones to follow by readers of every stripe. It is one thing to note that the canto ranks among those most discussed by critics, the most "famous" among students of the *Commedia;* it is as telling, perhaps more so, to note that the scene where the sinner blames the sin on the work of art has been a scene recast ever after by other artists,[5] although few of them have, as a result, been thus characterized as themselves subscribing to the beliefs of Francesca, as Boccaccio has. On the contrary, the most reasonable deduction to draw from the proliferation of versions—interpretations all—of one of Dante's most compelling moments is precisely that it possesses the great fertility of ambiguity for other readers, other artists, even if we say that for Dante it can, ultimately, be properly interpreted in only one way.

The ambiguity, however, is a necessary part of the original scene precisely so the precision and clarity of ultimate revelation can distinguish, in the light of retrospection, the difficulties of unenlightened reading and writing. Thus, nearly everything in canto 5 is at least slightly off, much is ambiguous, and the results are dolorous. And yet we have been asked to believe, by an exegetical tradition that makes of Boccaccio

5. One can safely guess that illustrations of the Paolo and Francesca episode outnumber those of any other single scene in the *Commedia.* And while both Pound and Eliot were obsessed with the *Purgatorio,* allusions to Francesca are far from absent in their work. Joyce, meanwhile, cites *Inferno* 5 more than any other (see Reynolds 1981).

an almost "mindless" reader of Dante, that Boccaccio not only accepts Francesca's damning judgment at face value but is willing to apply it unambiguously to himself and his text.[6] In this scheme of things the logical reading of the Francesca canto is the acceptance of her judgment that certain kinds of texts can be the cause of sins and thus are panders; moveover, that this is the interpretation of that passage that Boccaccio would have had; and finally, that Boccaccio would have seen and publicly proclaimed his own text to be one of those. This sequence of interpretations presents certain difficulties, not least among them being that Boccaccio is now casting himself, as well as his readers, as a particularly doltish Masetto: whatever the most obvious moral of the story is, that is what we accept it as being.

It is a risky and potentially boring enterprise to go where virtually everyone else has gone before, but nevertheless one is obliged to start from scratch and consider plausible interpretations for that most inter-

6. The pointed line about mindlessness is from Hollander: "This unlikely position [that the "young Boccaccio" was not yet an adequate reader of Dante] forces its followers to assert in public, that Giovanni Boccaccio, who had been reading Dante from the time of his earliest efforts as a writer, and who would become the first paid professor of Dante studies, from the age of thirty-seven to forty, was a relatively mindless reader of Dante's texts. It is not difficult to come to a firm conclusion as to who is a mindless reader" (1986:281–82). Hollander has recently written extensively on Boccaccio's relationship to Dante; see the cited piece, "Boccaccio's Dante," and also his 1977 and 1981–82 studies. One of Hollander's most important observations, with the customary encyclopaedic documentation of both earlier and contemporary scholarship characteristic of his studies, is that alluded to in the quote above, namely, that critics have tended to distinguish neatly between Boccaccio the professional Dantista and the "younger" Boccaccio, the author of (among other things) the Decameron. Curiously, but not, finally, surprisingly, Boccaccisti have assumed the direct criticism to be the real thing and have neglected or dismissed the Dante in the Decameron. One could argue the exact opposite, of course: the literary reflections are far more telling, more "truthful" than the discursive ones. Durling 1983 concludes in a fashion comparable to Hollander: "It [this reading] means that we must give up once and for all the traditional view of Boccaccio as an amiable but essentially dull-witted reader of the Commedia . . ." (286).

preted of Dante's cantos.[7] But the interpretation to be focused on here
will explicitly shy away from any kind of certainty or absolutism, partly
because the vast and varied history of interpretation of that canto itself
belies any such possibility. Part of the answer to the riddle is simply
that Boccaccio, exemplary reader of Dante in the *Decameron,* explicitly

7. For reviews of the vast bibliography see Paparelli [1954] 1975, Hollander
1977, Della Terza 1981 and, more recently, Noakes [1983] 1986. The range of
interpretations has, not surprisingly, run the gamut from (to focus on one of
several possible parameters) Francesca as pitiable victim to Francesca as a cold
solipsist who cannot accept the blame she deserves. More recent criticism, as
Noakes points out, has focused on the conspicuously metaliterary aspects of the
passage, that specific attribution of blame to the book itself and its author:
Poggioli, in a 1957 *PMLA* article that (as is the case, in a different sphere, with
Bernardo's Petrarch article two years before) can be seen as representative of then-
current critical stances, concludes that the acts of reading and writing certain
kinds of literature are highly problematic. This is exemplary of what might be
called the "pornographic" interpretation of the passage, although there is inevita-
bly a great range in the texture and sophistication within this grossly defined
category, and it has been since the fifties by far the dominant explicative mode. The
second approach, more recent and perhaps less popular, for which one could take
Popolizio 1980 or Noakes herself as exemplary, focuses instead on the reader
and/or her modes of reading, and in general concludes in one way or another that
Francesca was a deficient reader—that, to quote Noakes, "When read with these
characteristics in mind, the line 'Galeotto fu il libro . . .' emerges as an ironic
comment on the woman depicted as speaking it" (152), and that the entire episode
offers a model of misreading (166). In Hollander 1969 we find a reading that,
logically, dwells on the intersection between the mode of reading and the text: he
sees Francesca as a sort of anti-Augustine, and the line "quel giorno più non vi
leggemo avante" as an echo of Augustine's "Nec ultra volui leggere" (113).
Mazzotta 1979 points out, however, that the network of commentary on Au-
gustine, as well as the *Aeneid,* is considerably richer, and his extended discussion
(160–70, including further bibliographical contributions), far too rich to summar-
ize here, is characteristically the most thoughtful and wide-ranging. For a perspec-
tive from outside the field see Fontana's study of Morris's "Defense of Guenevere,"
where he concludes that Morris's text "suggests that Dante's theological and moral
critique of romantic fiction as pimp is itself a fiction, that natural passion is more
authentic because more intense than any law . . ." (292).

chooses a remarkably seductive—and no less remarkably problem-atic—splice of the *Commedia,* thus casting his own text, from the outset, as one that will be as difficult to deal with, and as variously dealt with, as the Galeotto passage itself. The suggestion lurks about, even, that seduc-tiveness itself is little more than ambiguity—and the potential for such strongly contrary opinions. In associating his own book, typologically, with the single passage of the *Commedia* that will elicit the most (and the most varied and contradictory) interpretations, Boccaccio is suggesting, quite accurately of course, that he and his text will do no less. But the difference, once again, is that while for Dante the variations and vagaries of interpretation are necessary limitations of the human condition, for Boccaccio, already bemused by the confusions and varied certainties provoked by the title, uncertainty is itself a good thing, a Truth.

The *Decameron* offers a vision of the human condition in which absolute truth and absolute interpretation, in practical terms usually one and the same thing, in either life or literature, are dangerous and usually elusive pursuits—not because they do not exist but because they cannot be grasped or articulated by most mere mortals. It is through this prism, in considerable measure, that the *Decameron* reads and interprets the vision of poetic truth and revelation of the *Vita nuova* and the *Commedia;* and from the outset, with the depiction of a cruel and often merciless plague that claims unambiguously innocent victims, to the near end, the Griselda story of, once again, unmerited punishment and cruelty, we are being admonished not to believe that things necessarily mean what they appear to mean, not to fall into the Masetto trap. But Dante's Francesca and her Galeotto await yet one more interpretation.

The Francesca episode of the *Commedia* includes the enormously provocative scene in which "love" and "literature" are utterly confused and fused: the kiss that exists for the readers, for Francesca and her lover, because it is in the book of Lancelot and Guenevere. The melding together of the two phenomena, of a book and a certain acting out of love, is indicated beyond the kiss as well: Francesca is kissing Lancelot, one cannot help but suspect (and that her own lover is never given the dignity of a name and is referred to with some disdain ratifies our suspicions); in that infamous line, she fuses Galahad, the book's go-

between, and the book itself, and both are deemed guilty of being the
go-between in her own tragedy; the critical line about the truncated act
of reading (too often forgotten or passed over as merely suggestive of the
sexual act[s] that followed the kiss), "quel giorno più non legemmo
avanti" (and that day we read no further), is not only critical for an
understanding of what Dante's moral appreciation of the episode might
be, but also, of course, suggests a further fusion of "life" and "litera-
ture," the point at which one need read no further because one has
become part of the story.

The reader is, or thinks she is, no longer a reader (and thus need not
read any further) but a character in the story—and Francesca, that
character so astonishingly powerful she has made us forget she too is
"only" a character, is in all of these assessments about the relationship
between life and literature, both right and wrong. And it is precisely in
the interstices of this right and wrong that Dante and Boccaccio are at
odds, as writers, and that Boccaccio's reading begins to distance Dante
from us. Dante's Francesca is only ever apparently right, and then, at
best, only within a moral and poetic system that is itself problematic.
From this perspective Francesca is both victim and snare in the universe
of love literature that constructs itself as its own end and center, the
universe of solipsistic and circular love, in other words, that the young
Dante of the *Vita nuova* was a part of until he saw the light. The canto is
allusive of the preconversion ideology of the *Vita nuova* in a number of
ways: from the lovely stilnovistic verses recited by Francesca herself to
the weepy lover by her side, so reminiscent of the annoying young artist
of the *Vita nuova*. Most strikingly, of course, the emblems of this ideology
Dante has left behind in the earlier work (and is about to leave behind
here, once again, in the *Commedia*) are those that clearly mark a "love"
that is the literature itself and nothing beyond it. Francesca is the
ultimate simulacrum of such an ideology, unable to distinguish, in the
end, between a kiss in the book and a kiss in her life, between her lover
and Lancelot, between Galahad and her own temptation. Pellico trem-
bled in great fear, and, in the "innocent" Zanze's kiss upon the Bible,
tells us why he must walk away from such literature—and Dante
himself faints at the spectacle. The horrors are everywhere: there is

horror at the trap he just barely managed to escape, the sin that Arnaut will be purged of in the purgatorial fires; and there is the infinite regret that he is thus abandoning that most remarkable creation of his, a Francesca of compelling passion, a lover beside whom Beatrice will fade, as Borges has made us see. And, as Pellico makes us see, the greatest horror of all may be the doubt about his own text, for even as it mirrors truths, in the conversionary process many traps will be laid for the reader, traps only some will avoid.[8]

The lessons seem transparent and inexorable: literature is not its own center, and the poetry that is never able to write beyond that conceit and constraint is a lesser poetry, however beautiful it may be. Francesca is thus the best example of that of which she is, within her own story, a victim: the extraordinary beauty and power of a poetry that is infatuated with itself, and a "love" that exists, paradoxically, both in failure and in repetition, the repetition perfectly embodied in Francesca's recounting of her love story—a recounting, one strongly senses, that takes place repeatedly and obsessively.[9] This is, then, the remarkable narcissism of a poetic ideology that calls itself love when it loves only itself, and the perfect fusion of the kiss and the book is the most extraordinary literalization, like Narcissus's own literalizing kiss, though, it is the kiss of death. One might argue again that what is condemned is neither what Francesca is reading nor how she reads it but, far more simply, what she is. After all, in a canto filled with other remarkable and already well-

8. As Mazzotta has put it: "He faints in the intense awareness, furthermore, that he, as an author, might trap readers into the illusory self-enclosure of romance, just as the stilnovistic poetry, which Francesca quoted in her speech, trapped her" (1979:169).

9. In a highly suggestive article Valesio notes: "Poiché ciò che questo discorso fondamentalmente ci dice è che l'unico modo di vivere una storia d'amore è quello di rivivirla in una ricostruzione verbale" (Valesio, 1981:125), and "Questa ripetizione è funzionale al processo per cui una storia d'amore esiste come tale in tanto in quanto è ripetuta—e specialmente in tanto in quanto il suo inizio (la 'prime radice') è ripetuto con variazioni" (131). Valesio, in other words, is making the same point: that it is not the love affair but the love story that "counts," even for the lovers themselves.

known, even infamous literary characters, Francesca is quite starkly unknown (although we have forgotten this now) and conspicuously Dante's creature, his own addition to the illustrious line of Didos and Gueneveres.[10] She is herself gloriously sinful poetry that, infatuated with itself and its own great beauty, tolerates, defines that kind of love that sings and begets great love poetry. It is she, of course, who is the pander—at least in Dante's frame of reference, both creature and creator. Of course Dante feels some self-pity at having to leave such a remarkable creation behind—not just Francesca herself, of course, but the immense power of the love-poetic tradition that has enabled her to be. In some ways he had good reason to grieve, good reasons to regret abandoning the hold and the passions that that kind of poetry has always had, unparalleled, on both readers and writers.

Petrarch, who so craftily and ably restored imitability and fertility to the love lyric, might well note, if he could be coaxed to speak so directly, that the abandoned Francesca of the love and literature surpassed and overcome, supplanted, in the *Commedia,* has in fact been by far the most prolific and productive and entrancing of all of Dante's poems, having become for so many an independent poem, a beautiful little lyric to be recited at dinner parties and sighed over from time to time. And that same Petrarch would not be unfair to point out that the violence thus done to the *Commedia* by the vulgar rabble was all too predictable. The dismemberment that we see of the text here is no less crucial a part of the Francesca story, that part where she stops reading, where she cuts off the text in hand. It is not profound, perhaps to note that this means that she simply did not finish reading the book, but as has been pointed out, the end of the book being read is, in fact, critical to an appreciation of its meaning. The story being read, of course, is one in which the adulterous kiss is catastrophic, and the story itself is, when read to the end (of course), an unambiguous example of the dire consequences of adulterous love—an adulterous love which has become the narrative and narrated version of the poetic solipsism of the lyric, unproductive

10. This crucial insight is John Freccero's, although it is nowhere in print as far as I can ascertain—unless some enterprising former students are preparing a *Cours.*

("sans issu," as we hear in the *Tristan*) and destructive of overriding social values.

In fact, although Noakes has argued convincingly that the actual text Dante is citing is the *Lancelot en prose,* "a religious attack on chivalric values," it matters little because there are few medieval texts (or for that matter modern ones) which present adultery in an unambiguously "romantic" or positive light. In fact, one would be hard pressed to cite the text that Dante could have used, or that we could use in recasting the scene today, that would serve as a "positive" example. The central attraction of such love and its poetry, as I have argued, is its very failures, its circularities and hermetic traps: the fates of the Emma Bovaries and the Anna Kareninas are not exceptional but exemplary of this tradition. And the highly fluid Lancelot tradition, like the Tristan one also evoked in *Inferno* 5, is one in which the multiple failures of the love between Lancelot and Guenevere are never far from sight and lead, at their most explicit ends, to catastrophic ruptures in the social fabric. So, when Francesca simply stops reading the story at the point at which an erotic adulterous moment captures her in the same gesture (and she never returns to the other story) she becomes a critical lesson in Dante's construct, for she exemplifies as clearly as possible the absolute need to grasp texts in their entirety. In the *Commedia,* of course, with its conversionary structure and its ever-increasing clarity and clarifications, to leave off in the middle, especially at a moment of indulgence such as canto 5—and that too is Dante's fainting spell—is to guarantee a misreading, a misapprehension. This too, then, is a Galeotto: a text that in fact demands the patience of the long haul, the vision only available at the end, but whose lyrical bits and pieces here and there, whose marvelous little stories and memorable scenes tempt us, the rabble, to see and love only them, to drop the book when the good parts are over. Once again, Francesca has become what she reads, a Galeotto, the tempting lyrical moment, the seductive scene, remembered by itself.

Thus, the first of what I believe are the two crucial "meanings" of the Galeotto as the "surname" of the *Decameron,* is as historically prescient as one could say Francesca's book-closing was, and the critical fates of the texts are thus remarkably inscribed from within: the *petites histoires* of the *Decameron,* its incomparably good stories—almost all of which fall well outside the bounds of the canonically moral, in one sphere or another—have understandably overwhelmed the whole. Boccaccio is alerting us that just as Francesca's lyrical moment is far more easily grasped than the full Truth vision of the Commedia—although of course her fate cannot be fully understood except in the end—the *Decameron* too is a heavy book to hold all at once, and because of that there will be many readers who will play the part of Francesca and use it as pornography.[11] But the critical difference, as I began to set out above, is that this foible of the reader, which Dante is intent on overcoming— or overriding—is an essential part of the second meaning of Galeotto for Boccaccio, the meaning that the *Decameron* will gladly cloak itself with: contingency is the most essential feature of all reading and thus of all texts, and the Galeotto is the text that is radically contingent, whose interpretation is a proof of relativism itself.

I V

LOQUITUR: En Bertrans de Born. Dante Alighieri put this man in hell for that he was a stirrer up of strife. Eccovi! Judge ye! Have I dug him up again? . . . (Pound, "Sestina: Altaforte")

You'd have men's hearts up from the dust
And tell their secrets, Messire Cino,
Right enough? Then read between the lines of UcSt. Circ,
Solve me the riddle for you know the tale. . . .
(Ezra Pound, "Near Perigord")

The first contingencies that present themselves are the several veils of Boccaccio studies, for, of course, most of our reading is strongly de-pendent on the expectations fostered by layers of traditions of criticism,

---

11. In an unpublished study, Leo Steinberg traces the genealogy of a distinct series of portraits of women with dropped books—which he interprets as em-blematic of a post-masturbatory state—to the vision of Francesca, as she herself recounts her falling into sin.

although often that knowledge is at the very edges of consciousness. The first of these we noticed briefly, above: it is too often the later Boccaccio and Boccaccio as *dantista* who is cited, although (because?) those "interpretations" are almost without exception genuinely straightforward and at times conspicuously uninspired. Boccaccio's "reading" of canto 5 in the *Esposizioni,* for example, can count as little more than an exposition of fundamental background material for the seriously uninitiated, dwelling as it does on the culpability of the original go-between responsible for the ill-fated union of Lancelot and Guenevere.[12] But, as I have suggested above, our contemporary compartmentalization of poets and critics—and a consequent belief in the revelatory, positivistic power of the critic—perhaps skews our perspective on the division of reading labors embodied in Boccaccio's different writings that reflect on Dante. In fact, the *Esposizioni* serve, by and large, a necessary task of education for a public and a readership whose fundamental grasp of literary (and other) history was not—conspicuously so with Dante—the same as the author's.[13] Moreover, with its subtle emphasis on the distinction between history (or histories) and the story Dante gives us, Boccaccio is

12. It is interesting to note, given that he is frequently considered the original "novelizer" of the Francesca material, that Boccaccio's comments here are quite limited in their scope. See the observations on this in Quaglio, who finds it very "di marca boccaccesca" that the commentator merely "corrects" Dante's presentation of Francesca da Rimini and makes sure we understand that the version in the *Commedia* is in fact Dante's own creation (16).

13. This, of course, is what some might consider the paradox of Dante's text and a major factor in Petrarch's reading of the *Commedia:* it is a "popular" text in being, most transparently, written in a language that is accessible, in principle, to a vast range of listeners and readers—and yet, of course, it is far from "merely" or simply a popular text and appears to any scholar to require fairly massive exegesis. (In "The Aleph" and its commentary, Borges also suggests that it is not the poetry of the Aleph itself but what pedants do with it that makes texts inaccessible.) The *Commedia,* however, is in this far from unique (one thinks immediately of authors like Dickens as his successors and, of course, the vernacular Testaments as antecedents), although it is a rather spectacular example of the ability of certain kinds of literature to be appreciated, loved and understood without scholarly mediation and yet be endlessly fertile terrain for exegesis.

not only "educating" the public, feeding it the historical "background" it lacks and needs, but, for the more subtle student in the audience, hinting at the far more delicate and slippery issue of multiplicity of versions. Like all fine teaching, Boccaccio's comments will be clear to the point of banal for the worst in the class but strongly suggest the difficulties for the brighter ones. But, as Hollander and Durling, among others, have established, Boccaccio's finest criticism and most subtle interpretation of Dante is a largely separate matter: it is inscribed within his own masterpiece.

The second principal critical contingency, prevalent until rather recently and far from gone today, is that complex of prejudices that make medieval literary studies much of the time a heuristically different enterprise from other "kinds" of literary studies.[14] The quarrels, the divisions, are simple: historians of medieval literature and their canonical readings have made of the texts they study objects ontologically different—Other—from those of later periods. The edifice of diachronic literary history, one of the most elaborate creations of the positivist philological enterprise, is in great measure constructed on the developmental principle that, among other things, views the broad range of types of intertextual relations as relatively straightforward, and certainly outside the orbits of modern neuroses.[15] It is not part of the

14. A special issue of *Speculum* (1990: 65) devoted to precisely these issues appeared after I had completed all but minor revisions of this book. Although I have not been able to fully integrate the frank and provocative views offered there by a number of scholars, especially those expressed by Patterson and Block, I am pleased to note that their global appreciation of the limitations of the "old" philological mode are largely congruent with those I have set out here.

15. Thus, to take the most simplistic of examples, a Freudian analysis of a medieval text would be considered "anachronistic" by many medievalists—as if Freud had invented the unconscious rather than given us the ability to name it. (Of course, perhaps in this a number of medievalists are just radically nominalist.) Or, equally distressingly, one frequently hears reflections of views among medievalists themselves that echo Bloom's unfortunate accusation of antediluvianism—that, for example, anxiety itself is a modern phenomenon, as if "medievals" were a more primitive species, lacking the psychological depths and complications, and their textual reflections, of true "modern man." Additionally, new terms are heard with

purpose of this book to become embroiled in those battles, but I draw attention to the contingency of contemporary criticism here particularly because it concerns Boccaccio so directly. The "truth versus fiction" paradigm—in this case in the guise of the "moral versus immoral" variant—has given the *Decameron* much of its texture. And what has been largely lost, in the meantime, is what is reflected in that simple epithet at the outset: the *Decameron*'s stark concern with its own ontological status and, critically, with the crucial problem of accounting for variants in interpretation. Boccaccio begins his class by throwing out the most vexing of interpretative problems of the text he is teaching and saying—again with a smile on his face—and what do we make of that? And, in the end, he will never let up, never himself give in to what he sees as the easy horrors indulged in by others, the strong temptation to be right, to be wrong. In the room where Boccaccio sits, philology has not yet become an imitation science, it does not yet believe in its own rigors, and Pound's and Vico's voices can still be heard, pleading that time is not so simple and reading trickier still: they probe the old scandals, say de Born is dead, talking of *trobar clus* with Daniel. But we have been elsewhere, by and large, and our literary understanding of medieval texts has, logically enough, unflinchingly reflected the premises of the textual criticism that has preceded and informed it. And, here too, certainty—the presumption of possible certainty that is our most conspicuous conceit—has insisted that there is an "original" there, a single and authentic original, and that the scholar's task is to find it and establish it. Variant readings, corruptions, of course, belong in footnotes.

But medieval texts are now often edited according to the once radical proposition that the definitive text is an elusive goal, probably even a fictional construct. We now have a variety of different perspectives that suggest, in different registers, that we look more closely at the issue of determining meaning that Boccaccio himself says, nearly everywhere, is the problem at hand—and that is itself highly dependent on our

---

alarm and, it seems to me, inordinate suspicion, as if "meta"-something were somehow intrinsically more obscure or more jargonistic than a Latinate rhetorical term.

perception of the relations between different writers and their texts.[16] But already one can hear the suggestions of "anachronism" (a concept dependent for its validity, at a minimum, on a belief in the simple truth of diachrony, of course), and the simplest answer is certainly that it is the conceit of modernity—or of its construct of what precedes it—that is "out of time": devout Christianity (or devout anything else), even in a medieval text, scarcely requires the same kind of belief in literal and transparent truth toward which the *Commedia* urged its readers. The distinction between what we now call fundamentalism and a faith that can doubt and be self-reflective has always existed. Even less, of course, did faith require—then or now—writing that believes only in itself.[17]

The *Decameron* is filled, quite literally from beginning to end, with characters and stories that push us inexorably to the conclusion that things are rarely all they seem to be or only what they seem to be, that categorical interpretations are fraught with possible error or certain hubris: from Ciappelleto and his false confession (which can fool other

16. The most explicit works on the self-awareness of the *Decameron* are certainly the fine and lucid Marcus and the more recent Mazzotta 1986 (despite the apparent chronology it is evident that Marcus's work derives from Mazzotta's teaching). Between them they establish the groundwork for a new understanding of the *Decameron*'s obsession with other literature, its metaliterariness, which is in turn an essential element in what Mazzotta will call its "playfulness." Of considerable and complimentary value is Almansi, with its perspicacious emphasis on the *Decameron*'s consciousness of the storytelling activity it is engaged in. Finally, I have found Durling 1983 of inestimable value and will return to his reading of 6, 9 as a commentary on the rigidity of Dante's interpretation criticized by Boccaccio.

17. For other examples of the same complex exploration of the difficulty of texts and their meaning(s) in a context where God and faith are ever present, one need only glance at the huge and massively popular tradition of framed tales of so-called Oriental provenance (they are, of course, European many generations over) that are kissing cousins in numerous ways to the *Decameron*: the *Thousand and One Nights* and its "variants" or derivatives, such as the *Sendebar,* the *Disciplina Clericalis;* and the *Kalila and Dimna,* to name just a few of the most prominent. These texts share the same irksome "problem": how can the reader construe—as he is almost invariably exhorted to do—"moral" meanings from stories that are as troublingly difficult, in terms of our concepts of morality, as the Masetto story?

mortals but is no less untrue for that; that the narrator and his audience know it to be false is the supreme indication, certainly)[18] to the intractable Griselda, the emblem of the human dilemma when faced with inexplicable, uninterpretable injustice. From this perspective Griselda is the counterpoint not only to Ciappelleto but, more poignantly and pointedly, to the cornice's story of the plague, the trials that we cannot understand, the suffering that has no rationally excusable explanation, and yet it will all ultimately, and only ultimately, be revealed. Too often Boccaccio's pointed demonstrations of the incoherence, in traditional moral terms, of stories has been assumed to be a rejection of (or obliviousness to) traditional Christian values and beliefs. This is the classic absolutist position: facts are true or false, beliefs are held or disbelieved. God exists or he does not. In such schemes, contingency does not really come to bear on a whole series of rock-bottom issues.

But Boccaccio's no less persistent fascination with the problem of how we interpret stories, life, outcomes, argues more forcefully that he is far from an unbeliever; rather, he is once again, perhaps ironically, the most devout sort of believer, one who believes in the face of the remarkable difficulty of belief, because the Truth will not be seen to be believed in the human life and telling of it. Boccaccio's stance—and it is unabashedly, from the title on, written with and against Dante—is one in which the Truth vision, let alone the writing of it, is merely the most common of human delusions. Interpretation, which is no different, of course, is no less contingent: every facet and variable of the reading experience will produce an interpretation. But it is not that they are equally valid in absolute or abstract terms; that is the typical absolutist caricature of contingency. Instead—and this Boccaccio retells strikingly in all of his most overtly metaliterary moments (the introduction to the Fourth Day, the Author's conclusions)—the value of the Truth (or the

18. This is the example used by Almansi, but the problem, of course, is that Almansi's conclusions assume, as Durling has rightly pointed out (1983:299–301), that we are supposed to be duped into believing the false confession, and that thus the reader is being urged to be a Masetto (or, as Durling puts it, to be like Betto and his *brigata* in 6,9).

interpretation) will vary according to the shifting values which condition it, dictate it. And in the face of the remarkable inconsistencies and mysteries of the human condition, and of the stories which narrate it and invent it, to be absolutely sure of the right solutions is to risk being as egregiously foolish as Masetto. For the "moral" of the Masetto story is just that: that his punishment (reward, of course) does not fit the crime, that life and its stories often do not work within the kind of logical parameters we would like to see. Truth, Justice, and Correct Interpretations (and Definitive Editions, one might add) are often evanescent, unknowable. It all depends:

> Chi non sa ch'è il vino ottima cosa ai viventi . . . e a colui che ha la febbre è nocivo? Direm noi, per ciò che nuoce a' febricitanti, che sia malvagio? Chi non sa che 'l fuoco è utilissimo, anzi necessario a' mortali? Direm noi, per ciò che egli arde le case e le ville e le città, che sia malvaggio? . . . Quali libri, quali parole, quali lettere son più sante, più degne, più reverende, che quella della divina Scrittura? E sí sono egli stati assai che quelle perversamente intendendo, sé e altrui a perdizione hanno tratto. Ciascuna cosa in se medesima è buona ad alcuna cosa, e male adoperata può essere nociva di molte; e così dico delle mie novelle.

> Who will deny that wine . . . is an excellent thing for those who are exceedingly hale and hearty, but harmful to people suffering from a fever? Who will deny that fire is useful, not to say vital, to man? Are we to conclude, because it burns down houses and villages and whole cities, that therefore it is pernicious? . . . What other books, what other words, what other letters, are more sacred, more reputable, more worthy of reverence, than those of the Holy Scriptures? And yet there have been many who, by perversely construing them, have led themselves and others to perdition. All things have their own special purpose, but when they are wrongly used a great deal of harm may result, and the same applies to my stories. (Boccaccio, "Author's Epilogue," *Decameron*)

198 Writing in Dante's Cult of Truth

Boccaccio takes Dante on directly in his story about Guido Caval-
canti, the abandoned *primo amico:* as Durling has so brilliantly demon-
strated, it is a novella that explicitly challenges Dante's apparent cer-
tainty of interpretation, in this case with respect to Guido. Once again,
as in the Masetto story, the perils and potential foolishness of definitive-
ness are enticingly acted out by the story's players: in this case it is
Messer Betto and his *brigata* who fall into the trap of "demanding
univocal meaning," as Durling has so aptly put it (291). But of course in
doing so they are only doing, in this case, what Dante himself has done,
and Boccaccio's strong suggestion here is that, at a minimum, in the case
of Guido, Dante's judgment should have been more equivocal. Boccac-
cio is, in this reading, grappling with the *sicurezza* of Dante's interpreta-
tion. He sees, first of all, that *Inferno* 10 itself is a "commentary on
interpretation: the mistaken philosophy of the heretics as a systematic
misreading of the data of experience . . . a dialogue in which the heretics
are shown misinterpreting what is said to them and in which the
interpretive mistakes are corrected by the superior interpreter, Dante"
(283). But, again, Boccaccio has a knowing smile on his face, for, of
course, Dante's own sureness about Guido's fate, about his Averroism,
about his poetic ideology or his politics, about how to interpret him, in
other words, is in the end just as problematic.

Messer Betto and the *brigata* are not only as sure of their grasp of
obvious truths as Masetto is, but they quite forcefully try and hem
Guido in, close him off. But Guido escapes, jumping over tombs that
remind us poignantly of those in *Inferno* 10 where Dante has so chillingly
conversed with the elder Cavalcanti. Closure, particularly interpretative
closure, is the choice of fools. We hear in the background Masetto's
cocky reading of his own story, a reading that so prematurely announces
closure. In both cases we see clearly what is evident elsewhere, every-
where, in the *Decameron:* the interpretative locus, and the concomitant
responsibility, is in the reader and his motivations rather than "defini-
tively" in the text itself. Perhaps part of the abundant laughter we hear
throughout the *Decameron* is at the endless tears and hours and lives
spent grappling with Alephs, how could we avoid laughing, and crying,
too, if we understood that the quarrels over the locus of Truth were so

vain and in vain? As Boccaccio will tell us explicitly in the *Conclusione,* there is no absolute text, and thus neither apprehensible absolute truth behind it nor determinable absolute interpretation to unlock it for the receptive reader. This too points us in the direction of the "Galeotto"— that text too could be and can be and is read in any number of ways, and Francesca herself made a perhaps unwise interpretative choice. But, again, how we chose to read her, to read the text she has become, and by extension the *Decameron* with which she, it, are now related, is also part of the story—part of all the stories.

But the lingering and tantalizing question, and the one that impinges most directly on Boccaccio's reading of Dante, is whether univocal meaning is ever more than a trap and enormous hubris, whether such degree of revelation is ever granted in the human life or ever readable in the human text. What is it we think we see in that dark basement, before the house itself is torn down? Is it, in other words, that Betto, like many others in the *Decameron,* are not as wise as we, are just bad readers? Or are not all humans Bettos and Masettos when they dare that which rightly belongs only to the Divine, Truth? And what is the point—or value—of literature in either case? Or, as Durling notes at the end of his article, "The ultimately important question is, how do *we* use the book?" (292). For the grossest misinterpretation of Boccaccio's relativism might well be to see him as lacking faith.[19]

Boccaccio does not lack faith or admiration for Dante, either, and his open delight in playing with Dante's text is mostly remarkable. But the differences are fundamental, as the Guido Cavalcanti story hints: Dante

19. The final chapter of Herrnstein Smith's brilliant *Contingencies of Value,* "Matters of Consequence," 150–84, is highly instructive in this regard. It begins with a passage that could well be directed at the sort of Boccaccio I have sketched out here: "It is recurrently said that the present analysis, specifically its questionings of absolute value and of the idea of objective standards, is 'quietistic' or . . . that the positions such questionings entail prevent one from opposing bad things and promoting good ones. Allegedly the author of this study must look on bad things benignly" (150). The rest of the chapter is a remarkable, and philosophically consistent, refutation of those accusations, of the (for a relativist, peculiar) notion that the recognition of contingency means the abandonment of beliefs.

has chosen a path, a kind of belief that makes Boccaccio squirm uneasily, nervously. It is not that he doubts Dante, not that he thinks Dante the fool, as such, that Betto is. But the voice of the *Decameron* makes it clear that one simply never knows and that many things are finally unknowable. To Dante's vision in which things can become clear and Truth is revealed and inscribed and interpretable, Boccaccio responds with a faith in the human ability to comprehend things that is far more guarded and skeptical. Ultimate interpretations are not to be found, clearly or necessarily, in human hands or texts.[20] It is not surprising, in this context, to find that he ends his own text with a transparent recasting of the most difficult of Biblical texts, the Job story, a text that is itself a warning about the radical difficulty—perhaps impossibility—of full and adequate human interpretation in the face of the Divine.[21]

But in the case of Griselda—and here there is a critical and telling difference from the sacred subtext being interpreted—we see the triumph over a kind of appalling ignorance and the assertion of faith in what is ultimately unknowable. And the "patient" Griselda is patient and noble—at least by her own standards—in the face of a grotesque injustice she has no way of explaining or understanding. Whether she is foolish by another's standards, or whether Gualtieri deserved such great loyalty (and Dioneo himself, followed even more strongly by Chaucer, will say he is a cad and she is a fool) is almost beside the point. For what makes Griselda a great reader, the most admirable and imitable of Boccaccio's readers, is that she suffers the story without drawing the "obvious" conclusions, conclusions others can easily jump to in a

20. "In a way, Dioneo's comment at the end of the last tale of the *Decameron* suggests that nothing is definitive and final in this narrative universe: the very end, conventionally seen as the privileged perspective from which the moral coherence and order of the text are constituted, is disclosed as a contingent and purely formal closure. By this expedient Dioneo implies that storytelling is an endless activity and that the 'right' finale lies elsewhere." Mazzotta 1986:129–30.

21. The Book of Job has occasioned great quantities of exegesis—and greatly varied exegetes, including Bloom and, in a brilliant tour de force, Jung—to grapple with its remarkably difficult "lessons." In this too, then, there is resonance with the Galeotto, which sits at the other, far end of the text.

minute. Many readers point out that the "problem" with this as a Job story is that the "God" figure is a mere mortal, whose hubris and other considerable deficiencies of character prompt him and allow him to play God. But it seems to me that that is ultimately the point: it is true that Gualtieri is "only" a man—an explicitly fictional construct, for that matter—and it is true that we thus hold his behavior to different standards than those of God. But in the human experience of both the divine and other humans, confusion and the inability to reckon things are often all one is left with. As Mazzotta has said, "It is a style whereby facts and fictions are not reassuringly separated for the readers' moral edification" (1986a:11). Gualtieri's actions, in that sense, are neither more just nor more comprehensible or excusable than God's in the opening story of the *Decameron* (or the Book of Job, for that matter), that of the plague: innocents at times, perhaps often, appear to be punished. And, as many of the stories make clear—and Masetto's can certainly be taken as exemplary—vice, from the petty to the grotesque, is at times rewarded. The most problematic of all conclusions is to leap into the abyss of clear and clean-cut interpretations. Among these one must count those canonical alternatives, the two visions of Boccaccio: he is either "for it or agin it." Perhaps Pound would not have abandoned Boccaccio's classroom nor forsaken his studies; but he, like most of us, has dealt with a different kind of literary history, one that has appropriated Dante as its own and whose pseudorationalism bristles at synchronicity.

But the *Decameron* offers a range of different possibilities, and in doing so radically undermines that reading of Dante that Dante says is true in *Inferno* 5, a Dante who abandoned the seduction, the heresy, of ambiguity—his delicious Francesca—and began a new cult, the cult of Truth. Boccaccio suggests, in fact, that the alternatives are always more challenging than the embrace or the abandonment, and his own book redefines the fundamental premises Dante has tried to inscribe: that there is a knowable Truth and a knowable and writeable God. This last question is not only at the root of and inscribed in the Galeotto conundrum but is, by extension, critical to how we interpret the work as a whole—or have interpreted it, even if and when the exact question was never asked explicitly. From the first words and the very naming of his text Boccaccio has asked us to look at and think about Dante's expressions of certainty and revelation. The Galeotto allusion, in fact, embodies a double certainty: it is, first and foremost, the damned Francesca's certainty that it is all the book's fault, but it is no less Dante's certainty that Francesca is in Hell, that the literature she is—again, I repeat that that is not synonymous with what she reads—is to be discarded, left behind. For a small, ugly moment—it is the same moment Borges struggles with, guiltily—Dante, dealing in unequivocal truths, is little better than his Francesca. But Griselda is a heroine where Francesca has failed: she has eschewed the temptation of the simple and obvious reading of a text, the temptation of thinking she knows how it all comes out, somehow, and acting on it. She damns not, she judges not. In this, ironically, Boccaccio can be seen as more traditionally devout than Dante, for his principal assumption about the Truth is that revelation can only come, indeed, in the afterlife, that as mortals we are condemned to seeing a very partial truth at any time, in any text, in any vision. Who can really pretend to see the Aleph? Who can pretend that if I create one anyone will recognize it?

Before the *Decameron,* a reader can sustain a belief in the clarity and transparency of the morals of Dante's Francesca story: she and the literary hubris that can create such creatures are luscious temptations, but ultimately false, because they cannot transcend themselves. Boccaccio, as in so many, perhaps all, of his stories, asks us to make sure that we are not dealing with the illusion and temptation of easy truths, with the kind of medicine doled out by Maestro Simone or heliotropes that aren't really there. And he does so, first and foremost, by nudging us, ever so delicately, into realizing that even a text like the *Commedia* contains the seed of its own doubts: suddenly, we are unsure whether it is Francesca herself that is at fault or what she read; whether Dante condemns or, somehow, secretly, sympathizes; whether, in sum, Dante is as transparent as he has told us he needs to be. Most of all, in attaching himself so explicitly to Dante, his text, and its fate, Boccaccio crucially contributes to the powerful subversion at play within the *Commedia:* he is the first of countless thousands who will follow to sense and render homage to the enormous power and creativity and independence, the astonishing unpredictability, of texts. God knows how they will be taken, what they will be read as. Dante may have damned Francesca, but she, most of all, was not to be forgotten. And Boccaccio's Galeotto thus gives us the best possible example of why writers, readers, and most of all texts, should tread ever so lightly when dealing with Truths and Absolutes and Judgments, for they have a way of turning on you.

Works Cited

Ackroyd, Peter. 1984. *T. S. Eliot: A Life*. New York: Simon and Schuster.

Almansi, Guido. 1975. *The Writer as Liar: Narrative Technique in the Decameron*. London: Routledge.

Anderson, David. 1979. "The Techniques of Critical Translation: Ezra Pound's Guido Cavalcanti, 1912." *Paideuma* 8:215–22.

———. 1983. *Pound's Cavalcanti*. Princeton: Princeton University Press.

———. 1985. "Pound alla ricerca di una lingua per Cavalcanti." *Lettere italiane* 37:24–40.

Apollonio, Mario. 1948. *Fondazioni della cultura italiana moderna. Storia letteraria dell'Ottocento*. Florence: Sansoni.

Auerbach, Erich. [1959] 1984. *Scenes from the Drama of European Literature*. Foreword by Paolo Valesio. Minneapolis: University of Minnesota Press.

Barolini, Teodolinda. 1984. *Dante's Poets*. Princeton: Princeton University Press.

———. 1989. "The Making of a Lyric Sequence: Time and Narrative in Petrarch's *Rerum vulgarium fragmenta*." *MLN* 104:1–38.

Bernardo, Aldo. 1955. "Petrarch's Attitude Toward Dante." *PMLA* 70:488–517.

Bernstein, Michael André. 1980. *The Tale of the Tribe: Ezra Pound and the Modern Verse Epic*. Princeton: Princeton University Press.

Bertacchini, Renato. 1974. *Ottocento*. Bologna: Calderini.

Binyon, Laurence. [1947] 1977. *The Divine Comedy*. In *The Portable Dante*, ed. Paolo Milano. New York: Viking/Penguin.

Bloom, Harold. 1973. *The Anxiety of Influence: A Theory of Poetry*. New York: Oxford University Press.

———. 1975. *Kabbalah and Criticism*. New York: Seabury Press.

Bloom, Harold, ed. 1986a. *Dante (Modern Critical Views)*. New York: Chelsea House.

Bloom, Harold, ed. 1986b. *Borges (Modern Critical Views)*. New York: Chelsea House.

Bloom, Harold. 1989. *Ruin the Sacred Truths. Poetry and Belief from the Bible to the Present*. Cambridge: Harvard University Press.

Boccaccio, Giovanni. 1966. *Decameron*. Ed. Cesare Segre. Milan: Mursia.

————. [1972] 1987. *The Decameron*. Trans. G. H. McWilliam. London: Penguin.

Borges, Jorge Luis. 1945. "El Aleph." *El Aleph*. Buenos Aires: Emecé.

Borges, Jorge Luis, trans. with Norman Thomas di Giovanni. 1970. *The Aleph and Other Stories, 1933–1969*. New York: E. P. Dutton.

Borges, Jorge Luis. 1970. "Commentaries." In *The Aleph and Other Stories*.

————. 1980. *Siete Noches*. Mexico: Fondo de Cultura Económica.

————. 1982. *Nueve ensayos dantescos*. Ed. M. R. Barnatan and J. Arce. Madrid: Espasa-Calpe.

Bornstein, George, ed. 1985. *Ezra Pound Among the Poets*. Chicago: University of Chicago Press.

Bowman, Frank. 1982. "Le statut littéraire de l'autobiographie spirituelle." In *Le statut de la Littérature. Melanges offerts a Paul Bénichou*, ed. Marc Fumaroli. Geneva: Droz.

Braden, Gordon. 1986. "Love and Fame: The Petrarchan Career." In *Pragmatism's Freud: The Moral Disposition of Psychoanalysis*, ed. J. Smith and W. Kerrigan: 126–58. Baltimore: Johns Hopkins University Press.

Branca, Vittore. 1956. *Boccaccio medievale*. Florence: Sansoni.

Brombert, Victor. 1949. *The Criticism of T. S. Eliot. Problems of an "Impersonal Theory" of Poetry*. New Haven: Yale University Press.

————. 1978. *The Romantic Prison*. Princeton: Princeton University Press.

Brownlee, Kevin. 1984. "Why the Angels Speak Italian: Dante as Vernacular *Poeta* in *Paradiso* XXV." *Poetics Today* 5:597–610.

Cambon, Glauco. 1969. *Dante's Craft*. Minneapolis: University of Minnesota Press.

Campbell, Joseph, ed. 1971. *The Portable Jung*. New York: Viking.

Chaytor, H. J. 1902. [reprinted 1974]. *The Troubadours of Dante*. Oxford: Clarendon [New York: AMS Press].

Cherpack, Clifton. 1959. "Is There Any Eighteenth-Century French Literature?" *French Review* 33:11–16.

Dante. [1947] 1977. *The Divine Comedy.* Trans. Laurence Binyon. In *The Portable Dante,* ed. Paolo Milano. New York: Viking/Penguin.

————. 1970, 1973, 1975. *The Divine Comedy.* Trans. and commentary Charles Singleton. Princeton: Princeton University Press.

————. 1973. *Vita nuova-Rime.* Ed. Fredi Chiappelli. Milan: Mursia.

D'Andrea, Antonio. 1980. "La struttura della *Vita nuova:* le divisioni delle rime." *Yearbook of Italian Studies* 4:13–40.

DeBonfils Templer, Margherita. 1973. *Itinerario di Amore: Dialettica di Amore e Morte nella "Vita Nuova."* Chapel Hill: University of North Carolina Studies in Romance Languages and Literatures.

————. 1980. "Quando Amor mi spira, noto . . . (Purg. XXIV)." *Dante Studies* 98:79–98.

Della Terza, Dante. 1981. "*Inferno* V: Tradition and Exegesis." *Dante Studies* 49:49–66.

De Man, Paul. [1964] 1986. "A Modern Master." In *Borges,* ed. Harold Bloom: 21–27.

————. 1979. "Autobiography as De-facement." *MLN* 94:919–30.

De Robertis, Domenico. 1970. *Il Libro della Vita Nuova.* Firenze: Sansoni.

Derrida, Jacques. 1981. *Dissemination.* Trans. Barbara Johnson. Chicago: University of Chicago Press.

DeSanctis, Francesco. 1971. *Storia della letteratura italiana.* Ed. Niccolò Gallo. 2 vols. Torino: Einaudi.

————. [1931] 1959. *History of Italian Literature.* Trans. Joan Redfern. 2 vols. New York: Barnes and Noble.

Dragonetti, Roger. [1977] 1982. "The Double Play of Arnaut Daniel's Sestina and Dante's *Divina Commedia*" [*Yale French Studies* 55/56:227–52]. In *Literature and Psychoanalysis: The Question of Reading: Otherwise,* ed. S. Felman. Baltimore: Johns Hopkins University Press.

Durling, Robert M., trans. and ed. 1976. *Petrarch's Lyric Poems.* Cambridge: Harvard University Press.

Durling, Robert M. 1983. "Boccaccio on Interpretation: Guido's Escape (*Decameron* VI. 9)." In *Dante, Petrarch, Boccaccio: Studies in the Italian Trecento in Honor of Charles S. Singleton,* ed. Aldo Bernardo and Anthony Pellegrini: 273–304. Binghamton: Medieval and Renaissance Texts.

Eliot, T. S., ed. and intro. 1918. *Literary Essays of Ezra Pound.* New York: New Directions.

Eliot, T. S. [1923] 1975. "Ulysses, Order, and Myth." In *Selected Prose of T. S. Eliot,* ed. Frank Kermode: 175–78.

————. [1929] 1950. "Dante." In *Selected Essays:* 199–237. New York: Harcourt Brace.

————. [1933] 1961. *The Use of Poetry and the Use of Criticism.* Cambridge: Harvard University Press.

————. [1946] [1950] 1973. "Ezra Pound." In *An Examination of Ezra Pound,* ed. Peter Russell: 25–36.

————. [1950 talk] 1983. "What Dante Means To Me." Printed as "A Talk on Dante." In *Dante in America,* ed. A. Bartlett Giamatti: 219–27.

————. 1970. *Collected Poems: 1909–1962.* New York: Harcourt, Brace, Jovanovich.

Eliot, Valerie, ed. 1971. T. S. Eliot. *The Waste Land. A Fascimile and Transcript of the Original Drafts Including the Annotations of Ezra Pound.* New York: Harcourt Brace Jovanovich.

Ellis, Stephen Paul. 1979. "Dante in Pound's Early Career." *Paideuma* 8:549–61.

Ellman, Maude. 1987. *The Poetics of Impersonality. T. S. Eliot and Ezra Pound.* Cambridge: Harvard University Press.

Fernández, James. 1988. *Strategies of Self-Defense: Episodes in Nineteenth Century Spanish Autobiography.* Princeton University dissertation.

Finocchiaro Chimirri, Giovanna. 1985. *La "Francesca da Rimini" nella produzione teatrale del Pellico.* Catania: C.U.E.C.M.

Fish, Stanley. 1989. "Being Interdisciplinary Is So Very Hard To Do." *Profession 89:* 15–22.

Fitzgerald, Robert. 1981. "Mirroring the *Commedia:* An Appreciation of Laurence Binyon's Version." *Paideuma* 10: 489–508. Also in *Dante in America,* ed. Giamatti: 390–410, and in *Dante Among the Moderns,* ed. Stuart McDougal: 153–75.

Fletcher, Jefferson. 1920. "The 'True Meaning' of Dante's *Vita Nuova." Romantic Review* 11:95–148.

Fontana, Ernest. 1979–80. "William Morris's Guenevere and Dante's Francesca: Allusion as Revision." *English Miscellany* 28/29: 283–92.

Foscolo, Ugo. 1823. "A Parallel between Dante and Petrarch." In *Essays on Petrarch:* 164–208. London: John Murry.

Forti-Lewis, Angelica. 1986. *Italia autobiografica.* Rome: Bulzoni.

Freccero, John. 1975. "The Fig Tree and the Laurel." *Diacritics* 5:34–40.

————. 1986a. *Dante. The Poetics of Conversion.* Cambridge: Harvard University Press.

————. 1986b. "Virgil, Sweet Father: A Paradigm of Poetic Influence." In *Dante Among the Moderns,* ed. Stuart McDougal: 3–10.

Gallup, Donald. 1970. "T. S. Eliot and Ezra Pound." *Atlantic Monthly* 225 (January): 48–62.

Gaskell, Ronald. 1985–86. "Eliot and Dante." *Agenda* 23: 167–79.

Giamatti, A. Bartlett, ed. 1983. *Dante in America. The First Two Centuries.* Binghamton: Medieval and Renaissance Texts.

González Echevarría, Roberto. 1983. "BdeORridaGES (Borges y Derrida)." In *Isla a su vuelo fugitiva:* 205–15. Madrid: Porrua. Also in English in *Borges,* ed. Harold Bloom: 227–34.

Greene, Thomas M. 1982. *The Light in Troy: Imitation and Discovery in Renaissance Poetry.* New Haven: Yale University Press.

Greene, Roland. Forthcoming. *Petrarchan Experience and the Colonial New World.*

Hall, Donald. 1962. "Ezra Pound: An Interview." *Paris Review* 7:22–51.

Harrison, Robert Pogue. 1988. *The Body of Beatrice.* Baltimore: Johns Hopkins University Press.

Haughton, Hugh. 1989. "The Pent and its Venting." *TLS* March 17–23: 285–86.

Headings, Philip R. 1982. *T. S. Eliot* (revised edition). Boston: Twayne Publishers.

Hegel, G. W. F. [1910] 1967. *The Phenomenology of Mind.* Trans. and intro. J. B. Baillie and intro. George Lichtheim. New York: Harper and Row.

Herrnstein Smith, Barbara. 1988. *Contingencies of Value.* Cambridge: Harvard University Press.

Hiscoe, David W. 1983. "Dante's Poetry, Daedalus' Monster and Arnaut Daniel's Name." *Italica* 60:246–55.

Hoffman, Daniel, ed. 1983. *Ezra Pound and William Carlos Williams. The University of Pennsylvania Conference Papers.* Philadelphia: University of Pennsylvania Press.

Hollander, Robert. 1969. *Allegory in Dante's "Commedia."* Princeton: Princeton University Press.

————. 1974. "*Vita Nuova:* Dante's Perceptions of Beatrice." *Dante Studies* 92:1–18.

————. 1977. *Boccaccio's Two Venuses.* New York: Columbia University Press.

————. 1981–82. "Boccaccio's Dante: Imitative Distance (*Decameron* I 1 and VI 10)." *Studi sul Boccaccio* 13:169–98.

————. 1986. "Boccaccio's Dante." *Italica* 63:278–89.

Holloway, Julia Bolton. 1985. "The *Vita Nuova:* Paradigms of Pilgrimage." *Dante Studies* 103: 103–24.

Jay, Gregory. 1983. *T. S. Eliot and the Poetics of Literary History.* Baton Rouge: Louisiana State University Press.

Jung, Carl. [1951] 1971. "On Synchronicity." In *The Portable Jung,* ed. Joseph Campbell: 505–18.

———. [1956] 1971. "Answer to Job." In *The Portable Jung,* ed. Joseph Campbell: 519–650.

Kenner, Hugh. 1971. *The Pound Era.* Berkeley: University of California Press.

———. 1983. "Poets at the Blackboard." In *Pound and Williams,* ed. Daniel Hoffman: 3–13.

———. 1985. "Ezra Pound's *Commedia.*" In *Dante Among the Moderns,* ed. Stuart McDougal: 39–56.

Kenny, Paul. 1988. "A Text with a Voice." *TLS* January 1–7, 1988:18.

Kermode, Frank, ed. 1975. *Selected Prose of T. S. Eliot.* New York: Harcourt, Brace.

Kirkham, Victoria. 1981. "Love's Labors Rewarded and Paradise Lost (*Decameron* III, 10)." *Romanic Review* 72:79–93.

Klemp, P. J. 1984. "The Women in the Middle: Layers of Love in Dante's *Vita Nuova.*" *Italica* 61:185–94.

LaCapra, Dominick. 1989. "On the Line: Between History and Criticism." *Profession* 89:4–9.

Langbaum, Robert. 1985. "Pound and Eliot." In *Ezra Pound Among the Poets,* ed. George Bornstein.

Marcus, Millicent. 1979. *An Allegory of Form: Literary Self-Consciousness in the Decameron.* Saratoga, Calif.: Anma Libri.

Mazzaro, Jerome. 1981. *The Figure of Dante: An Essay on the Vita Nuova.* Princeton: Princeton University Press.

Mazzotta, Giuseppe. 1978. "The Canzoniere and the Language of the Self." *Studies in Philology* 75:271–96.

———. 1979. *Dante, Poet of the Desert.* Princeton: Princeton University Press.

———. 1983. "The Language of Poetry in the *Vita nuova.*" *Rivista di Studi italiani* 1:3–14.

———. 1984. "Dante and the Virtues of Exile." *Poetics Today* 5:645–67.

———. 1986a. *The World at Play in Boccaccio's Decameron.* Princeton: Princeton University Press.

———. 1986b. "The Light of Venus and the Poetry of Dante." In *Magister Regis: Studies in Honor of Robert E. Kaske,* ed. A. Groos et al. New York:

Fordham University Press. 147–69. Also in *Dante,* ed. Harold Bloom: 189–204.

————. 1988. "Humanism and Monastic Spirituality in Petrarch." *Stanford Literature Review* 5:57–74.

McDougal, Stuart. 1972. *Ezra Pound and the Troubadour Tradition.* Princeton: Princeton University Press.

————. 1985. "Dreaming a Renaissance: Pound's Dantean Inheritance." In *Ezra Pound Among the Poets,* ed. George Bornstein.

McDougal, Stuart, ed. 1986. *Dante Among the Moderns.* Chapel Hill: University of North Carolina Press.

McDougal, Stuart. 1986. "T. S. Eliot's Metaphysical Dante." In *Dante Among the Moderns,* ed. Stuart McDougal: 57–81.

McMahon, Robert. 1987. "Homer/Pound's Odysseus and Virgil/Ovid/Dante's Ulysses: Pound's First Canto and the *Commedia.*" *Paideuma* 16:67–75.

Melli, Elio. 1959. "Dante e Arnaut Daniel." *Filologia romanza* 6:423–48.

Mombello, Gianni. 1962. "Breve nota su 'Mes Prisons' de Verlaine." *Studi francesi* 17:292–93.

Moody, A. D., ed. 1974. *The Waste Land in Different Voices.* London: Edward Arnold.

Musa, Mark. 1973. *Dante's Vita Nuova: A Translation and an Essay.* Bloomington: Indiana University Press.

Nelson, Lowry, Jr., ed. and trans. 1986. *The Poetry of Guido Cavalcanti.* New York: Garland Press.

Noakes, Susan. 1983. "The Double Misreading of Paolo and Francesca." *Philological Quarterly* 62:221–39. Also in *Dante,* ed. Bloom: 151–66.

Nolan, Barbara. 1970. "The *Vita Nuova:* Dante's Book of Revelation." *Dante Studies* 88:51–77.

Olney, James. 1980. "Autobiography and the Cultural Moment: A Thematic, Historical, and Bibliographic Introduction." In *Autobiography. Essays Theoretical and Critical,* ed. Olney. Princeton: Princeton University Press.

Paparelli, Gioacchino. [1954. "Galeotto fu il libro e chi lo scrisse."] 1975. "Ethos e pathos nell'episodio di Francesca da Rimini." In *Ideologia e poesia di Dante:* 171–200. Florence: Olschki.

————. 1979. "Due modi di leggere Dante: Petrarca e Boccaccio." In *Giovanni Boccaccio Editore e Interprete di Dante:* 73–90. Ed. Società Dantesca Italiana. Florence: Olschki.

Patterson, Lee. 1987. *Negotiating the Past. The Historical Understanding of Medieval Literature.* Madison: University of Wisconsin Press.

Pellico, Silvio. [1832] 1983. *Le mie prigioni*. Milano: Longanesi.

―――. [1832] 1986. *Le mie prigioni*. Ed. Angelo Jacomuzzi. Milan: Mondadori.

―――. 1885. *My Prisons: Memoirs of Silvio Pellico*. Intro. by Epes Sargent. Boston: Roberts Brothers.

―――. [1963] 1978. *My Prisons*. Trans. I. G. Capaldi. [New York: Oxford University Press] Westport: Greenwood Press.

―――. 1985. *Francesca da Rimini*. In Giovanna Finocchiaro Chimirri, 1985. *La "Francesca da Rimini" nella produzione teatrale del Pellico*. Catania: C.U.E.C.M.

―――. 1905. *Francesca da Rimini*. Ed. and trans. Joel Foote Bingham. London: Henry Frowde.

Perloff, Marjorie. 1985. "The Contemporary of Our Grandchildren: Pound's Influence." In *Ezra Pound Among the Poets*, ed. George Bornstein.

Petrarca, Francesco. 1985. *Letters on Familiar Matters*. Trans. Aldo Bernardo. Vol. 3. Baltimore: Johns Hopkins University Press.

Petrie, Jennifer. 1983. *Petrarch: The Augustan Poets, the Italian Tradition and the Canzoniere*. Dublin: Irish Academic Press.

Picone, Michelangelo. 1979. "I trovatori di Dante: Bertran de Born." *Studi e Problemi di critica testuale* 19:71–94.

Pipa, Arshi. 1985. "Personaggi della *Vita nuova:* Dante, Cavalcanti e la famiglia Portinari." *Italica* 62:99–115.

Poggioli, Renato. 1957. "Tragedy or Romance? A Reading of the Paolo and Francesca Episode in Dante's *Inferno.*" *PMLA* 72:313–58.

Popp, Carol. Forthcoming. "Psychic Energy in the Analytic Relationship." *Chiron*.

Popolizio, Stephen. 1980. "Literary Reminiscences and the Act of Reading in *Inferno* V." *Dante Studies* 98:19–33.

Pound, Ezra. [1910] 1952. "Il miglior fabbro." In *The Spirit of Romance*: 22–38. Norfolk, Conn.: New Directions.

―――. [1910] 1952. "Dante." In *The Spirit of Romance*: 118–65. Norfolk, Conn.: New Directions.

―――. [1910] 1952. *The Spirit of Romance*. Norfolk, Conn.: New Directions.

―――. [1934]. "Hell, A Review of Dante's *Inferno* translated into English Triple Rhyme, By Laurence Binyon." [1954. in *Literary Essays*, ed. T. S. Eliot.] In *Dante in America*, ed. A. Bartlett Giamatti: 175–86.

―――. 1954. *Literary Essays*. Ed. and with an introduction by T. S. Eliot. Norfolk, Conn.: New Directions.

―――. 1954. *Translations of Ezra Pound*. New York: New Directions.

―――. 1956. *Selected Poems*. New York: New Directions.

———. 1985. *Forked Branches. Translations of Medieval Poems.* Ed. Charlotte Ward and with an introduction by James Laughlin. Iowa City: Windhover Press.

Praz, Mario. [1958] 1966. "T. S. Eliot and Dante." In *The Flaming Heart:* 348–74. Gloucester Mass.: P. Smith.

Quaglio, Antonio Enzo. 1973. *Al di là di Francesca e Laura.* Padova: Liviana.

Reynolds, Mary T. 1981. *Joyce and Dante: The Shaping Imagination.* Princeton: Princeton University Press.

Russell, Peter, ed. 1973. *An Examination of Ezra Pound: A Collection of Essays.* New York: Gordian Press.

Ruthven, K. K. 1987. "Ezra's Appropriations." *TLS* 4416 (November 20–26, 1987): 1278, 1300–1301.

Said, Edward. 1975. *Beginnings. Intention and Method.* New York: Basic Books.

———. 1983. *The World, The Text and the Critic.* Cambridge: Harvard University Press.

Scaglione, Aldo. 1984. "L'autobiografia in Italia e i nuovi metodi di analisi critica." *Forum Italicum* 18:203–16.

Shapiro, Marianne. 1974. "The Fictionalization of Bertran de Born (*Inf.* XXVIII)." *Dante Studies* 92:107–16.

———. 1980. *Hieroglyph of Time: The Petrarchan Sestina.* Minneapolis: University of Minnesota Press.

———. 1982. "*Purgatorio* XXX: Arnaut at the Summit." *Dante Studies* 100:71–76.

Shaw, J. E. [1929] 1976. *Essays on the Vita Nuova.* [Princeton: Princeton University Press] Millwod, N.Y.: Kraus Reprint Co.

———. 1947. " 'Ego tanquam centrum circuli etc.' *Vita Nuova* XII." *Italica* 24:113–18.

Sherry, Vincent. 1988. "Cannon Fodder." *TLS* August 19–25:914.

Singleton, Charles. 1945. "*Vita Nuova* XII: Love's Obscure Words." *Romantic Review* 36:89–102.

———. 1946. "The Use of Latin in the *Vita Nuova.*" *Modern Language Notes* 61:108–12.

———. [1949] 1977. *An Essay on the Vita Nuova.* [Cambridge: Harvard University Press.] Baltimore: Johns Hopkins University Press.

Smith, Nathaniel. 1980. "Arnaut Daniel in the *Purgatorio:* Dante's Ambivalence toward Provençal." *Dante Studies* 98:99–109.

Soldo, John J. 1982. "Eliot's Dantean Vision, and His Markings in His Copy of the *Divina Commedia.*" *Yeats Eliot Review* 7:11–18.

Spengemann, William C. 1980. *The Forms of Autobiography: Episodes in the History of a Literary Genre*. New Haven: Yale University Press.

Stefanini, Ruggiero. 1980. "Dante in Borges: L'Aleph, Beatriz e il Sud." *Italica* 57:53–65.

Steiner, Wendy. 1986. "Collage or Miracle: Historicism in a Deconstructed World." In *Reconstructing American Literary History*, ed. Sacvan Bercovitch. Cambridge: Harvard University Press.

Stillinger, Thomas. 1988. *Authorized Song: Lyric Poetry and the Medieval Book*. Cornell University dissertation.

Sturm-Maddox, Sara. 1985. *Petrarch's Metamorphoses: Text and Subtext in the Rime Sparse*. Columbia: University of Missouri Press.

Tanturli, Giuliano. 1985. "Il disprezzo per Dante dal Petrarca al Bruni." *Rinascimento* 25 (2d ser.): 199–219.

Thiem, Jon. 1988. "Borges, Dante, and the Poetics of Total Vision." *Comparative Literature* 40:97–121.

Updike, John. 1985. "Eliot Without Words." *The New Yorker*. March 25, 1985:120–30.

Valesio, Paolo. 1981. "Regretter: Genealogia della ripetizione nell'episodio di Paolo e Francesca." In *From Linguistics To Literature: Romance Studies Offered to Francis M. Rogers*, ed. B. Bichakjian. Amsterdam: John Benjamins.

Valesio, Paolo. 1984. Foreword to Erich Auerbach, *Scenes from the Drama of European Literature*. Minneapolis: University of Minnesota Press.

Van Slyke, Gretchen. 1982. "Le narrataire et l'autobiographie." *Francofonia* 2:19–33.

Vickers, Nancy. 1981. "Re-membering Dante: Petrarch's 'Chiare, fresche, dolce acque.'" *MLN* 96:1–11.

———. 1988. "Vital Signs: Petrarch and Popular Culture." *Romanic Review* 79:184–95.

Von Hallberg, Robert. 1986. "American Poet-Critics since 1945." In *Reconstructing American Literary History*, ed. Sacvan Bercovitch. Cambridge: Harvard University Press.

Wallace, Emily Mitchell. 1983. "Youthful Days and Costly Hours." In *Pound and Williams*, ed. Daniel Hoffman.

Waller, Marguerite R. 1980. *Petrarch's Poetics and Literary History*. Amherst: University of Massachusetts Press.

Wilhelm, James J. 1974a. "Guido Cavalcanti as a Mask for Ezra Pound." *PMLA* 89:332–40.

————. 1974b. *Dante and Pound: The Epic of Judgement.* Orono, Maine: University of Maine Press.

————. 1977. *The Later Cantos of Ezra Pound.* New York: Walker and Company.

————. 1982. *Il miglior fabbro: The Cult of the Difficult in Daniel, Dante, and Pound.* Orono, Maine: National Poetry Foundation.

Wilkins, Ernest Hatch, revised by Thomas Bergin. [1954] 1974. *A History of Italian Literature.* Cambridge: Harvard University Press.

Yowell, Donna. 1989. " 'Trop amar' vs. 'Ben Amar': Redemptive Love in Arnaut Daniel and Dante." *Romance Philology* 42:385–95.

Index

About the Author

María Rosa Menocal received her degree in Romance philology at the University of Pennsylvania and has written on a broad range of medieval literary and linguistic topics, including a previous book, *The Arabic Role in Medieval Literary History: A Forgotten Heritage*. She has taught at Bryn Mawr College and the University of Pennsylvania and is currently Associate Professor and Director of Graduate Studies in the Department of Spanish and Portuguese at Yale University.